TIME MANAGEMENT
FOR TEACHERS

Techniques and Skills
That Give You
More Time To Teach

TIME MANAGEMENT FOR TEACHERS

Techniques and Skills That Give You More Time To Teach

Cathy Collins, Ph.D.

Parker Publishing Company, Inc.
West Nyack, N.Y.

© 1987 by

PARKER PUBLISHING COMPANY, INC.

West Nyack, N.Y.

Library of Congress Cataloging-in-Publication Data

Collins, Cathy.
  Time management for teachers.

  Includes bibliographies and index.
  1. Teachers—Time management.   I. Title.
LB2838.8.C65 1987   640'.43'024372   87-2431

ISBN 0-13-921701-0

Printed in the United States of America

This book is dedicated to Michael.

About the Author

Cathy Collins received her Bachelor of Science Degree from Lamar University (Beaumont, Texas) and her Masters of Science Degree from North Texas State University. She completed her Doctorate at the University of Wisconsin–Madison in the fields of Curriculum and Instruction and Educational Psychology.

Dr. Collins is an associate professor in the School of Education at Texas Christian University (Fort Worth). During her more than 16 years' experience in education, she has served as a public and private school teacher in grades K–12, as an assistant professor at Southern Illinois University, and as a research assistant at the Wisconsin Research and Development Center for Cognitive Learning at the University of Wisconsin–Madison. Dr. Collins has also served as a teacher center associate and as a consultant for numerous school districts across the country, during which she trained many faculties to improve and increase their time management skills. She is also the co-author of *The Stanford Early School Achievement* and various publications concerning instructional program improvement and classroom teacher advancements. She has authored systemwide assessment tests and curriculum guides and has served and been a member of numerous professional organizations.

In the fall of 1985, Dr. Collins was selected as the TCU Chapter of Texas Student Education Association's Distinguished Professor.

How This Book Will Help You Effectively Manage Your Time

As you pick up *Time Management for Teachers*, you may ask yourself, "If I read this book, will it really help me be a better teacher? Will it help me to enjoy my work and be more valuable to my school?"

Then some of you may go on to think . . .

"My job *is* demanding more of my time. The entire education process is more complex and requires more management skills than ever before. District policies and curriculum content are changing frequently, and I have less time to plan good lessons and to *teach*. I wish I could learn skills to increase my effectiveness."

"I work hard enough already, and if I learn time management skills, I might learn how to do more! Won't this *increase* rather than *decrease* the stress I have?"

"I'm already in so much control at work that I'm getting bored. I may even be getting burned out! Do I need a career change?"

"Although I'm the kind of teacher who's always hurrying around, I never seem to get things done that are very significant."

"I'm under so much pressure! I work and work, but never get to do the things *I* want to do."

Time Management for Teachers was written to eliminate these problems and more. It was designed so you can more easily put the time management principles, first identified in the fields of business, sociology, and psychology, into practice in your own classroom.

More specifically, those who will probably profit most from reading this book are

1. Teachers (of preschoolers to adults) who wish to improve their professional skills.

2. Teachers who have a serious time management problem to solve.

3. Practicing teachers or administrators responsible for developing inservice training programs for teachers in their districts.

4. Teachers who wish to increase the time-use skills of their students.

5. Professors, corporate human resource managers, staff training directors, and continuing adult education instructors responsible for adult inservice training and skill development.

6. Preservice teachers who have not been trained in classroom time management skills or who have experienced the problems this lack of skills could produce.

Research in time management has increased remarkably within the last few years, and many teachers are not aware of new time management methods and the impact these can have on their lives. Yet, teachers who are introduced to and practice the skills report that they receive more pleasure from their work, do more significant, satisfying tasks, and take more pride in who they are.

HOW TO USE THIS BOOK

Time Management for Teachers can be used in a variety of ways. When used as a daily, self-study program, you can guide your reading by first learning the skills of your greatest interest. You can take notes in the margins to preserve the reflections, conditions, and techniques that accompany your growth. These notes could also be reviewed to determine how long it took to reach the level of skill you desired or how long it has been since the skill first became a "habit."

A second way the book can be used is as a manual for inservice and preservice training programs. Directors can select different readings, to be combined in a variety of ways, to meet specific group needs in large- and small-group presentations.

A third purpose is to serve as a reference book for yourself and your principal. That is, whenever a problem arises and you are not reaching a goal, you could read the sections of the book designed to eliminate that difficulty. Whenever your principal faces a problem with another teacher, a specific discussion giving background information concerning the problem could be given to the teacher.

HOW THE BOOK IS ORGANIZED

Time Management for Teachers is divided into 11 chapters, each focusing on one set of time management principles. Following an introductory discussion of the skill, practice exercises and reproducible worksheets are provided to help you more easily and rapidly develop the habit of using the techniques.

Chapters 1 through 4 demonstrate that good time management will only begin when you consciously reawaken your sensitivity to those goals, values, and talents that are most important. Then you advance your development by creating a program whereby you practice time management techniques. In reaching this point, you will also learn to schedule time effectively on a daily, weekly, and yearly basis. You will eliminate habits that drain your personal and professional resources.

Once these changes have occurred, Chapter 5 will help you learn to avoid future overcommitments. In Chapter 6, you can enhance the skills of creative problem solving that will, in turn, become the first step you take to "make time" for yourself, your work, and others. In the process, you will find out in Chapters 7 and 8 how to spend more effective time in groups and to set aside time for continued self-improvement.

Chapters 9 and 10 address two major problems faced by teachers: burnout and mounting paperwork. Chapter 11 discusses numerous methods you can use to set students' and colleagues' time management skills in motion.

BEFORE YOU GO FURTHER

Let's take a moment and employ one of the tricks of our trade. We will learn the skills in *Time Management for Teachers* if we each set a personal goal and expectation we hope to accomplish by reading it. Use the following lines to write the goal you wish to have reached by the time you finish this book, the method you plan to use in reaching it, and what you can see yourself doing once the goal has been reached. I wish you success!

_____

_____

_____

_____

_____

_____

Cathy Collins

Acknowledgments

This book is written from the input and guidance I have received from many people:

Kim Massey, Jane White, Lisa Barlow, and Jane Hart typed the manuscript. Evelyn Fazio is a remarkable editor who dedicated herself to this book from beginning to end; she is a dynamic person and professional. Billie Jarrell, my sister Donna Zinke, my stepmother Dorothy Zinke, Charlene Bice, Elene Demos, and Lynn Rhoades most encouraged me to write the book. John Mangieri and Cherie Lohr gave me the resources to write it. Dale Young has shown me new ways to dedicate myself to the profession and put moments of joy in my life. Wayne Otto has inspired me to grow and is a part of this book in many ways. Mary Louise Long is a special friend who helped solve problems before I asked. Christine Combs, my best friend, took out frivolous words, challenged ideas, and worked many hours to help me refine the first draft. My sister Wanda Zinke worked on each revision and gave continued support through long hours of work and typing, and my mother JoAnn Zinke gave her many talents to the project and worked countless hours, doing everything possible to help the book be the best it could be. But it is because of Michael that the book was written.

Table of Contents

Chapter 6

CREATIVE PROBLEM SOLVING: MAKING MORE TIME FOR TEACHING AND LEARNING   *145*

Chapter 7

SPENDING QUALITY TIME IN GROUPS *164*

one

Getting Started: Better Objectives and Plans for Yourself, Your Students, and Your School

A Teacher Comments on Chapter 1

No two people are alike, as we all know. However, I can say that Chapter 1 is for all teachers, regardless of the circumstances they face or the unique characteristics they have. After reading Chapter 1, I was amazed at how good I felt. It helped relight an appreciation of self that I had let dim.

This chapter will revive your mind and senses. As I read it, I became aware that I can definitely better myself! I have become a better teacher already, and it was so easy. I now use more teaching talents that I had previously not known to be a part of me.

Jan Worthington Reid
Elementary Teacher
Boone, North Carolina

I find the great thing in this world is not so much
where we stand as in what direction we are moving.

—*Oliver Wendell Holmes*

No other profession in our society charges each professional with as many diverse responsibilities in the working environment as does the teaching profession. As a teacher, you are charged with the responsibility of creating, managing, and evaluating the space, resources, materials, and time invested in the classroom to increase your talents and skills as well as those of your students! In this respect, you can be justly compared to a "king," a ruler who earns his subjects' devotion through the wisdom he exhibits in advancing his domain.

Chapter 1 will add four resources to your management repertoire, namely, (1) setting and reaching better classroom, personal, and schoolwide goals; (2) selecting the best methods to reach goals; (3) turning work to results; and (4) planning powerful lessons. You will learn to control classroom space, to make more time for teaching by identifying your strongest teaching skills, and to write clear, motivational objectives. These, in turn, will significantly increase your (1) availability to students, (2) output for the school, and (3) time to achieve personal goals.

YOUR CONTROL OF CLASSROOM TIME

Did you know that there are ten reasons why you lose control in your classroom? The first step to regaining complete control is understanding the reason for the loss. We begin our study of time management by exercising introspection. As you continue reading, work to identify the reason why you lose control in your classroom. With this information in hand, we can move on to set a specific goal and method for minimizing the times it occurs for you in the future.

Reasons for Loss of Control

1. You may lose control of your class because you feel overwhelmed, spending your time confronting one crisis after another. When this occurs, your goals are not being accomplished. Alternatively, someone else could be establishing too many of your goals. The crisis-to-crisis experience will be greatly reduced as you learn the skills in this chapter and Chapter 5. Concentrate on the sections that delineate the reasons why it is so difficult for you to say no.

2. You may lose classroom control when activities lack a clear focus. If you do not have good estimates of the amount of time needed to complete

tasks, your room will tend to be cluttered at the end of the day. Absence of a clear focus can also reflect an inability to plan effectively. Chapter 3 will be of great benefit toward eliminating both of these underlying causes.

3. Classroom control can be lost because classroom activities have no satisfactory end. That is, activities appear to be very carefully planned but, due to your "overcommitment," few are completed conscientiously before several others are underway. This "overcommitment" could be valid, and you will learn to avoid it in the future, or it could be a disguised representation of two other underlying causes: your classroom may be out of control because (a) you create incomplete cycles through limited guided and independent practice sessions (e.g., the learning, incubation period is not long enough for the students in your room) or (b) you lack skills in diversifying the weekly schedule. Because this reason for loss of control is the most complex, several sections of the book are allocated to helping you reduce the causes.

4. You may not sense the underlying continuity to the passage of activities and feel that the rhythm of time is uncontrolled. As you begin to use the eight methods of time management presented in Chapter 2 effectively, this feeling of powerlessness will disappear.

5. Teachers who feel a disharmony between themselves and their students, are dissatisfied with themselves or their profession, or experience a disproportionate number of failures will lose control frequently. Disharmony is probable if you have set goals and led activities that do not capitalize upon your talents. If you see yourself as a teacher of this type, you will benefit from the work we'll do to increase good professional habits and eliminate ineffective ones. If you are overly anxious, fearful of attempting new things, or shy away from making a strong commitment to the profession, you may not yet use your full power. This book can assist you in using your maturity, the natural, evolutionary process of skill development, and the passage of time to change failures to successes. With practice, your newly developing skills will displace older, less productive ones.

6. A tense classroom wastes resources, energy, and time. Tension will exist if lessons are not planned in harmony with your biological clock and the "world rhythm." According to Michael Gauquelin, in his revised edition of *The Cosmic Clocks* (San Diego, Calif.: ACS Publications, 1982), the "cosmic rhythm" of all living things continually imparts universal information to each organism. When this sense of timing is violated, the by-product affects physical functions. But, even more important, our deeply embedded emotional responses to events become desensitized. Lasting learning cannot be built when students are experiencing some of these symptoms (Meerloo, 1970). Tension will rapidly decrease as lesson plans are made to complement the rituals within individual school buildings and the subtle rhythms of "the school week."

7. Teachers who lack strong, positive self-images or have not received adequate rewards for past innovations will overemphasize the importance of time. This is often true for teachers who do not recognize their significance or set goals that require all their expertise to achieve. As McCoy (1959) first communicated, we will never achieve a goal larger than the one we set for ourselves. That is, we can become the greatest limitation upon our own accomplishments. The success we desire may use only a few of our talents. Further, regardless of the amount of talent our goals leave dormant, we will not achieve beyond this predetermined purpose we envisioned before we began our work. Chapters 1 and 9 will be of particular value if you feel you are limiting your own contributions.

8. You may waste time and unintentionally interfere with classroom efficiency as a result of your (a) disagreement with specific school district policies, philosophies, or operating procedures; (b) antagonism toward a particular person or duty; or (c) attitude toward school-related sources of displeasure. Subsequently, and maybe even subconsciously, you may waste time because you believe that doing so will "get even with" the "negative force" you battle. Sometimes you waste time because you or someone in charge of your achievement lacks strong instructional leadership skills. You could have a limited ability to follow, and this ability is stressed by a particular principal, administrator, or program director. Chapter 7 will help you to develop skills to counteract this behavior.

9. You could be delegating too little time, responsibility, and space to students, aides, and colleagues. In turn, these people will only live up to the level of expectations you set. Your precognitions (i.e., telepathic awarenesses of other people's inner goals and their abilities to predetermine occurrences) are detected by others, who, if they sense negative assessments, will begin to waste their time and talents. This chapter and Chapter 11 will help you to raise your level of expectations.

10. In classrooms where students assist in planning their own lessons and/or complete creative or self-directed activities, aspects of classroom control will be lost unless you use special management skills. This seems to be a more frequent problem for inexperienced teachers who become anxious when, upon the lesson's end, they fear that they will be unable to return students to the normal routine and structured rules for discipline. Thus, they begin to exert strong control and use fewer creative activities in the pursuit of order. The discussions concerning discipline in Chapter 7 and the work on managing creative activities in Chapter 11 will remedy these conditions.

Present Classroom Time-Control Assessment

To assess your present skills in controlling your classroom, refer to Figure 1-1. Complete the assessment in this figure by shading in each index to a point that

Figure 1-1

MEASURE OF A TEACHER'S CONTROL OF THE CLASSROOM

Directions: On the top half of each row, shade the row to the point that best indicates the degree of influence each cause for loss of control has upon your class or is experienced in your class in a typical week. Leave the bottom section blank; it will be shaded with a different colored pencil or pen as a post-assessment later in the book.

Typical Week's Time Units
M T W TH F

**Indices That Denote
Losses of Classroom Control**

You feel as if you move from one crisis to another.

Too often someone else sets your classroom goals.

Activities lack a clear focus.

Each activity does not have a good ending.

Your classroom seems to be out of control.

You feel disharmony with your students.

You feel dissatisfied with your teaching performances.

Classroom environment seems tense.

You have received inadequate rewards for your work.

There are periods of wasted class time.

Your expectations of student ability was too low.

Time was misused by students and/or aides.

Time was wasted when students were engaged in creative or self-directed activities.

symbolizes the number of times each will influence your classroom in a typical week. For example, if you feel the effect of a specific cause daily, you should shade the representative row from Monday through Friday. If you experience the impact approximately every other day, you will shade the index one-half of its length or to the midpoint.

Later in the book we will do a second self-assessment of your classroom. Then you can determine how much the work you have done has improved your classroom climate and control.

As you begin to develop your first time management skill, consider the following two quotations as added motivation:

> Birds don't fly because they have wings; they have wings because they fly. (Anonymous) Geniuses [and great teachers] don't have more control and time because they are great; they have greatness because they manage their time [and their classroom time] more wisely. (Cox, 1926, p. 139)

Further, since "Mediocrity is self-inflicted; genius is self-bestowed" (Russell, 1974, p. 19), we will now begin learning and *self-bestowing*.

GOAL SETTING: THE PROCESS OF INCREASING KNOWLEDGE ABOUT YOURSELF, YOUR STUDENTS, AND YOUR SCHOOL

It will be helpful if we realize that planning is a learned skill. It violates many natural tendencies and preferences in our lives. As a matter of fact, you may even find that human nature will work against you as you begin to use new, more efficient planning techniques. You might even wish to abandon all planning activities, as if predetermining any more of your life will limit your freedom. You might even have difficulty setting time aside to establish goals. You may even have been conditioned to respond to all of life on the basis of immediacy.

To use time for nonurgent tasks could take a reordering of priorities, concentrated attention, paperwork, commitment, and a well-established planning procedure.

Step 1

Learn to value and follow the words of the ancient French adage, *Reculer pour mieux santera*, "Move back, the better to jump." To set most productive classroom and personal goals and objectives, you may need to employ this phenomenon, now labeled "disintegration," more often. Specifically, as documented by MacKenzie (1975), the more time we spend in planning before executing an action, the less time the total execution process will take. As the following diagram illustrates, if you increase the amount of time spent and the quality of skills you use in lesson planning, you reduce the total amount of time spent in each learning experience.

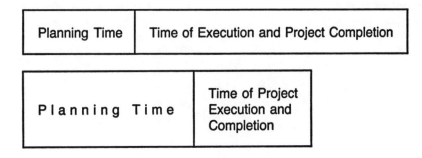

Planning Time	Time of Execution and Project Completion

Planning Time	Time of Project Execution and Completion

Step 2

There are eight methods that you can use to increase your planning and enhance your goal-setting skills. As you read each, select the one(s) that is (are) most appealing to you. Because each is designed to enhance a specific teaching style, the one that you judge to best match your working style will work fastest for you. You may choose to do each if you wish.

Undertake Self-reflection. Ask five questions of yourself, as if you could step outside of yourself and view your classroom objectively.

1. What is the most vital function of my work to me?
2. What do I see myself doing each day that is really significant?
3. What do I see myself doing each day that is really draining on me and unproductive?
4. Why do I do the things I do?
5. What is my long-range major goal and aim?

Write Talent-Centered Goals. While Chapter 2 will delineate the properties of procrastination, an inclination toward procrastination could indicate that you presently do not set goals that call upon your talents. Thus, the more you consciously evaluate your talents and improve your skills, you will begin to set goals to build a reputation that matches your best abilities. As you begin to enjoy teaching more and as you are called upon more frequently to exercise the talents you enjoy, your contributions will become more valuable and unique.

To begin, you can separate your present teaching actions into talent-centered and talent-foreign categories. To develop the skill of viewing actions in this manner, in the space provided list seven major types of actions you did the last few days that contributed to your most important goals and those that did not. In the right-hand column, list the things you enjoyed doing; in the left, those you avoided or dreaded.

The next step is to identify your talents more clearly. Writing the answers to each of the following questions with the first answer that comes to mind will aid in this process. Also, write today's date in the margin of the first question for future reference.

Activities that were Talent-Involved:	Activities that did not advance your goals:
1.	1.
2.	2.
3.	3.
4.	4.
5.	5.
6.	6.
7.	7.

1. What did you help "to go correctly" these past three days? _____
_____

2. What did you contribute to something that detracted from your most important, valuable, and enjoyable goals? _____
_____

3. What time of day did you start on the most important thing you did the last few days? _____
_____

4. What could you do to begin one of these important tasks earlier in the day tomorrow? _____
_____

5. What productive pattern do you tend to use most frequently to reach your most valued goals? _____
_____

6. What is your worst bad habit?_____
_____

7. Did you spend your first hour of the day doing important things?
_____ Yes _____ No

8. What part of the day was your most productive? _____
_____

9. What part of the day was your least productive? _____
_____

10. Who (or which group of people) accounted for most of your interruptions and/or activities that did not contribute to talent-oriented goals?
_____

11. What was the most frequent reason you changed or left a talent-centered goal and moved to a talent-foreign goal? _____
_____

12. How much of your time was spent on high-valued, talent-centered activity? _____

13. How much of your time was spent on low-value, unenjoyable activities that did not capitalize upon your strongest skills?_____

14. On which activities could you have spent less time and still produced as good a result? _____

15. Which activities could you have asked someone else to do, and specify the person that could have accomplished the task? _____

_____

The answers to the following questions are designed to expand your self-awareness.

1. Should I perform more of my duties with two or three of my colleagues so that combined talents would achieve greater results?
   Yes _____ No _____ Why _____

2. Should I begin to work more independently so my talents can be more fully developed to reach school district needs?
   Yes _____ No _____ Why _____

3. Should I involve more people in the goals I set?
   Yes _____ No _____ Why _____

4. Should I set goals that have more immediate results?
   Yes _____ No _____ Why _____

5. Should I concentrate more time on developing longer-range objectives, projects, and talent-focused goals?
   Yes _____ No _____ Why _____

6. Are 50 percent of the activities I do enjoyable and are they making me successful?
   Yes _____ No _____ Why _____

7. Are 50 percent of the activities I do wasting my time or calling upon skills that I do not wish to develop further? Yes _____ No _____
   Why _____

8. To do a better job, do I need to devote more time for:
   Sleep: Yes _____ No _____
   Hygiene: Yes _____ No _____
   Self-development: Yes _____ No _____
   Learning about new machines: Yes _____ No _____
   Amusement: Yes _____ No _____
   Physical exercise: Yes _____ No _____
   Cultural or aesthetic appreciation activities:
   Yes _____ No _____
   Relaxation: Yes _____ No _____
   Other: _____ Why? _____

_____

On a sheet of paper, write four actions you wish to take before you set your new goals. These actions will reflect decisions you have made concerning the value of your present goals/time when measured against your potential. Here are examples from a director of curriculum:

1. "I now realize that I receive greater satisfaction from accomplishing many small goals instead of one large goal. Each time I set a new goal, I write it as if it is a series of smaller subgoals so I can increase the amount of satisfaction I receive from doing it."

2. "I enjoy beginning projects early. I now realize that I am very skilled at planning for upcoming events. When called on to take part in a new committee, I am going to volunteer to lead planning types of activities, as opposed to the normal job I used to select—being recorder/documenter."

3. "I will ask my friends *why* they are asking me to do something before I agree to do it. I am not sure "why" I am constantly asked to do the simple things. I'm going to find out why I am asked to be involved in so many different and unchallenging activities. Maybe I'm not showing my true potential to others."

4. "I will set a new goal. I will never close a faculty conference concerning a problem without asking the other party(ies) involved to generate at least six alternative actions that we could take. By each person thinking positively about the problem before our next meeting, we can reach consensus earlier and gain more information about the problem."

Make a Time Journal. In business, time logs are one of the most widely used tools for training employees to write and actualize talent-centered goals. Robert Rutherford (1981) and Merrill and Donna Douglass (1980), three leading consultants in corporate time management, ask their workshop participants to keep logs for three days. They document their major areas of activities.

You can use this method by filling in the 18 items on the Teacher's Time Use Journal (Figure 1-2) just before you leave the office today. (Be sure to make two copies of the form.) Two examples of journals are also given so you might better understand the task before you begin. Figure 1-3 was kept by the same director of curriculum whose self-analysis was used as the example earlier. Seeing his journal could also assist your understanding of the facts that preceded these self-reflections. Figure 1-4 was written by a middle school speech therapist.

You may keep the journal each day for a week to record the best information upon which to base future goal-setting activities for yourself and your classroom activities.

Recognize the Things You Do Well. Do you know the ten things in your life and work that you most enjoy? Can you list ten things that you really do well in your work? If you have never thought about these two questions, you will be amazed at the ease with which the answers bring increased, often surprising self-awarenesses.

Figure 1-2

TEACHER'S TIME USE JOURNAL

Date _____ Day of Week _____

Name _____

Today:

1. I felt good doing/completing/beginning _____
   _____ .

2. I was not pleased with _____ .

3. I said "yes" when I could and should have said "no" when _____
   _____ .

4. I said "no" when I could and should have said "yes" when _____
   _____ .

5. I felt that I was wasting time or using it inappropriately when _____
   _____ .

6. The high points of my day were: _____
   _____ .

7. The low points of my day were: _____
   _____ .

8. I was unable to do or did not complete these tasks: _____
   _____ .

9. I spent too much time doing _____ .

10. Agreements made with myself that impacted my time positively were: _____
    _____ .

11. Agreements made with others that impacted my time positively were: _____
    _____ .

12. Agreements made with others that impacted my time negatively were _____
    _____ .

13. Insights I gained today about using my time were _____
    _____ .

14. Things I could, should, and would have done today if I had managed my time
    more efficiently were: _____
    _____ .

15. Ideas and thoughts I had today were: _____
    _____ .

16. In the time I allowed for myself today, I _____
    _____ .

17. The three most time-consuming tasks or goals that I cannot control the
    amount of time they take are: _____
    _____ .

18. Analysis of the day's activities in light of talents used and enjoyment/outputs
    gained reveals that: _____
    _____
    _____ .

Tomorrow spend 10 minutes completing another copy of this form. Keep separate notes
without referring back to this worksheet.

Revised from Time Dialogue Journal in R.D. Rutherford's *Administrative Time Power* (Austin, Tex.; Learning Concepts, 1978) and Daily Time Record Log, in Merrill and Donna Douglass's *Manage Your Time, Manage Your Work, Manage Yourself* (New York: Amacon, 1980).

Figure 1-3

TIME JOURNAL OF DIRECTOR OF SECONDARY CURRICULUM

Today:

1. *I felt good about doing* the last hour of catch-up correspondence before leaving the office for the weekend.

2. *I was not pleased with* the number of extended conversations I had on the phone.

3. *I said 'yes' when I could and should have said 'no'* to reviewing all the Math Grant before the first draft was complete.

4. *I said 'no' when I could and should have said 'yes'* to allowing someone to pay for my lunch, when they really should have.

5. *I felt that I was wasting time or using it inappropriately when* I didn't spend more time on my practicum plans for September's inservice.

6. *These were the high points of my day:* seeing colleagues I hadn't seen for several months.

7. *These were the low points of my day:* spending too long and not reaching a conclusion to the problem one of my principals is having and worrying about not getting a good start on my practicum plans.

8. *I was unable to do or did not complete these tasks:* work enough on my practicum; practice my speech for the board meeting; spend much time with my assistant; discuss and direct the new reading minimum-competency objectives.

9. *I spent too much time doing* low-priority letter writing.

10. *Agreements made with myself that impacted my time positively:* meeting colleagues coming in for lunch.

11. *Agreements made with others that impacted my time positively:* meeting with Linda Jo at the administration building to help her get some information regarding the September curriculum practicum.

12. *Agreements made with others that impacted my time negatively:* agreeing to give the introduction for a friend at a monthly meeting that I normally do not attend; agreeing to sing at a wedding of an acquaintance.

13. *Insights I gained today about using my time:* I seem to lack patience in handling individuals' personal problems that I feel are not high-priority problems.

14. *Things I could, should, and would have done today if I had managed my time more efficiently:* I would have spoken to the high school counselors about the TABS test, completed more of my review of the ninth grade texts, and practiced my speech for the board meeting.

15. *Ideas and thoughs I had today:* it's great to have friends, how much I appreciated my wife and daughter; and how little time there seemed to be in a day.

16. *In the time I allowed for myself today, I* relaxed; thought about and felt excited about the potential that the educational practicum holds as a method of improving our inservice in September.

17. *The three most time-consuming tasks or goals that I cannot control the amount of time they take were:* meetings required to attend by the superintendent; emergency/crisis interruptions, and time/resources being wasted by others in our district.

18. *Analysis of the activities, in light of talents used and enjoyment/outputs gained:* being Friday seemed to help my attitude even though the day was very short of time as far as getting things completed that I wanted to do. I did utilize my time to the fullest most of the day and did have the feeling that things were accomplished.

Figure 1-4

TIME JOURNAL OF A MIDDLE SCHOOL SPEECH THERAPIST

Today:

1. *I felt good about completing* the resource/reference book I planned to read.
2. *I was not pleased with* the mess on my desk.
3. *I said "yes" when I could and should have said "no"* to manning the phone while the secretary went to the dentist office.
4. *I said "no" when I could and should have said "yes"* to go to faculty subcommittee on language arts curriculum changes.
5. *I felt that I was wasting time or using it inappropriately when* I have to always write my name, address, and title on all correspondence instead of getting some labels.
6. *The high point of my day was* going to lunch with Joyce and Roberta.
7. *The low point of my day was* not being able to give Mark all the comfort that he needed.
8. *I was unable to do or did not complete these tasks:* taking notes and finding ways to implement what I learned from the books; buy that new set of word cards.
9. *I spent too much time* grading the work in the workbooks.
10. *Agreements made with myself that impacted my time positively:* to close the door and read.
11. *Agreements made with others that impacted my time positively:* to observe John's speech in Ms. Reynold's class.
12. *Agreements made with others that impacted my time negatively:* to be a "substitute" secretary.
13. *Insights I gained today about using my time:* writing times down helps to give sense of accomplishment.
14. *Things I could, should, and would have done today if I had managed my time more efficiently:* cleaned desk, worked on new plans for John.
15. *Ideas and thoughts I had today:* democratic-type relationships are satisfying.
16. *In the time I allowed for myself today,* I realized that active listening involves facial expressions and encouragement; I need to learn to respond to a person's statements and to take them a step farther.
17. *The most time-consuming tasks or goals that I cannot control the amount of time they will take were* time that students spend getting to class and the number of times they were absent and records that are due on the same day I receive the forms.
18. *Analysis of the activities in light of the talents used and enjoyment/outputs gained:* I say "yes" too much to things that bore me and that do not require my talents.

In the first column below list the specific activities, and the conditions surrounding these activities, that most please you. In the second column, identify ten of the most important things for which you hope to be remembered professionally.

Before you begin, note that most people can usually list five in both categories. The last five require more thought. The results justify the work. Be patient with yourself. You will be surprised as to the items that appear as entries 8, 9, and 10 on your list.

Activities I Most Enjoy or Do Well	**I Would Most Like to Be Remembered for**
1. _____	1. _____
2. _____	2. _____
3. _____	3. _____
4. _____	4. _____
5. _____	5. _____
6. _____	6. _____
7. _____	7. _____
8. _____	8. _____
9. _____	9. _____
10. _____	10. _____

Any time you establish goals that do not call upon talents you enjoy or wish to develop, attaining that goal will be more difficult. Further, it will be more difficult for you than for others you may be watching who are exercising talents as they work toward that goal.

Many educators have not had an opportunity to study the characteristics common to the most successful and famous people in our society. These people report that they purposely refrain from spending time pursuing works outside of their areas of personal strength (Goertzel and Goertzel, 1962; Cox, 1926; and Thomas, 1980). The majority stated that they concentrated all their activities in single areas of expertise.

You may desire this level of commitment. To achieve the successes you most value, you must modify your teaching so that it calls upon more of your unique skills. The list you just completed will help.

Establish Priorities and Allocate Emphasis and Time Used on Each Goal. Teaching priorities can be set in several ways. The first is to decide how many hours you would like to spend in activities concerning each of your present priorities. For example, you may want to increase the amount of time you spend (1) planning, (2) reevaluating and modifying instruction each week, (3) growing professionally, (4) developing student character, and (5) assessing student learning.

During the time you set aside for professional growth, take a few minutes at the end of the week to total the number of hours you spent in each goal area. That is, keep a note in your lesson plan book that would resemble the following:

Planning Act	Professional Growth	Student's Character Development
Monday, ¼ hour	1 hour	0 hour
Tuesday, ½ hour	½ hour	⅓ hour
Wednesday, etc.		
Total _____	_____	_____

After looking at the weekly tally, you can schedule time during the next week to give attention to the priorities of most need. In this way you give the time needed to do quality work in each category. With this system, if pressures in one or two areas inhibit reorganization of priorities in the upcoming week, you can continue to give the necessary overemphasis to one area until the pressures subside without worrying that you are neglecting others. When the unit of study or the difficult period has ended, you can then take extra moments to do a more in-depth evaluation of your use of time and block out time to get caught up at an unhurried pace in the other areas of importance. Without this system, you might neglect priorities and tend to engage in ritualistic, unproductive behaviors.

In addition, by recording time use in this way you can avoid weeks becoming filled with "nonurgent," "unimportant" tasks. That is, you will have already blocked out your working week goals and times to complete them before a less important request is made of your time. Having evidence that you have already committed your time will be an important aid in avoiding overcommitment, as we will study in Chapter 5.

To use this system, find a place in your calendar or lesson plan book where you can write your goal categories. (The place one educator uses is the blank space in the first Sunday of each month's calendar.) In this space write down five goals or goal categories. At the end of each week do the recordings described earlier. At the end of each month, compute the total number of hours spent in each category of activity. If you discover that five categories is too few or too many or you need to reproportion time allocations, you can begin your next month's plans with your new alterations.

Spend Time by Categories. Another method of blocking out time is to superimpose a balanced sense of time by using "different types of time." That is, you divide your day into units that use time in the following important ways (Hill, 1983):

1. *Evaluation time.* Schedule time at the end of your day to plan ways of getting tasks done in less time. Plan and assess the day's activities with thoughts of improving the efficiency and effectiveness of your work.

2. *Withdrawal time*. Set aside time to recover, reflect, and plan; you need time, frequently, to recover from fatigue or overstimulation and to create new teaching and problem-solving methods.

3. *Ritual time*. Set aside time to recognize and affirm yourself and others, which can be as short a period as 15 minutes or as extended as a weekend. This time keeps you from drifting too far from the central values and ideals you seek.

4. *Pastime*. Take time to make a history with your colleagues, to share special talents, hobbies, and the like. This is the time you invest to enhance your most cherished human qualities and to redevelop your appreciation of each person's uniqueness.

5. *Intimate time*. The time you spend in open, honest expressions of affection, unburdening concerns or confronting conflicts and issues is equally important to the other five types.

6. *Work time*. Time you spend in accomplishing goals is your working hours.

If too much time is being allocated to one of these areas, one of the following school climates will probably exist:

1. The school is tense; everyone must look busy.

2. People in the building avoid work and problems, as indicated by the increased incidences of use of avoidance mechanisms such as griping, discussing unrealistic ideals, and running personal errands.

3. "Real" agendas appear masked and greetings become more phoney.

4. During pastimes, interactions become superficial and employees begin to play games, for example, using problems to "get" someone else's attention or to make someone feel bad.

5. Inner circles form, with the possibility that one will be favored by a principal.

Use the Power of the Subconscious and Synectics. On a sheet of paper, write down

The most important change I want to make to improve myself is
_____. The benefit it will give to me is
_____. The benefit it will afford others is
_____. The change I'll make for others (students/
colleagues) that either I can do or I can help them to do for themselves is
_____

By putting this piece of paper in a place where you won't reference it for a month, your subconscious will work to accomplish the goals you wish to achieve. You may wish to become an expert in the goal you set. You can read books and take special training. You can then share your knowledge by conducting inservice training sessions in your district and in surrounding areas.

Engage in "Guided Fantasies." "Guided fantasies," are where you visualize people you most admire, is designed to help you explore your preferences and inclinations.

> Picture how the people you wish to emulate would act in your most difficult situations. Then visualize in a different direction. Ask yourself what it would be like to be the first expert in an area within our profession. Imagine the type of experiences you would have and how you would teach these to others. Then return your thoughts to the person(s) you first visualized. Place that person(s) in your room and imagine the steps they take as they reach this "expert" status and solve the problems you face.
>
> To begin this procedure reread the preceding paragraph, this time pausing briefly between sentences to feel the first images that come to mind. Then, each time you face a new problem or begin to set a goal, exercise "guided fantasy" first.

Step 3

After each goal is set, identify potential obstacles. Obstacles could include personal weaknesses; other people's weaknesses; the type and number of people your goal will affect; tendencies of students, administrators, and the community; your self-defined standards; the information you had available at the time of decision, time available; resources needed; and personal possessions and hobbies. If you assess the needs that control the people influenced by your decision, you will move closer to probable success. People need to feel personal growth and professional development. Some need to help others, have freedom, be liked, dominate, be recognized, impress others, be rewarded for being creative or intelligent, be involved in solving difficult situations, or avoid crisis situations and conflicts. You'll learn how to do this assessment of people's needs in Chapter 11.

Step 4

Once talents have been identified, you can set specific objectives for yourself and your students in the daily lesson plans you write. These are two separate objectives. You should always build in a way to reward yourself and to accomplish a new professional goal that is unrelated to students' learning the objective of the lesson you taught. This second objective can motivate and challenge you to improve daily.

As you write each objective, describe how the objective will be accomplished—exactly how will students determine that they met the objective and what distinguishable, measurable, visible outcome will they be able to see as a result of their learning? Include these three elements in the goals you write for yourself as well.

Before we leave the discussion of setting talent-centered goals, let's summarize our main points:

1. The purpose of spending more time planning is that it reduces the total time that will be spent in executing classroom tasks.

2. "The ordering of our thoughts and images makes them amenable to reason and conquers doubt and fear," according to Spinoza (1677), Italian philosopher. By identifying your strengths and talents, goals will be more easily achieved and accomplishments will be more significant.

3. Douglass and Douglass (1980) found that success is *not* a "natural state." Success will not be achieved by following our natural tastes, habits, and human tendencies. Success is based on development of skills. As Napoleon Hill stated, in *Think and Grow Rich* (1965), the biggest secret to success is to plan time to develop good habits. These good habits are the key ingredients because they enable you to do the actions that "failures" avoid and find too difficult to begin.

4. Successful teachers manage student learning effectively by (a) creating better plans, (b) developing yearly plans for each subject, and (c) planning with their students. In addition, these teachers report that they plan *their* time carefully, even though some acknowledged that it is difficult for them to do so (Tschudin, 1978; and Weade, 1985).

5. Most successful teachers have the ability to wait for long periods of time to see their plans bear fruit.

6. Good planners set aside time to analyze their time use to uncover better time uses even though the analysis can be difficult and time consuming. On the other hand, less successful teachers tend to be satisfied "with whatever results they can obtain by just doing the things they like to do" (Douglass and Douglass, 1980).

7. In planning you can set the highest of goals and strive for the very best. But even if your best efforts fail, do not become disappointed. Some planners even allow for setbacks in deference to Murphy's law: "If something can go wrong, it will."

GETTING YOUR GOALS IN GEAR

The following list specifies nine methods of beginning to work on large classroom goals more rapidly and profitably. Place a check before the method(s) that most appeal to you.

_____ 1. If you have difficulty taking control over time, begin by selecting one thing that you will exchange from your normal daily plans so as to have time to work in your new area of specialty or goal, for example, delegating the watering of class plants and cleaning the aquarium so you can begin to set up the new science kit.

_____ 2. If you consider yourself to be highly structured, you may find it easier to categorize your new goals and block out segments of time to work on a new goal. You may also like tying the new habit or goal to a second, student-related priority. To illustrate, a secondary physical education teacher wanted to improve her own physical fitness level, so she built a unit on aerobic dancing for her students, and worked out with them daily.

_____ 3. If you tend to overcommit, you may plan to reach new goals by finding a better way to do regular tasks. To begin, you can ask close friends to tell you what they perceive that you are spending too much time doing. Then you could ask them to tell you what they might do to save time in that activity.

_____ 4. If you enjoy team teaching, working in professional projects, or frequently use small groups for instruction, you may find that you accomplish new goals more easily when you begin a "buddy program." Suppose you and a friend set aside 15 minutes or more a week, usually during your planning periods, to discuss your weekly plans to reach new goals. These "buddy talks" center only on the new goal each is striving toward and are timed. You will support and motivate each other to continue.

_____ 5. If you enjoy challenges or working alone, you may want to make your goal into a game. By taking a risk and by giving yourself big rewards, you can set up an individualized system or record-keeping system for keeping track of your progress. When new goals are reached, you can establish a new challenge and a new record-keeping method and design a new reward.

_____ 6. If you have a close relationship with your principal or supervisor, you may want to write down your goal and describe the plan you want to use to your principal (or supervisor). The principal gives his or her approval and suggestions for improving the plan. The principal, then, keeps the plan you wrote and later "informally checks" with you to see if your goal was met as scheduled. A more subtle approach is to write down your goals and plan and fold and staple them to the date in your lesson plan book on which it is to be accomplished. This goal would be a personal goal for your professional development.

_____ 7. If you have artistic ability, you could graph your goal, using colors and symbols to depict the degrees of difficulty you anticipate.

_____ 8. If you enjoy leading others, you may accomplish more by planning to work on your goals as if they were group projects. Your goals will be actualized by guiding your students and colleagues. Your leadership may create a positive, productive climate and build the confidence and successes of others in the process.

_____ 9. If you accomplish more when you initiate several activities at a moderate- to low-risk level, you can mark out a column in your lesson plan book to record your special goals and their plan. You may also benefit from systematically making a list of yearly goals in the back of your lesson plan book.

By selecting a method from this list and trying this technique, you have already taken the first step to increase your job productivity and satisfaction. Before reading the rest of the chapter, pause. Write one talent-centered goal so as to review all you've learned to date. Practice this new skill this month using one of the nine methods just listed. Remember that good objectives must answer, "What do you really want?" "What skills and talents will you enjoy using to get what you want?" and "What sign will be the clearest to you that you indeed reached your goal?" Write this goal on a separate sheet of paper. Place this paper in Chapter 7. We'll refer to it then.

THE DO'S AND DON'T'S OF MAKING LISTS

Many educators make daily lists of things that need to be done. Many do not. The decision about which method will be the best for your self-improvement in teaching and time management will be one that you will make, based on your analysis of personal teaching style, as you read this section of the book.

One leading psychologist, Dennis Waitley (1981), cites the following benefits one can receive from making daily lists:

1. Small tasks can be organized into groups so they can be completed more rapidly and with less effort.
2. The mind and desk can be cleared of lower-priority items that might otherwise be forgotten.
3. Priorities for the day can be more easily established.
4. Goals will become more concrete as you will probably have written down steps you will take to accomplish them. You feel accomplishment as you check each goal off.
5. Each time you look at the list, you will be called back to thinking about your priorities for the day, possibly causing you to make better individual decisions concerning your use of time.
6. The list helps to refocus your attention on your goals so you become more like a rifle shot of efficiency than like a shotgun of diversification.
7. When lists are composed mentally, at the end of the previous day and in reference to weekly goals, you may give yourself a psychological head start for the coming day.
8. Daily lists may help you to modify the amount of emphasis you give to weekly goals, continually updating them and making them more realistic.

Alternatively, daily lists can cause the following effects for teachers:

1. They can serve as a method of procrastinating; as a substitute use of energy, "list making" could take away time and energy needed to begin work on the tasks themselves.
2. Daily lists can limit one's abilities to recognize and respond to spontaneous opportunities of the moment and the joys resultant from the unexpected.
3. Daily lists can force one into a "1–2–3" structure that limits creativity.
4. Writing daily lists ignores the force of natural highs and lows of energy levels very often.
5. Daily goal-setting activities decrease some people's motivation and time use skills; by spending the first 10 minutes of each day drawing up a "to do" list, some depress their drive to begin, psychologically convincing themselves that the day is probably going to be rushed.
6. Daily lists can inhibit one's flexibility, as most people are inclined to do the daily activities in the written order they created, doing them as separate units, limiting management experimentation.
7. "To Do Today" lists can serve as justifications for never doing the tasks on the list. That is, sometimes just by writing an item on the list people can demonstrate that they "Really want to do the task but they just don't have time to do it."
8. Putting something a person does not like to do on a daily list can subconsciously force the person to do the entries listed above that item more slowly, ensuring that time will not be available to do that undesirable activity.

You may wish to experiment before you decide if daily lists are good for your teaching performances. By trying days when you do and do not use lists, you can analyze your accomplishments more specifically.

I find that I benefit from daily lists on days when my mind is cluttered with minor, unrelated, low-priority items. However, on days when I have major projects to complete, I take care of smaller priorities as they occur so I can return to the project with a clear mind. On days when I don't use lists to guide me, I find I improve my ability to say "no" effectively. That is, without a list of items that may contain something I'd really rather put off, I have less need to say "yes" to new lower-priority demands so as to avoid starting the next item on my list. As I decreased my use of daily lists, I increased my ability to remember important mental lists I make. I can place more trust in my own mental capacity to do what is important and what I've promised.

This is the type of analysis you will do as you decide whether or not daily lists increase your teaching performances. Each analysis will be different, and each will help to separate teachers in separate ways. As stated previously, the choice "to do" or "not to do" daily lists is yours. Some types of days a list could be used and others not.

PUTTING YOUR PLANS AND GOALS TO WORK

Now that we have several methods of implementing goals, we must break the natural inertia and move thoughts to outcomes. In the final analysis, success will mean that we've acted.

I have used each of the following actions to nudge myself from "the dreaming" to "the being" stage, from talking a good plan to beginning to act. Others have told me that they work for them as well. I hope they assist you as much:

1. Sometimes when you've been thinking about doing something for a while you may need to just get up and turn off the TV and, while standing, literally "take the first step to action." This is easier to do since the first step has already been taken (the walk to turn off the TV). It may seem trivial, but mentally labeling a simple, unrelated task as the first step in pursuit of a goal makes the first step of the goal process begin faster.

2. If you try to identify which habits detract and which compliment your new goal, you can make your goals more habitual. Taking this mental notation can help you accomplish more. The increased self-knowledge is multiplicative as you will be able to apply this greater self-knowledge to the next goal you attempt.

3. Sometimes it may help you to continue toward your goal if you recall this definition: "Courage is being afraid to do something but going ahead and doing it anyway." You may have also have learned that waiting to build a commitment to something is not necessary before you take an action toward a goal. In some cases commitment will come only after you have begun working, and then, during the process or even after the work and investments have been completed, commitment toward the goal will have been created. Sometimes the commitment comes through your appreciation of the increased talents that working on the task unexpectedly created for you.

4. As early as 1959, McCoy named one method of beginning plans. He discovered that the most progressive managers in business are those who practice "selectivity." They have a keen ability (apparently developed through practice) to identify the goals, tasks, and systems of personal evaluation that are becoming obsolete. They dispense with these practices without remorse, as soon as possible.

5. A very effective method of beginning is to delegate a section of the work to someone else who would grow from completing the task. This approach is effective because many people are motivated by a desire to develop others and are stimulated by the company of someone else who is enjoying the work.

6. Dr. Robert Tennov, (1984) a behavioral consultant and professor of psychology at the University of Bridgeport-Connecticut, pointed out that beginning projects at your peak level of your "biological clock" makes "the beginning" almost effortless. The five personal performance levels are described next. They fluctuate with each person's physiological and psychological well-being. The peak is when you have most mental energy to learn new things and when new ideas evolve rapidly. By beginning important projects at these times, you can capture and use thoughts that cannot be generated at lower points in the day.

The *good level* is when one is aware that most things are done well and easily. The *average level* is most easily identified by the fact that you can complete complex tasks and behaviors well, but when new aspects are introduced you do not seem to pick them up easily. The next to the lowest level is the *relaxed, pleasant level*. At this stage you can function well if the tasks are easy. *Low levels* can be identified when you do not want to think about something, think about something any longer, or wish to delay making decisions.

When are the peak times of your day? _____
When are the good periods? _____
The average periods? _____
The relaxed periods? _____
The low periods (for most people between 4:00 and 6:00 P.M.)? _____

7. If you have an unrealistic view of yourself, you may set goals that are too high. You will also often be afraid to act because you are convinced that your work will not be perfect. The key to avoid these unrealistic fears is to learn to use a new personal assessment of your skills or plans. You may want to ask your principal what strengths he or she feels should be used to complete a particular task.

8. Have you ever found yourself saying "I wish I had the time to . . . " If so, you might want to begin to try the following self-talk as a substitute: "I'll take the first step right now." That is, in the future when you are tempted to wish for more time, make yourself follow every "I wish I had time to" statement with the words "I'll take the first step now, by doing . . . ." Make yourself do one small part of your goal the moment you are tempted to tell yourself you can't. For example, a secondary English teacher wanted to have more time to share poetry with his students. The next time he went to the library, he "took the first step now" by taking a minute's time to check out a good poetry book. As he led students back to the room, he selected a short poem and then read it to the class as soon as they all returned. Then the next few weeks as he walked to and from the library he carried and read that book so he could practice the next poem he would share with the class. The class began to enjoy poetry, and he felt like a more accomplished teacher.

9. Some teachers find that they accomplish more if they write out a plan and read over it at the beginning of the day. Then they review the plan

at the end of the day, evaluating their progress and writing, in detail, parts of the plan that were difficult for them. You may even benefit from posting reminders to yourself at appropriate spots in your lesson plan books or teacher's manuals so as to improve your ability to implement certain sections (e.g., ''Remember to monitor seatwork better today.'').

LESSON PLANS: THE KEY
TO ALL SUCCESS

Teaching is one of the few professions where every moment has a scheduled activity. That is, for optimal goals to be reached, teachers set complete agendas for each day. Even business executives report that they do not plan activity for 50 percent or more of their time. Because planning skills are such an integral component of the teaching repertoire, good teachers most often use exceptionally well-prepared lesson plans.

While there are many types of lesson plan formats, there is a major difference among plans used by most and least successful teachers. The difference is not in the format followed but in the fact that the less successful spend less time thinking and may have spent more time than the successful teachers writing elaborate formats and detailed activities within a lesson plan.

A master lesson plan is shown in Figure 1-5. This format results from a culmination of several research studies designed to identify the elements that best stimulate learning. This form can be reproduced and placed as a marker in your lesson plan book. This will enable you to reference it frequently until the format becomes automatic. It will also serve as a reminder of sections that you have not yet implemented as well as you would like. While each lesson will not be as detailed as the form illustrates, all thoughts represented on the form should be considered in each lesson delivered.

Research has also uncovered that teachers who followed the principles outlined in the following format (1) were significantly better lesson planners, even to the point of giving students long-range calendars of assignmetns and posting daily assignments; (2) were more prepared; (3) gave better academic presentations, such as giving the rationale for lessons and rules/procedures needed to follow; (4) explained concepts in more concrete terms; (5) guided students in practicing the concepts more frequently; (6) retaught concepts when necessary; (7) provided new information often; (8) divided complex tasks into simpler tasks easily; and (9) used concrete examples more frequently (O'Neal, 1984; and Wyne and Stuck, 1982). Also these teachers demonstrated to project positive benefits to enhance the students' desire to begin the lesson (Green and Rasinski, 1985).

Before you study the Master Lesson Plan Format, determine if you have any of the following problems in delivering lessons. If you do, the actions in the left-hand column have increased the effectiveness of lessons. These suggestions are adaptations of time management principles used in business.

Moving from one topic to another too rapidly or putting in too much trivial or extraneous information

Make an outline of content and stick to it; hold back complexities until main points are developed.

Giving too many directions or presenting too much too quickly

Give everything in steps, for example, step 1, step 2; check for understanding before proceeding.

Being ambiguous or indefinite such as saying "maybe," "more or less," "you know," "not always," "sort of"

Refer to concrete objects or examples; state what is correct and what is not correct and why.

Moving too rapidly to next topic because time is short or because no student asks a question

Ask one or two students to summarize the main points or to make up a question to ask the remainder of the class to see if the class is understanding the main points being covered.

Having time covering all the lesson plan in a single period

In the left margin of each lesson plan, write down approximately how many minutes each section will take as you write the lesson plan.

SUMMING UP

In summary, if you had to cite three important skills you gained from reading this chapter, they would be

1. _____
   _____

2. _____
   _____

3. _____
   _____

My list includes (1) to plan on a daily, weekly, "rhythmical," and yearly basis; (2) to strengthen my conscious use and awareness of the need to identify my talents; and (3) to increase my lesson planning skills.

Figure 1-5

MASTER LESSON PLAN FORMAT

Begin lesson on time.

Preplanning Thoughts:

— Is this lesson one of the essential elements I am to cover this year?

— Can I use this lesson as a means of varying the size of the group, the room arrangement, use of concrete objects, holding class outside or in another room to increase learning potential?

— Does the lesson provide for students with auditory, visual, tactile, and kinesthetic learning modalities?

— What method of grading (to check to be sure students have learned) will be fastest in giving good feedback to students and eliminate the amount of time I have to spend grading papers?

— Consider how your time should be spent during this lesson. According to Davis (1951), first-line supervisors should spend 30 percent (15 minutes every 50-minute period) managing and delegating the learning process and 70 percent or 35 minutes doing/leading/creating the learning process.

— What level of mastery do I expect?

— What amount, depth, and variety of coverage do I expect and need?

— What are the affective needs of the class?

— What attention span needs will this lesson demand and does this match with the time of day and year that this lesson will occur?

— What type of pacing is demanded by the logical analysis of the content and what perceptions do I have of the amount of group cooperation I can expect?

Mental Set: Accomplished by one of three ways: Students will be motivated to learn by (1) planning a mental set that shows relevance of the lesson to their lives, (2) pointing out how this lesson will explain a discrepancy in past learnings or past experiences they may not have been able to explain before, or (3) arousing their curiosity.

Rationale: This section presents a need for future use of the concept they will learn.

Objective: This is one of the two most important sections of the lesson plan. This should be written or stated in terms you will use to tell students exactly what they are going to do, how they will do it, and how they will know they have been successful.

Input: This is the second most important part of the lesson. This is the section that most influences the amount students learn and the section that is easiest to do a poor job of delivering. This is where the concept is taught, not merely where instructions for how to do a problem are given to the class. Many teachers never *teach* the concept. Some tell how to do or how students can try to learn something, but they never create the learning for their students through planning a specific method of giving input about the concept. In Chapter 7 there are 62 activities you can use in this input section. The following listing is a collection of strategies that create learning experiences and teach students concepts. You can use the list to identify which of the strategies best matches the features of the concept to be taught. The strategy can be used to clarify the strategy, processes, objects, symbols, and critical attributes so that students will be clearly able to identify the

Figure 1-5 continued

concept during the modeling, guided practice and independent practice sessions of the lesson plan, when examples and non-examples will be used in the instruction. If you chose to use a discovery method in this input section, you could (1) lead the students to discover the process or principle involved, (2) ask questions or lead the student to perform the skill or concept, (3) have students verbalize or question what is to be done or what they are attempting to discover, (4) skillfully highlight "correct" questions and answers so teacher cues and guided questioning can be reduced, or (5) delineate the possibility that students will make a wrong deduction as they begin to learn something brand new. To select an item on the list, you match the attributes of the concept to be taught to one of the strategies that would best illustrate those attributes.

1. Undertake peer reteaching.
2. Use examples and non-examples.
3. Model the concept.
4. Tell an interesting series of facts about the concept.
5. Conduct peer teaching in small groups.
6. Ask students to write down questions over material read that classmates will answer.
7. Incorporate a question and answer period.
8. Institute student-led discussion period.
9. Assign simulations.
10. Role play.
11. Schedule demonstration teaching by a student who has a special talent concerning the topic to be learned.
12. Schedule reciprocal teaching with a colleague.
13. Conduct research.
14. Brainstorm.
15. Encourage students to make decisions about what should be learned next concerning a topic.
16. Conduct small-group discussions.
17. Create a seminar: students present formal papers as if speaking at a professional association meeting.
18. Review case studies.
19. Write plan and design a new curriculum.
20. Make displays.
21. Develop a task force.
22. Develop creativity.
23. Undertake problem solving.
24. Do laboratory work.
25. Offer a critique of one's teaching strategy.
26. Offer a critique of peer's teaching strategy.
27. Offer a critique of expert's teaching strategy.
28. Engage in team teaching.
29. Give audiovisual presentation.
30. Give workshop.

continued

Figure 1-5 continued

31. Do independent study.
32. Do a research project.
33. Visit within one's building.
34. Visit within one's district.
35. Interview consultants.
36. Make a film or videotape.
37. Participate in a professional organization.
38. Interview students/colleagues.
39. Interview community resource people.
40. Have classroom officers design lessons and create new activities to meet individual/group/student needs.
41. Employ a learning point system.
42. Use timings or time limits (as detailed in Radicchi, 1984) where students practice a particular activity for a set amount of time and challenge them to run a contest between themselves to see if they can get more done within the same amount of time in repeated timings.
43. When using dittos or a standardized handout for the entire class, make hand-written headings, summaries, or funny/motivational comments to increase student interest and attention, or write in adjunct questions individualized to this class's experiences.
44. Use the "keywork method" of teaching major concepts (concept is paired with as attribute that begins with same letter and cartoon is drawn whereby two people talk about concept and attribute).
45. Use "fish bowl" or expanded-groups method whereby a small group of students interact with you to learn a concept and the remainder of the class sits in a semicircle around the group and watches but does not participate.
46. Divide students into two pairs representing the pro and con sides. This method promotes more verbal rehearsal, exchange of assigned material, more concern that students learn the assigned material, more active search for more information about the topic being studied, more reevaluation of one's positions, more attitude change, more liking for the subject matter and the instructional experience, higher self-esteem, and more accepting and supporting relationship among handicapped and nonhandicapped students than did debates or individual study where students were given all the information on both the pro and con sides of the argument.

Modeling: Teacher shares an example of the concept to ensure that the first transfer the students make is correct.

1. Show the student the process.
2. Apply the rule to an event that occurred in class.
3. Draw an inference that shows the concept in a form in which it normally occurs in our world.
4. Make a metaphor or visual image or find a picture that illustrates several attributes of the concept.
5. Draw an analogy or tell a story that is in a setting where the concept's use would be familiar.

Figure 1-5 continued

6. Act as if you are talking to yourself and "thinking through" the way you first learned or the way you presently use the concept.

7. Walk through an example of the concept together except you ask no questions of the class, only of yourself, to ensure that the first experience with the concept involves 100% correct information.

Guided Practice: The students work as many samples under your direction as they feel they need to understand it well enough to begin to practice it and use it by themselves. The types of samples to use include

1. Questions or activities concerning the concept using each level of thinking on Bloom's taxonomy (knowledge comprehension, application, analysis, synthesis, and evaluation levels).

2. Introducing a general thematic area and to enliven the learning process by evoking a feeling of student's personal relevance to learning and self-motivation to continue to learn more.

3. Arousing a sense of disequilibrium in students so they begin to initiate their own questions about the concept because of the unusualness of the examples used in the guided practice or the discrepancies that were introduced.

4. Increasing the student's motivation to read on or to attend to the concept more actively.

5. Interpreting the general concept more by giving several concrete examples, vivid evidences, tests of the truth of the statements, and use of counter examples if limits of the concept need to be clarified so that transfers of the material become evident when future generalizations are cited.

Independent Practice: Sufficient time is provided for students to learn, practice, use, and remember the skill without interruption from you or other students. Students should come to you only to ask questions about aspects of complicated applications of the concept or to ask questions concerning an incorrect connection they made between two attributes of the concept. This section is really the test of your effectiveness in teaching the concept. If the students' questions concern material you covered on key or basic aspects of the concept, then you know your *input section* was not as effective as you had hoped. You may want to plan a new, mini-input reteaching lesson, using a new strategy for the next day. The feedback you give during the independent practice segments differs significantly from the types given during guided practice. In independent practice, feedback is in the form of questions about why the students think they are having difficulty with the section they ask about, questions about why they feel they are unable to work a particular part alone. Any explanations a teacher gives should involve how to figure out the underlying concept rather than how to figure out the particular example of the concept about which the student inquires. The teacher should ask students to begin to call upon their own reasoning in moments of doubt and uncertainty by asking themselves questions at the application and analysis levels, e.g., How is this similar to the ones we worked together earlier in our lesson? Tell me what you think you need to know to be able to do these by yourself?

If a student asks if an answer is correct or not, ask him or her why he or she is asking you to verify or ask what part of the concept is still not clear. Alternatively, ask the student to take a position, to decide if he or she thinks it is correct and then to justify that position/decision.

continued

Figure 1-5 continued

Generalization/Summary/Restatement of the Objective/Diagnostic Progress Test: In this section of the lesson, you or the students restate the objective as a review, a teaching strategy to enhance retention, and a means of completing the gestalt of the lesson. Alternatively, this can be a testing setting, where students can demonstrate to you and themselves how much they have learned.

Transitions: Use of an established routine to move from one lesson plan to the next or the use of overlapping activities to move from one to another activity.

Additions That Can Be Made to the Lesson Plan Format: Based on the types of interactions you intend to have with students, the level of your own competence, and the type of teaching environment in which you work, one or more of the following additions may be needed in a lesson plan:

1. List of the individual needs of students that will need a scheduled time to reteach the concept at another time during the day or week.
2. Work for early finishers.
3. Criteria for grading.
4. Prerequisites necessary for the lesson.
5. System whereby one can check off the parts of the lesson students learned.
6. Types of reinforcements that will be used.
7. References one will make to help students make associations to past learnings or personal experiences.
8. Tests of retention.
9. Creative, effective, efficient evaluations to be certain learnings have transferred.
10. Good motivational lead-ins.
11. Where this lesson can be stored to be best referenced in the future.
12. Something nice that you can tell the students about themselves and their performances that you will tell them that day.
13. Checklist of a variety of methods and materials that one wants to be sure to use during the year.
14. Specific reactions to lesson plans students stated, for example, specific comments made concerning what helped them learn the most or what they enjoyed the most.
15. Rescue methods, ways to reach the objective if an interruption occurs.
16. Resource gathering.
17. Developing student self-management skills in producing their own learning.
18. Notations of obstacles to avoid the next time the lesson is used.
19. Personal, professional development objective that is for one's own development and is unrelated to the objective the students are to learn.

REFERENCES

Cox, Carol. "The Early Mental Traits of Three Hundred Geniuses." In L. Terman, ed., *Genetic Studies of Genius*, Vol. II. Stanford, Calif.: Stanford University Press, 1926.

Davis, Robert. "Time and Motion Study of First Line Supervisors in Four Job Types," *Journal of Human Resource Management*, Vol. II, No. 4, Spring 1951 pp. 47–59.

Douglass, Merrill, and Donna Douglass. *Manage Your Time, Manage Your Work, Manage Yourself*. New York: Amacon, 1980.

Goertzel, Vernon, and Marie Goertzel. *Cradles of Eminence*. Boston: Little, Brown, 1962.

Green, Judith L., and Timothy Rasinski. "Teacher Style and Classroom Management: Stability and Variation Across Instructional Events." Paper presented at the annual convention of the American Educational Research Association in Chicago, April 1985.

Hill, Arthur. "Time Use." In Pearson, P. David; Barr, Rebecca; Kamil, Michael; Mosenthal (ED) *Handbook of Reading Research*, New York: NY: Longman, Inc., 1984, pp 60–79.

Hill, Napoleon. *Think and Grow Rich*. Chicago: Combined Registry, 1965.

MacKenzie, Alec. *The Time Trap*. New York: McGraw-Hill, 1975.

McCoy, James T. *Management of Time*. Englewood Cliffs, NJ: Prentice-Hall, 1959.

Meerloo, Joost A. M. *Along the Fourth Dimension: Man's Sense of Time and History*. New York: John Day, 1970.

O'Neal, Sharon. "Staff Development Strategy for Improving Teacher Practice (One Plan Does Not Fit All)." *R & DCTE Review: The Newsletter of The Research and Development Center for Teacher Education*, Vol. II, no. 3, September–December 1984, 3–5.

Radicchi, Judy. "Use of Timings and Time Spaced Learning in the Elementary Classroom." In Pearson, P.D., Barr, Rebecca; Kamil, Michael & Mosenthal, Peter (ED) *Handbook of Research on Reading*, New York, NY: Longman, 1984, p. 32–64.

Russell, Walter. *Reflections on Humanity*. New York, NY: McGraw-Hill, 1974, p. 19.

Rutherford, Robert. *Just in Time: Immediate Help for the Time-Pressured*. New York: Wiley-Interscience, 1981.

Spinoza, Benedict. *Ethics*. Everyman Edition, translated by Andrew Boyle, Part IV, 1677.

Tennov, Robert. "Working With Your Biological Clock," personal communication, 1984.

Thomas, John. "Agency and Achievement: Self-management and Self-regard." *Review of Educational Research*, Vol. 50, No. 2, 1980, 213–240.

Tschudin, Ruth. "Secrets of A+ Teaching." *Instructor*, Vol. 88, September 1978, 65–74.

Waitley, Dennis. *The Psychology of Winning*. Los Angeles: Dynocal, 1981.

Weade, Regina. "Lesson Construction and Instructional Management: An Exploration of Social and Academic Content Demands Within Lessons." Paper presented at the annual meeting of the American Educational Research Association, Chicago, March 31–April 4, 1985.

Wyne, M. D., and G. B. Stuck. "Time and Learning: Implications for the Classroom Teacher." *Elementary School Journal*, Vol. 83, No. 1, September 1982, 67–75.

two

Eight Ways
to Manage Your Time

A Teacher Comments on Chapter 2

In the teaching profession, it is easy to feel that we haven't accomplished much, that everything we've done is no better than anyone else in our position could do. I have always been intrigued at how fast and effectively teachers must work to be able to present a lesson that produces solid results.

High-quality teaching requires clear thinking. If we can "automate" certain routine movements in the classroom, our minds can be working and organizing thoughts. Chapter 2 taught me to think before I do my work and to analyze the way I organize my work. It has shown me why some teachers are truly able to be the best.

Ana Colón
Special Education Teacher
San Juan, Puerto Rico

Time is a constant we pass through;It cannot be stopped or expanded.But when we manage the way we use time,It becomes the priceless resource it was designed to be.

—Cathy Collins

You've already come a long way in managing your time and becoming a stronger educator. I hope you are more confident and clear about the goals and talents that are most important to our profession, your students, your colleagues, and yourself.

Now we'll add power to these goals. *You'll put time to work.* In this chapter we'll learn the eight most important methods of managing time. Through them we will not only learn to stomp out procrastination but to finish every task. We'll also learn to delegate time. By developing these skills we will no longer fall prey to the force of unmanaged time.

Before we begin, let's see if we agree on a few points about people and time:

1. When we've been given a big task to do, we know we should begin to work on it immediately, but we usually put it off, at least for a while. True_____ False_____

2. Whenever we've failed at a task, we tend to remind ourselves that we might fail again, and we defer acting on that task. True _____ False _____

3. If we are assigned a task that we've never done before, or one that isn't clearly defined, we do simpler tasks first in an attempt to delay the difficult assignment. True _____ False _____

All these statements are true. Psychologists label the reasons why we respond in these ways as "fortifications against foes." These tendencies are natural. We use these defenses as our "gathering of arms" to guard against (1) the perceived dangers of failure, risk, and ridicule; and (2) the ramifications of (a) doing something wrong, (b) being hurt, (c) having to change, (d) suffering discomfort or embarrassment, or (e) losing prestige. When we have finished this chapter, we will no longer need to hope that, if we just wait, our task will become less difficult or cause us less discomfort. Instead, we'll begin our work quickly, delegate time to our most advantageous skills, and substitute newly mastered time management skills for the unproductive defenses we now use in our fight against time.

The remainder of this chapter has eight parts. Each begins with the introduction of a major time management method. Each concludes with practice sessions. Feel free to read the entire chapter now, in one sitting, or spend as long as you need practicing one method before reading the next. By the end of this chapter, you'll know exactly what to do when you feel ineffective because (1) you are uninspired, (2) you are asked to do something that is outside your areas of expertise, (3) you are beginning to do things with less quality than you demand, (4) you are bored, or (5) you have left something before it was completed.

BEGIN NOW, BUT NOT AT THE BEGINNING

To become the most effective and efficient educators, we must know where to begin a task. New, "dreaded," or vague tasks should not be started where logic tells us to begin. Higher-quality products are produced in the shortest time when we begin our work with either clearly defined sections or ones we can already do well. Ironically, these sections will not be the opening sections of the task. These sections are usually characterized as statements of focus or purpose. As such, they cannot be completed without thorough familiarity with the content's scope and sequence. This is the exact knowledge we lack when a task is new to us; thus structuring a beginning at the beginning of our work is next to impossible. As a result, we often have only two recourses: we procrastinate and not begin at all, or we grow anxious and try to do something but fail.

Henceforth, as soon as a new, or not clearly defined, task is assigned, you will begin (1) at a point that is interesting to you, (2) with something you've done before, or (3) with a part that calls upon one of your talents. We'll view this new task as a series of small, conquerable pieces. The project will become increasingly more distinct, and the tendency to procrastinate will vanish.

Second, as we select work sections, on the basis of one of the preceding choices, rather than by the order in which they will appear in the finished project, we will help the big task "get going." Further, because this plan allows us to accomplish several, talent-filled work sections quickly, we can finish a large amount of work without having to risk very much or experience failure.

In the time it will take others to convince themselves that the task "really *is* hard," you, armed with several successful accomplishments, will have accumulated content familiarity and mounted several skill-producing experiences, self-confidence, commitment, and drive to tackle the task's hardest aspects. Concurrently, you will have increased the amount of time you want to sustain involvement with the work. This increased level of involvement will be necessary when the more complex, general, or difficult sections are tackled.

Third, by using the *begin now, but begin not at the beginning* method, you will rapidly reach a point of sustained attention where you will not want to stop and you will learn that big tasks can be accomplished.

There are five steps to take as soon as difficult, vague, and/or creative tasks are assigned.

Step 1: Identify Why You Aren't Enthusiastic About Doing the Assigned Task

When we begin our "big tasks," we should begin with the thought, "What single, easy task can I do right now?" or "What would I like to do right now?" instead of asking, "Where in the world will I find the time to do this 'really tough job'?" Factors that diminish our enthusiasm include the facts that we (1) prejudge the task as one that is just too enormous to do in the time available, (2) have a fear of failure, (3) are unsure as to the design of the end project, and/or (4) need to be inspired or creative on the task.

We must pinpoint exactly what we are dreading. This realization sets our subconscious in motion. It will help us to overcome the fear.

Step 2: Do What You Can That's Easy Right Now

We will begin to work on something related to the task just as soon as the task is assigned. That is, the instant a task is assigned, instead of saying "O.K. I'll do it" and laying the materials on the desk, you will begin to do something related to the task even before you lay it aside for the first time. In this way, the work becomes your own. You will become committed to the possibilities it holds, and you will not procrastinate in the future. Then, before you set the task aside, you will block out a future time when you will return to it.

Step 3: Set Aside Blocks of Time to Work and Do Not Set Specific Objectives to Finish

Success, in first working sessions with this type of task will be measured by whether we stayed with the task for the period of time we committed to rather than how many things we completed. This method of scheduling work is akin to the way people make creative monuments, that is, people who conceived and began work on Mount Rushmore first just had to work for eight hours a day chipping away chunks of rock. (While we will take little breaks when needed, we will never leave the task until the time we've set aside has elapsed, regardless of whether we can begin to see the end product or not.) It's only after the parameters of "big tasks" are established that we can begin to assess the time needed to complete specific parts of a task (e.g., only when the "heads" on Mount Rushmore were carved could the sculptors begin to establish a reliable estimate of how long it would take to complete the "noses".)

In the past, in the early working stages of big tasks, if you set specific objectives to accomplish, you, inadvertently, built in your own failures. That is, due to the vagueness of the time required to complete such objectives, you would either have gotten frustrated because it was taking so long to do so little and you'd stop or the task would take such a surprisingly short amount of time that you'd want to work longer but wouldn't want to put forth the effort or know what objective to do next so you'd quit "early" and waste time, or begin to procrastinate.

Alternatively, in the early working stages of big tasks, you should plan to set aside a block of time to work on the project and work that full amount of time regardless of how much or how little work was completed.

Serendipitously, when you plan your work in blocks of time this way, you really begin to enjoy the work and you do your best. You complete what you set out to complete! You do not pressure yourselves to do the impossible. You work diligently for as long as you had established you wanted to work. When you're done, you set your next block of time to return to the project and then walk away, feeling proud that you stuck to your goal.

Step 4: Pause to Think When an Impasse Is Reached

Never leave a task when you don't know how to proceed. Instead, think about how much has already been accomplished. Replay each part of what has been done. Then think about methods of resolving the specific problem you faced and brainstorm. Dissect the problem; see all parts separately. Apply all your talents to each section. Using this step means, that occasionally during your blocks of work time, you'll just sit, seemingly doing nothing. But, in reality, at the very least, if the thinking time does not resolve the problem, you will have used the unexpired time to develop self-discipline and put the subconscious to work so your next work session will be more productive. Others may get stumped, leave, and delay their work. But not you. You will learn to sit still and think because you've set aside a block of unexpired time that you're controlling.

Step 5: Remember That the First Time You Attempt a New Plan or Task, Your "Perfect Self" Will Rarely Be Viewed and You Will Rarely Reach Your High Level of Performance

By growing more accustomed to the way you feel, look, and act in new situations, you will place yourselves in more growth-producing situations and continue to expand your skills.

Right now, we all have some task that needs this time management method, I believe. It could be a school talent show, science fair, track meet, annual report, school newspaper, art motif, class schedule, curriculum guide revision, field trip arrangements, establishing an honor society, initiating a parent education program, beginning a Reading Is Fundamental Free Book program.

Why are you delaying? What is the worst thing that could happen if you began right now to work on it? . . . Now, let's get to work. What can you do on the task right now?

By practicing this method often you'll almost automatically find yourself beginning certain tasks at points other than the beginning. You'll experience significant increases in productivity. I am glad you are beginning to use it now.

LEAVE IT LYING AROUND

Alan Lakein, a leading time management consultant, discovered that certain tasks have to be "seen often" before you make a commitment to complete them. Thus, you should leave some things just lying around. This is especially true for those tasks where some parts have merit but you aren't exactly sure what you want to do with them. It is important that "lying-around tasks" are convenient, easily accessible, and seen daily. By frequently seeing the task or a note of reminder, you will be nudged to complete the task. Also, because your task is so accessible, in times when you normally would be doing nothing, you will tend to work on the task, even if for just a few minutes.

The main psychological impact of lying-around tasks is that they help to remind us that time is under our control. That is, you will gain confidence that you will work on the task when the time is right and each time you choose. You begin to realize that you are in control of the tasks. Before you set lying-around tasks in view, you might have convinced yourself you were not "capable enough," "smart enough," "disciplined enough," or "in control of your time enough" to do the things you value.

To use this method, leave materials as they were when you last worked on them, if at all possible. Materials are not restacked, but neatly, purposefully arranged, inviting you back to work. By leaving the materials available, you do not waste time putting materials up, then getting them back out again, reorganizing, refocusing on where you were, getting ready to begin, then, getting out of the mood, deciding to stop, restacking materials back together again in their "storage order" (as opposed to their "working order"), and then wondering when you will ever have enough time to get to this really important thing done that you want to do.

Instead, each time we use the lying-around method, we see our task and think about it a little more. Each time we do, we, mentally, if not actually, work on the part we last left. Even if we work on the task only a few seconds a week, the evenly spaced work, over an extended period of time, causes the quality of the tasks to improve. In addition, a need for closure develops and gives added momentum to complete the work.

We, as teachers, have a tendency to abuse this method, however. Only 5 percent of all tasks can pass the test of "qualifying" to become good "lying-around tasks" (Leas, 1978). That is, before a task should be left out, it must be

1. A task we are anxious to complete.
2. A task we look forward to completing.
3. Valuable to us and a priority in our professional lives.
4. Capable of being neatly and attractively arranged in the space available.
5. A task we feel pressured to complete.

Tasks that respond well to this method are (1) to-do lists; (2) checklists; (3) books to be ordered; (4) new props or equipment to be made or repaired; (5) new teaching methods being created; (6) routine cleaning tasks, such as leaving the scrubber needed to clean the aquarium in view near the desk; (7) things you enjoy doing but have to be in the mood to begin; and (8) role sheets or forms to be completed.

This method is very successful. Because you work on lying-around tasks when you want to work on them, the quality of your work rises. Because you only work when you enjoy working, your thinking is more flexible and innovative.

It's important to note that tasks of this type may lie around for a long time before the right moment comes along to begin work. You can judge if you are using the correct method with the task if the passage of time only increases the value of the task and makes it more appealing to you.

In closing, do not throw old, unfinished lying-around tasks away. By filing them, they can be referenced when a new purpose or piece of information is available. You may be amazed at how quickly lying-around tasks are finished when the right moment finally arrives. To illustrate, a high school geometry teacher was using this method, working on a task, sporadically for seven months. Suddenly, the long-awaited "insight" to complete it arrived. He was finished in 15 minutes. He later told me that had he forced himself to work on the task one moment sooner, it would have taken him weeks and it would have been completed with less quality. This story illustrates one of the most fascinating principles of time management: sometimes time management means that you don't make time for something but that you recognize and capture the right time for things.

What lying-around task would you like to create today? It might be as simple as beginning the plant growing project by digging out the radish seeds package from the back of your desk drawer and "laying it around" (placing it on top of your desk). It might be as comprehensive as relocating the trigonometry text and beginning to write a proposal for an honors class, placing this book and the outline you just wrote on the unused, student desk in the corner of the room. Former students of time management report that by using the lying-around method with one task *as soon as* you learn about it, you will learn how to apply it faster and more effectively. You may wish to select a task right now.

ESTABLISH APPROPRIATE DEADLINES

Yes! No! What response do you give when a deadline has to be met? Our work today will give you increased skill in meeting deadlines others have set and skill in recognizing the types of tasks that need deadlines to be completed in the most efficient manner. Four skills will accomplish both objectives.

Learn to Select Methods for Meeting Deadlines

All tasks have explicit or implicit deadlines. Implicit deadlines can be statements, such as "It seems as if I'll never finish" or "I wish I had finished this long ago." Therefore, the skill we must develop is not to establish deadlines. Rather, *we must learn to select methods to meet deadlines*. That is, we must learn to assess accurately the amount of time needed to complete a task and to exercise the flexibility of using more efficient means of reaching goals. We must have a method of matching time available with a technique that utilizes only that much time.

To begin, you must recognize when a mismatch between the method you are trying to use in completing a task and the deadline for the task has occurred. Three clues make this skill an easy one to develop. First, whenever a task "nags" at you continuously, or it has not responded to the first two methods of time management, a mismatch has occurred. You may even begin to feel guilty or uneasy. A task will seem to echo constantly in your ear: "You should be working on me right now! I'm not going to let you enjoy anything until you're finished with me."

Second, tell someone else or yourself that you will do something but do not tell that person when to expect it.

Third, make up unjustified excuses as to why you haven't finished a task.

Unless you develop these skills, you may have no recourse but to respond to task deadline mismatches by increasing your stress, losing your temper, losing patience with your students, and wasting additional time doing less important things, to release your stress, as the deadline draws nearer.

Analyze Your Response to Deadlines

You must analyze your response to deadlines, as some personality styles do not respond well to the pressure and decreased freedom some deadlines create. To develop this skill, complete the self-analysis of your behaviors when you faced pressing deadlines in the past. Below, list the negative and positive reactions you had to deadlines. To assist in your understanding of the task, review my self-analysis before you begin yours.

Positive Responses:

1. I feel a sense of satisfaction, as if a weight has been lifted off my shoulders, when the deadline has been reached.
2. I do better quality work under the pressure of a deadline because I must concentrate more and I force myself to use my best, most intense, and highest levels of thinking skills continuously.
3. I do not need to reorient myself to the task when I'm under the pressure of a deadline, so I save time. All my time seems to be spent in advancing my thoughts and not trying to retrack former thoughts.
4. The results of my work are more timely.
5. I do not overkill an idea, as I tend to do when I have unlimited time to work on something.

Negative Responses:

1. I overeat to keep with tasks so I can meet the deadline when I set unrealistic deadlines.

2. I tend to become short with people if I'm interrupted from meeting a pressing deadline.

3. I underestimate the amount of time a deadline will take.

4. I neglect my physical well-being.

5. I need to improve my ability to break my normal routine to meet a deadline without as much pressure.

Complete your listing now.

Positive Responses I've Had to Deadlines:

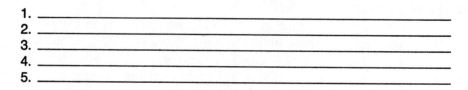

Negative Responses I've Had to Deadlines:

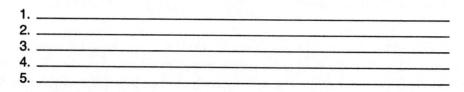

What insights does this listing provide for you? For example, because I did this activity, I now realize that my response to deadlines is more positive than I had suspected. Before I did this analysis, I had almost convinced myself that to do my best work I should set as few specific deadlines as possible. I now realize that by (1) focusing my priorities in areas of talent; (2) taking more frequent, yet earned breaks; and (3) saying "no" to activities of little priority, I have greatly reduced the number of negative responses I have to deadlines. I now *really enjoy* the challenges and successes of creating appropriate matches between methods and deadlines. Your enjoyment and ability to meet deadlines will also increase as you learn the four skills you are developing now. Write and date your self-analysis in the space here. _____ (date) _____

_____

_____

Understand the Value of Deadlines

If you understand why deadlines reduce the amount of time it takes to complete a task, setting them may become easier for you. First, deadlines help you to make yourself accountable. Because deadlines establish a time when a product will be delivered, you will work more diligently, to save face and avoid disappointing others. Deadlines, thus, increase the value of tasks, as with them you will not only work to get the work done, but you work to be certain you demonstrate your competence.

Second, deadlines save time. They reduce the amount of time you spend "dreaming" about the end product. Without deadlines, you can fool yourself. That is, you can just think about how good it would be if the goal were finished and convince yourself that you were indeed "working" on a goal. In reality, you were really putting forth very little energy toward the work required to actualize the goal. To state it in a slightly different way, deadlines pull our ideas about a task from our limitless terrains of imaginings into the world of reality. They force us to begin drawing up a plan of action and to question whether this goal is worth our hard-earned time.

Third, deadlines increase efficiency because they increase the immediacy of the task and timeliness of the goal. That is, they increase the likelihood that the tasks we do will be among the first of their kind. When you are tempted to not set a deadline, it might help you to move ahead if you remind yourself that people really reward those who finish first. That is, when two new products are being created to serve the same function, only one will be labeled an innovation. This product will have been made by the person who set and met their deadline first. Our society also most values "being first"—consider all the English words for this concept: winner, discovered, avant-garde, innovator, brand new, and so on. There are no synonyms for finishing in fifth place.

Deadlines ensure that energy and time will not be wasted in tension-relieving activities. People tend to do unproductive things to avoid work. In addition, until the work is complete the task will demand some of our psychological energy and resources continuously, whether or not we consciously realize it. To prove this point, think of the last time you met a deadline and experienced the feeling of "a weight having been lifted from your shoulders." This lift is to have been freed from the continuous cognitive and psychological attention that the unfinished task had used.

In summary, you will have developed the third skill in establishing appropriate deadlines when you experience and develop a positive value for establishing deadlines. You must no longer perceive them as negative, external pressures. Deadlines are valuable, time-saving tools that can be used masterfully.

Establish Action Plans

You need to develop the skill of establishing action plans. First, you must learn to set a deadline as soon as a task is assigned. Then you must break the larger task into smaller, scheduled units so you can move from point A to point Z. According to the research of Kozoll (1984), the ability to develop this "action plan" is one of the most distinguishing characteristics of highly successful professionals. Less successful teachers spend time trying to figure out "how to move from point A to point Z in one fell swoop."

Once the deadline and method of work have been established (by matching time of method to time available), you should shift your thoughts toward selecting the first four things that must be done. Then begin working on these things and do not think any further about the beauty of the eventual goal.

Kozoll also discovered that the most successful teachers enjoy working on the plan they created. They enjoy the process used to reach deadlines, realizing what the process is doing to help them become stronger and more professional.

They inadvertently are establishing an integral relationship between accomplishment and self-discipline. They attribute the successes they experience to the plan of action they follow. After deadlines are reached, they identify what they did exactly to be successful. They learn to expect, deeply appreciate, and frequently enjoy their experiences with success. You can increase the likelihood of your future successes by strengthening your skills in controlling the action plans you create. This entire process will soon become a habitual, rather than an occasional, behavior.

Most successful teachers also report demanding excellence of themselves. That is, they use a high estimate of personal potential as they make plans. This power and potential has been proven to arise from the state known as *eustress*.

Eustress is the mental energy state whereby one becomes totally engaged in an activity and does not want to withdraw from it. Eustress enables people to become a part of the "flow" of productive energy. People who experience eustress complete more tasks. Developing an action plan enhances the possibility that state of eustress will begin.

To review the steps of skill 4 and to be more specific;

1. As soon as a task is given, estimate how long it will take to finish it. Until you develop skill in matching methodology time to time available, add 25 to 50 percent as much time to the plan as you had originally estimated.

2. Write the deadline on the calendar. Then, back up on the calendar and block out time to work on the task. These time blocks will be appointments you set with yourself that are as important and inflexible as is a meeting called by the principal.

3. At the beginning of the week, schedule all deadlines that will occur that week as your highest priorities. Block out time to work on these tasks before the week begins, so lesser priorities will not absorb the valuable classroom minutes you can truly call your own. By blocking out deadlines by the week, each day becomes easier. That is, you will have one week of tasks to do (and five days to plan and complete them), instead of five separate days, with separate special projects/deadlines due each day. With only a small amount of practice, you will begin to take a few minutes every Friday afternoon or Monday morning to survey the week, see it as a single unit, and write in blocks of time for you and your students to do the work and meet the deadlines you have set.

4. Frequently practice setting appropriate deadlines and using the skills learned today. They *will* become automatic. Select the task that has been bothering you the most, or a task you need to finish for someone else but you hadn't specified when. Set a deadline after selecting the method that matches the time you want to spend on the task. (Refer to the lists of methods in Chapter 1, cited in the Input section of the Master Lesson Plan, to assist you in selecting the best method for the task.) Block out the hours in the day today and the coming week that you'll spend on the task. Take 1 minute now and do this.

DO IT BETTER

We've all heard the two conflicting quotations, "If anything is worth doing, it's worth doing well" and "Do something, even if it's wrong." We may believe that one is more valid than another. To be the best teacher, however, you may need to follow both of these principles simultaneously! How in the world can you do that? Doing so is the fourth method of time management. We'll learn how today.

The *do-it-better method* is to do your very best on everything and do everything within the time allowed, even if the time available is not enough for the method you prefer to use or have used traditionally. To do so, you may need to have the following beliefs. You may need to believe that everything you do deserves your full attention and best effort.

Second, you may need to believe that "doing something right" does *not* mean that you delay action until all conditions are present to replicate the way you've always done something in the past or that you procrastinate until you can approach the task with the most commonly used method. Next you have to accept the fact that doing something correctly may require rejecting the first, most comprehensive action plan you develop. Often, you will create a better, more creative, and more efficient method. You must learn to view each task as unique. With each time you do something, if you set aside a brief period to generate ideas as to how you can do the task better in the future, a self-improvement program will have become habitual. Last, you will always decide in the beginning that you will not do any task with less than your best effort, even though time or conditions prohibit approaching it in your usual way.

Many people establish arbitrary rules that guide their behavior in situations that they judge to be similar. These rules not only lead to compulsive behavior but limit creative thinking. The only reward such people can receive is to reaffirm that, while they miss deadlines, experience few innovative plans of action, and develop few new skills, they do stick to "the arbitrary and often irrelevant rule" they had imposed upon themselves! An even sadder aspect of this planning system is that there will always be exceptions to their rules. When these exceptions arise, these people will not be able to receive any rewards.

For example, let's assume that a teacher received three parent notes in a single day. Only one note required a typed response, one a handwritten explanation, and one no response, as it was a note of appreciation for something the teacher did well. The teacher, who is unskilled in this fourth method of "doing it better," will make many inefficient decisions as the task is completed. First, the teacher will be horrified to have received three letters at the same time! You see, the teacher has set an arbitrary, self-imposed rule: "a truly professional teacher will always type messages to parents. How would this teacher ever find time to be a good teacher today? How could she type three letters, today, of all days? This teacher's arbitrary rule prevents her from viewing each task as unique."

While we can, and do, applaud the goal of projecting a professional image, the inflexible method proposed in reaching this goal is self-defeating. If she chooses to follow "the rule" rather than the principle of method 4 "doing it better," the teacher may even tarnish the professional image she seeks. That is, because her arbitrary rule will guide her actions, the teacher may have to stay after school to type her letters. If this occurs frequently, she may begin to resent parents for the "amount of time she is having to spend on their concerns." She has other things to do that are more important. Alternatively, this teacher could choose grudgingly to break her rule, just this once, and type only one letter and handwrite the others. If this is the action she takes, she may become upset at herself. The self-imposed standard may have become so closely tied to her overall goal of professionalism that "not typing the other letters" will be interpreted, by her, as the first step toward unprofessionalism. The teacher then could become afraid that it will become easier in the future to lower her standards again.

To complete this scenario, neither alternative would have enabled the teacher to have responded to all three parents that day, perhaps a truer measure of professionalism. Alternatively, had the teacher used the "do-it-better" method and responded to each parent "better," all three letters could have been answered, and answered within the time available. Let's see exactly how Method 4 could be applied in this situation:

The bell rings, planning period begins. Our teacher gets the mail. "How interesting, three letters from parents," the teacher thinks. After getting her coffee, she gives her full attention to the first letter. The teacher soon realizes that the response needs to be comprehensive, typed, and approved by the principal. She then pens the response and sets it aside to give to the school secretary for the principal's revision and additions.

The teacher then turns her attention to the second letter. The teacher jots a handwritten response on the bottom of the parent's letter, as suggested by the parent, who wanted the response returned by his son that evening. The third letter is opened and the teacher smiles at the kind remarks and appreciation this parent expressed. She is so touched that almost without realizing it, she takes a piece of stationary from the desk drawer and writes the following words to mail to the parent: "Your letter made my day. Thank you." The teacher walks to the office, gives the first written response to the secretary and mails the third letter, and returns to her room for the work she had planned to do during the planning period. With method 4 three letters received answers, no overtime was expended, and "more tasks were completed better."

To "do it better," one will call this method 4 to mind each time a task leads one to say, "I need to do _____ , but don't have time to *do it* [in the traditional way]." When this self-talk exists, affirm *to do something* now. Begin by generating ideas about "how it can be done right" with the resources and time at your disposal. Then, plan to take the first step toward "doing something now" and "doing something well."

You will have countless benefits from using this time management method. These benefits increase as you feel more comfortable with the flexible thinking involved. To begin, identify the key phrase you have said in the past whenever you felt you should do something but you couldn't do it the way you normally would. Whenever you say that phrase in the future, may it remind you to use method 4 of time management! You will "do it better" than before.

As we discussed at the beginning of the chapter, we procrastinate at times because some tasks become tedious, boring, or menial. The next four methods increase our skills in efficiently delegating time to these tasks. Before we study these methods, it is important to understand why we have trouble with tedious tasks.

These tasks force you to act repetitively in a routine manner. You resist such mental limitation. These tasks also do not capture your full creative capacities and problem-solving potentials. Such tasks do not demand any growths in skill that may have only been recently acquired. They also limit your body movement. Thus, you become bored and (1) either slow down, increasing the amount of time spent on the task or (2) decrease the work's quality. Because one of the next four methods will probably be easier and more fun for you to master, feel free to experiment with each (and combinations of several) until you find the method that most effectively changes unpleasant, boring taks to ones you can enjoy and value. Each time these methods are used, they become more automatic.

CHIP AWAY WITH 7 AND 11

The *"7–11" method* saves time when used in association with monotonous tasks because it is based on the principle that one increases proficiency if attention is given to certain tasks for very brief periods at a time. The 7–11 method is designed to allocate only a few minutes twice a day for a boring responsibility. For example, you can allocate 7 minutes in the morning and 11 minutes in the afternoon to filling in report cards, completing records, or grading papers. With this method you can complete the task in less time than trying to sustain attention for a very long period at one setting. While there isn't anything magical about setting aside only 7- and 11-minute periods, it is important that you don't set aside more than a two 20-minute periods a day and that one is scheduled before and one after 12:00 noon. When you time your work in this way, you can also begin to compete against yourself by counting the number finished each day, seeing if you improved the quality and quantity of work you did. This method is valuable if you enjoy being engaged in several different tasks at one time or if you are very skilled at beginning some aspects of a job as soon as it is assigned.

This technique may be more difficult for you if you are uncomfortable when you have several things going on at once or prefer to work on one task until finished. One teacher gave this testimonial after learning this skill:

> I enjoy this method because I find that once I've told myself I "can" only work on this "wearisome" task for only a few minutes, I begin without procrastinating. I have also learned, through the 7–11 method, that the most monotonous tasks can become great "wasted time fillers." That is, I now take this type task with me wherever I go. In the 5 minutes wait for everyone to get to the faculty meeting or in the last few minutes of the day when I'm normally too tired to tackle anything big, I pull out my 7–11 task and finish two or three parts of this task in the time I would have previously just idled away in boredom. Even if I end up having only 1 minute

to devote to it, I feel fantastic; I'm one step closer to my goal of completing a task I've worked on, and I've not become angry at having to wait.

The tedious tasks you may enjoy using the 7–11 method to complete include

1. Filling in standard lessons and/or district codes.
2. Making lists or inventoring supplies and books.
3. Writing individual notes of praise to students and/or parents of the students.
4. Thinking of new, creative introductions to tedious lessons that bore students.
5. Filling out report cards.
6. Setting those large lifetime goals that you always want to have time to think about.
7. Thinking of a better way to improve your teaching.
8. Cleaning off desks and cabinets.
9. Designing a new method to eliminate the amount of time spent on grading papers.
10. Identifying a situation in which you want to learn to say no and preparing/practicing a "script" to deal with it.
11. Arranging the encyclopedias or desk materials.

Look on your desk right now. Work on the task that you most dread for just a few minutes. When you get in the habit of (1) nibbling away at these tasks, (2) taking a little bit of them with us when you may have to wait, and (3) setting two small periods, morning and afternoon, to work on them, you will complete your work faster and feel better. Begin your first practice session. Work for 7 minutes now and then read the next paragraph.

Now, write in your lesson plan book, one day each week where you will put "7–_____" and the "11–_____" (with the latter being after lunch, perhaps). In this way, as you plan each week, you will plan what tedious task you will keep with you and work on with the 7–11 method each week.

MAKE AN ASSEMBLY LINE

This method is excellent for completing boring tasks in one setting. As a matter of fact, the *assembly-line method* is the fastest way to finish tasks that have the same, repetitive mental demand. As implied in the title, this time management principle is best used with tasks that (1) have several parts requiring the same action, (2) can be easily divided into sequential sections, (3) require different skills or tools, and/or (4) have a wide variety of tasks to complete before the end is reached. With this method, all units that require the same decision, skill or task will be done before moving to the next section of each unit's work.

The success of this method is based on the principle that our capabilities and efficiency are increased by doing one activity repeatedly. Boredom and tedium are reduced as the larger task is divided into successive actions, because we learn to do each section more smoothly, efficiently, and accurately as we repeat each action. For example, the most efficient method of grading a set of essay papers (if we wish to complete all papers in one sitting) is to grade all answers to question 1 and then question 2. Because we will have only one criterion in mind, the memory load is reduced and the accuracy of our work increases. Last, the assembly-line approach delimits the possibility that we will stop before the task is finished as we will not have completed units tempting us to take a break upon each one's completion. Instead we will view "grading the papers" as a single unit, and we'll only experience closure after the last question of all papers has been finished.

To illustrate when this method will be the most efficient, we can contrast handmade and factory-produced objects. When several parts of things need to be treated equally, using the assembly-line, factory-made approach eliminates the likelihood that we'll show favoritism. The method also allows us to "free our brain's secretary," who otherwise would have to ask "Did you grade #3?" "What part of #7 did you want to be sure everyone mentioned?" "Were you too lenient with Susan's answers?" "Gosh, what do you do now, you've graded almost all the papers, given several A's, and George's paper, which you've just come across for the first time, is superior to all others?"

These questions, doubts, and indecisions cause extra work, waste time, expend a lot of mental energy, and reduce quality. This method also eliminates two other negative aspects of past work habits. When used appropriately, you will no longer feel forced to discard quality and rush to finish something.

In essence, unnecessary time will not be wasted when doing routine tasks if you ask a few questions before you begin: Do you want to finish it in one sitting? Does the task have sections that require different actions, or decisions? If the answer is yes, begin to create your own unique assembly-line method to complete the work. One assembly-line task might be completing

1. Report cards where you must grade the final, average the grades, and then record them on the reporting form.
2. A school newspaper for final printing.
3. The Seniors' honors banquet.
4. Special gifts or papers for individual students.
5. Film orders for each subject area.

BUILD A SET OF TRAINING WHEELS FOR ACHIEVEMENT

If you are postponing a task that is routine, important, and difficult, the task may be a little beyond your level of unassisted ability. This type of task requires that we build a "set of training wheels" before we begin. First, you must recognize when you have set goals that challenge you to grow and compliment yourselves for doing so. Then you must build a support to ensure that you will experience success.

One support is to ask someone else to help. Many educators have already learned how much fun tasks become when a friend is asked to help. For example, you know that in two weeks you are going to have to mail out report cards for the first time this year. You decide to ask your best friend, the teacher across the hall, and both teacher's aides to come to your room and sit at the back tables each day for the next four days during the planning period to "make out" report cards. You four (or two, if aides are not available) vow that no interruptions will sidetrack you for the next days. Someone might even suggest that each of you "take turns" at buying snacks or cold drinks for the "report card group."

What tasks would you like to do before the year is over that would be best accomplished if done with someone else, or in a group?

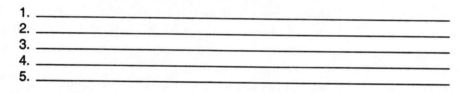

1. _____
2. _____
3. _____
4. _____
5. _____

Beside each task, jot down when and to whom you will speak to begin your plans for changing boring, put-off tasks to shared experiences.

CHANGE THE PROCEDURE TO SUIT THE TASK AND YOUR WORKING STYLE

There are times when it's not the job that bores us but, rather, the way we have to do it. The procedure we follow may have been suggested by someone else or set in motion because of tradition. Among your first indications that a procedure is inappropriate is that you'll have a negative attitude each time you approach the task. You have to force yourself to do it. This particular duty seems to always be preceded with a sigh and the same mental dialogue, "Well, I guess I'd better _____."

A change in the procedure also will be warranted if you begin to do the job less well than you desire. You then will notice that you justify the decreased quality by telling yourself that the task isn't important anyway.

Often we need merely to change a segment of the procedure and all negative attitudes disappear. To identify which structure of a task is causing difficulty, you must categorize the routine you dread. (The types of "dreaded tasks" listed in this category are distinct from those that best respond to the first method. These are not dreaded because they are new, but merely because you don't want to do them. You think they aren't worth the time you'll have to invest in them, but you are expected to do them.) Through task analysis you can isolate opposing aspects of the structure that interfere with your personal work flow and the normal rhythm tasks have when they are "working like clockwork." You experiment with new procedures and schedules until the arduous tasks become easy. As we complete the list in Figure 2-1, we focus on the similarities between tasks in each category. We can note these in the margins as we complete the worksheet. List three or four activities in each category.

Figure 2–1

SELF-ANALYSIS OF MISMATCHED WORKING ROUTINES

Category 1: Routines that bore you or are performed by methods that you have not deliberately selected:

1.
2.
3.

Sample answers I gave:

4. Completing student achievement reports.
5. Writing letters for professional purposes.
6. Fulfilling participant role that I take in committees that I don't chair.
7. Having to get permission from several different people before I can begin a new activity.

Category 2: Routines that have little value to you or that you do not do as well as you should:

1.
2.
3.

Sample answers I gave:

4. Checking roll.
5. Filing new research data and papers of new information that will be used in teaching.
6. Taking time to interact with colleagues on team-teaching plans.

Category 3: Routine duties that are approached experimentally in trying to develop an efficient, creative method to insert it into the daily routine that you already have:

1.
2.
3.

Sample answers I gave:

4. Grading papers.
5. Collecting mail from main office.
6. Recording grades.
7. Balancing changes in schedules or personal life with professional responsibilities.

Category 4: Routine tasks that you perform productively and creatively with a method that you value and possibly created:

1.
2.
3.

Sample answers I gave:

4. Class preparation time.
5. Method of handling student questions/problems.
6. Schedule time to complete written reports.

What dimensions of category 4 items can we insert into the routines that were listed in 1 and 2? Rewrite the activities in categories 1 and 2 as they would appear if you added the dimension of category 4 that reflects one of your talents. For example, refer to my analysis in Figure 2-1. After noting that I have talent in thinking on my feet and responding orally, I realized that I could change several activities in categories 1 and 2 to ones I would enjoy and value if I decreased the amount of writing I had to do. I have now changed the procedure I follow when I go to committee meetings: I no longer take three sharpened pencils and spend the time being an efficient recorder and note taker. I now think more and contribute orally. I like the change and value the committees on which I now serve more than ever before.

I'd like for you to make the same types of changes in your procedures. You will notice that when the correct procedure for the task is identified: (1) you will feel a sense of ownership over the activity, that is, feeling partly responsible for the benefits that will result, and (2) the procedure and task will become so effective that you will not have to give as much time to planning and maintaining the procedure, but this decreased time will not affect the quality. The energy and time you'll save, as well as the confidence that will arise from creating a good flow of work, will transfer into a desire to establish other efficient and productive routines.

I've worked on the analysis worksheet twice. Each time I gained a different set of insights. You can rework this analysis listing at any time you begin to dread a routine task.

THE IMPORTANCE OF ELIMINATING PROCRASTINATION

Research in the field of educational psychology has demonstrated that new behaviors often have to be practiced six times before the old behaviors are suppressed. Thus, to suppress the procrastination habit, you should build in motivators to cause you to work at your best. Before you put something off, you should seek to work with someone else, set a reward to gain, or identify reasons why something is as it is.

Research in the field of business has identified several characteristics of human nature that contribute to our desire to procrastinate. Specifically, we tend to (1) put off unpleasant tasks, (2) avoid things that are difficult, (3) neglect tough decisions, (4) protect ourselves from getting hurt, and (5) enter a profession outside our area of talent and interest because of low self-esteem, making career changes necessary and time-wasting. Business managers are trained to do their most unpleasant task first, attack debilitating fears and develop good decision-making skills. As an educator, you make thousands of decisions a day, but have not been trained in making decisions effectively. Let's be sure that you avoid the routine satirized in this poem (Davis, 1951):

> 9:00 to 9:15 A.M.
> I've dusted my desk and I've wound up my watch,
> I've tightened (then loosened) my belt by a notch.

I've polished my glasses, removed a small speck.
I've looked at my check stubs to check on a check,
I've searched for my tweezers and pulled out a hair,
I've opened a window to let in some air,
I've straightened a picture, I've swatted a fly,
I've shifted the tie clip that clips down my tie,
I've sharpened each pencil till sharp as a dirk . . .
I've run out of reasons for not starting to work.
Richard Armour

If this sounds familiar, you may have a problem with procrastination. Other diagnostic clues to undue postponing of tasks follow. That is, while procrastinating can allow a person time to generate new ideas, if procrastination occurs more than once on any task or someone uses tension-relieving activities too frequently, you can be relatively sure that the person involved has a procrastination habit that needs to be broken.

As a matter of fact, if you or a colleague of yours finds that work is less and less enjoyable and all professional tasks are being postponed, a change in career might be warranted, if the skills of this book don't change the productivity.

If you are saying to me, *"But* I procrastinate because I work better under pressure!" you may be using procrastination for one or two unproductive reasons. That is, you may be putting tasks off so you can justify setting aside time to be left alone to work or you use procrastination to gain more control, sympathy, or power at work. Neither reason will end in positive gain. If this is your problem, you must identify what rewards you are receiving by putting things off till the last minute.

When asked to make decisions, you may use the following crutches to make the decision process easier.

1. You may make a decision based on past experiences. These experiences may reveal elements of human nature that you took into consideration as you made your decision, decreasing the likelihood that you'll make an error.

2. Your past failures can make it easy for you to limit the possible choices to be considered before deciding.

3. Habitual skills and talents you have, through observing the successes of others, afford you the opportunity to solve some aspects of problems.

4. Your biases clearly specify how far you will go personally.

5. Your associations with others in your area of expertise make you more keenly aware of all the resources you can use to make and implement your decision.

With this in mind, practice making tough decisions in areas outside your teaching profession. Each time you have an impulse to avoid making a tough decision, tell yourself that your decision-making ability will grow, as will your feelings of satisfaction and accomplishment if you will use the skills you'll learn next.

The best defense against procrastination has been identified as an ability to protect blocks of time and to set aside time to do important tasks. When the important task is a difficult one, you should do the task when your energy level is highest. Be sure to protect the big blocks of time that you need to complete your important goals, for example, moving to a quiet place, closing the door when you begin. When is your best time of day for beginning your most important tasks? When is your energy level the highest? Write that information here. _____

A second strategy is that when you are tired, during a big task, change the type of activity you are doing from a convergent to a divergent one. That is, if you are constantly creating new ideas during a task, change briefly to a mundane, easy task so as to break the difficulty level and then resume thinking for a brief period. If you are having to do a lot of writing, or a passive activity, break for a moment to do an active task or talk to someone about the work.

Last, always remember that the easiest method of overcoming procrastination is not to allow the seed to bloom. To do this, identify what motivates you to *action*. Since procrastination has been defined by *Webster's New World Dictionary of the American Language* as "to defer taking action," identifying the most frequent reason you take an action may help you find what motivates you to begin a task you've been putting off. Think carefully. What causes you to do something? Is it that you enjoy helping others? Do you seek stimulation, change or reward? Do you want results, to make changes or to solve problems? Do you enjoy finding the cause or reason for things? One of these will usually stimulate each personality type to action. By identifying the one(s) that best motivate you, you will know what to add to your next task to make it easier to begin.

In summary, managers know that time problems *are* resistant to will power, but are easily solved with one of the eight methods of time management. The more we practice each method, the more you'll combine them and expand your efficiency. You must realize that different tasks demand different management strategies. Through practice, you can begin to appropriately use the techniques of (1) beginning "not" at the beginning; (2) leaving tasks out, inviting, calling us back; (3) setting deadlines; (4) doing tasks in the best manner in the time assigned; (5) using several free moments to complete monotonous tasks; (6) developing assembly lines; (7) building training wheels for ourselves; and (8) changing the procedure to better match task demands and personal working style.

Because procrastination has the potential of entering every goal you establish, it has been labeled the greatest of thieves. In 1980, Jack D. Fenner developed a Procrastination Rater to determine how much time buisness experts waste. Rather than spend time determining how much procrastination is in our work presently, let's study indicators of procrastination and make mental notes of methods we can use to combat this force. For the next few moments, apply what you've learned in this chapter. Each of the following sentences is an example of how procrastination enters our work. Complete each statement with a skill or method you will use to conquer this thief of time:

1. Instead of inventing reasons and looking for excuses for not acting on a tough problem, I'll (e.g., practice making tough decisions by facing

them when my energy level is high) _____
_____

2. Rather than trying to pressure myself into getting on with a difficult assignment, I'll _____
_____

3. I've thrown away the old method I used to use of taking half-measures to avoid or delay unpleasant tasks; now I'll substitute the time management skill of _____

4. I can no longer use the excuse that I have too many interruptions and crises that interfere with my big tasks because I _____
_____

5. When pressed for an answer to an unpleasant decision, I am forthright because _____

6. In the past I may have been guilty of neglecting follow-up aspects of important plans or actions, but I'll never neglect these important details again because _____

7. Instead of getting others to do unpleasant tasks for me, I _____
_____

8. I now find that I schedule fewer big jobs late in the day or take them home because I'm beginning to develop the skill of _____

9. The best way I've learned to overcome the tiredness, nervousness, or tension associated with beginning difficult tasks is to _____
_____

10. While I used to always finish all simple tasks before I began a tough job, I now _____

With these time management methods in hand, we're going to direct our attention to our scheduling skills. In Chapter 3, we'll learn how to overcome the "rushing around" habit and how to avoid being busy *without* being productive. We'll take a look at all types of schedules we use in teaching. The intent will be to learn to connect the time management skills we're developing together so the day will flow smoothly, so our days will become more fun filled, productive, beneficial, and satisfying.

Before we learn how to tie all our time management activities together, I would like to challenge you for a second time. Do you think you've learned the eight basic time management methods in the chapter? I think you have. Let's see if we're right. Answer the questions in Figure 2-2. If you answer eight out of ten correctly, you have learned when to use each management technique! Good luck.

Check your answers, using the answer key provided. If you scored 80 percent or better, congratulations. Before you begin the next chapter, reread the method(s) you missed. The few moments this will take will have amazing results, as your review will come so close to the time you first learned it that your retention will be greatly increased.

Figure 2–2

TEST OF THE APPROPRIATE SELECTION AND USE OF THE MAJOR TIME MANAGEMENT METHODS

Directions: In the blank that precedes each task, designate which of the methods of time management most productively addresses each task. Make your designation by placing the number of the method in the blank that precedes each item. These methods are

Method 1: "Start Certain Type Tasks at Places Other than the Beginning"

Method 2: "Leave It Lying Around"

Method 3: "Set a Deadline and Block out Working Periods"

Method 4: "Do It Better"

Method 5: "Chip Away with 7 and 11"

Method 6: "Make an Assembly-Line"

Method 7: "Build a Set of 'Training Wheels' for Superachievement"

Method 8: "Change the Procedure to Suit the Task and One's Own Working Style"

In the blank that follows each item, specify why the selected method completes the task most efficiently.

_____ 1. Three students, simultaneously, ask you to be their sponsor for their talent show number. You only have time to give up one planning period a week for this activity, and it took that long to sponsor only one person/act last year. _____

_____

_____ 2. *The Wall Street Journal* is running a series on the ramifications of capitalism upon democratic governing principles. You know the information could become one of the most exciting parts of the next semester's government class, but you don't know how to find time to collate all the separate articles and then to build methods of teaching. _____

_____

_____ 3. The instructional specialist asks your advice about how to begin. He or she has been asked to compare achievement scores in math, reading, spelling, and science for grades 2, 4, 6, and 8 in the six schools in the district. The instructional specialist is to analyze the comparisons and make a report by grade, subject, and building as to areas of strength and weakness, with explanations as to why areas were judged as they were. _____

_____

_____ 4. You've been asked to design the bulletin board in the foyer for the Public Schools' Week Open House? "But," you ask, "what do you want more specifically?" _____

_____

_____ 5. No one else knows that I want to spend more time in one-to-one conferences with my students, so I shouldn't get so mad when I keep saying yes to the requests others ask of me. Why can't I find the time to hold individual student conferences? It's so important to me. _____

_____

_____ 6. It really is important to you to write a special comment on the bottom of the 20 failing notices you have to send out by Friday of this week. While every note will be individualized, you essentially want to say the same thing to each student: tell each student (a) how many points he or she must earn to pass, (b) which assignments he or she missed and should begin to work on, and (c) which

continued

Figure 2–2 continued

behavior he or she might want to modify to better ensure that they will not fail again. _____

_____

_____ 7. You are one of three poeple who has been assigned to write a grant proposal to begin a new program for the gifted and talented students in the building. Traditionally, in committee work you have always played the role of the "worker bee," doing all the typing, editing, and running errands. You have grown professionally and wish to assume more responsibility. _____

_____

_____ 8. You want to make a display in the hall for Public Schools' Week. You aren't sure of the theme. You have two great ideas and the materials to use, somewhere. You wish to do a fantastic job, and you are looking forward to the challenge. _____

_____

_____ 9. "I am so nervous. This is my first time to speak before all the teachers in the district. Not only that, but I have to host and plan the banquet. I've never planned anything for 2,000 people before. I'm flattered the superintendent has confidence in me, but where do I begin? Why did she ask me? What does she see in me that makes me qualified for this enormous responsibility?" _____

_____

_____ 10. You divided the math class into an advanced and an average to below-average group. Members of the group are to work at their own pace throughout the week, completing at least ten problems a day, with the pages covered being guided by the pace and learning speed of each student. It's Friday and time to grade the papers. _____

_____

Answer Key

1. 4. You can find a way to sponsor all three in one 45-minute period when you create a "better method" of sponsoring.

2. 2, if you have done such a project before; 1 and/or 2, if you haven't.

3. 6 or 7. Because the tasks require repetition and various levels of specificity are needed before the task is complete.

4. 1. As the end product has not been clearly defined.

5. 3, if the task is important to you and you lack time because time has not been budgeted to complete it. Or 2, if you read the task as one that was not necessarily needing to be finished.

6. 5 or 7. While the 20 units appear to be identical (demanding use of the assembly-line method), none of the three parts of each handwritten section requires the same repetitive thought; they require individualized "handmade" responses. The 7–11 method or building a set of training wheels would be the most productive.

7. 8. You will change the procedures and structure of the committee so as to better suit your talents to the task and better assign tasks according to your most productive working style.

8. 2. This task is not a tedious one and does not have distinct, separate skills. Lying around method for new, big, creative tasks will most efficiently complete this task.

9. 1, if you intend to do it yourself. Or 7, if you want to include others.

10. 7, if you ask others to help (e.g., students grade papers from another group to be exposed to concepts they didn't work on themselves). Or 5, if done by yourself.

If you missed more than two exercises, I suggest two steps. To ensure more rapid learning and strengthened automaticity in using these methods, spend two days seeking as many opportunities as you can to apply each method in this chapter. Then when you decide to test your learning again, take the five-item review check shown in Figure 2-3.

When we finish this paragraph, we will conclude our introduction of time management methods. Depending on the grade earned on the test, you will do one or two additional tasks I've suggested to refine your learning. Henceforth, refer to Chapter 2 discussions at any time you procrastinate or are afraid to begin a task. Often, just referring to the list of methods that appears in the directions of our test will enable you to take the first step in managing the activity before you. Try to be patient as you learn these new skills. What you are attempting to do is to develop a new way of thinking about time, a new process of delegating time and resources to your work, and to appreciate time and the power it affords, in ways you've never done before. Now, after grading your test, you may want to pause and create a plan of how to continue learning these time management techniques.

REFERENCES

Davis, Robert. "Time and Motion Study of First Line Supervisors in Four Job Types," *Journal of Human Resource Management*, Vol II, No. 4, Spring 1951, pp. 47–59.

Fenner, Jack D. *Successful Time Management*. (New York: John Wiley, 1980).

Kozoll, Charles E. Speaker at the educational forum conducted by Texas Christian University, April 10, 1984.

Lakelin, Alan. *How to Get Control of Your Time and Your Life*. New York: New American Library, 1973.

Leas, Speed B. *Time Management: A Working Guide for Church Leaders*. Nashville, Tenn.: Abingdon, 1978.

Figure 2-3

FIVE-ITEM REVIEW CHECK

Directions: In the blank that precedes each task, designate which of the methods of time management most productively addresses the task. Make your designation by placing the number of the method in the blank that precedes each item. These methods are:

Method 1: "Start Certain Type Tasks at Places Other than the Beginning"
Method 2: "Leave It Lying Around"
Method 3: "Set a Deadline and Block out Working Periods"
Method 4: "Do It Better"
Method 5: "Chip Away with 7 and 11"
Method 6: "Make an Assembly Line"
Method 7: "Build a Set of 'Training Wheels' for Superachievement"
Method 8: "Change the Procedure to Suit the Task and One's Own Working Style"

In the blank that follows each item, specify why the selected method completes the task most efficiently.

_____1. "I didn't know we were supposed to have this turned in to your office yesterday." _____

_____2. The Classroom Teachers Organization or Association has asked you to chair a committee charged with combining the Professional Growth Committee and the Instructional Improvements Committee into one. You are the chairperson of the Professional Growth Committee, and you are very familiar with every task and deadline under their direction. You don't know any of the people or tasks of the Instructional Improvements Committee. You also have to study the bylaws of the organization, as there are strict rules to follow when a committee is dissolved. You don't know where to begin or what to do. _____

_____3. "Gee, these directions to make an active volcano model seem very simple and fun. I really would like to make it for the science class, but where will I ever find the time? I bet it would take 5 hours to finish." _____

_____4. "What in the world did she mean, 'Write up a tentative schedule for the high school tournament'?" _____

_____5. "I really need to make a new bulletin board. I've wanted to begin it for 2 weeks and now it must be finished in 1 week." Or it's the Christmas season already, and you haven't begun to make the gift you usually give to your students.

Answers Key

1. 3. Definitely and possibly 8, if the procedure followed by the principal is diametrically opposed to your working style or the demands of the task. The person had not set a deadline for himself or herself, had not developed an action plan, and did not block out time to work on the task.

2. 1. You will have to add new goals for the new, combined committee. If you choose 3 or 6, you overlooked the fact that the new committee will have to have new goals and revised tasks.

3. 2. If you intend to do it yourself. And 4, in addition, if you are going to change the directions so you can use students and other resources to make it.

4. 1. Because you are unable to get clarifications of the task and end product.

5. 3 and 4. Because the task is a new one, involving creativity.

three

Improving Schedules Within and Between Days and Classroom Lessons

A Teacher Comments on Chapter 3

Chapter 3 is not just a "how to" discussion. I recommend these activities to other teachers because I gained by using them. Many books for teachers on the market are too theoretical. They are difficult for teachers to use.

This chapter sparked my creativity and provided a basis for organizing my classroom! It made me a more efficient teacher all around. I was also made more aware of how crucial scheduling skills are if students and teachers are to succeed!

Rhonda Wilson
Elementary Teacher
Germantown, Tennessee

I am a prisoner of hope when I hope someone is
going to make me do for me what I must choose to
do for myself.

—Anonymous

I never realized how important scheduling skills were until I read the research of Barr (1980), Sanford (1983), and Evertson et al (1984). These researchers discovered that 80 percent of the difference in student achievement can be explained by the amount of content covered and how efficiently it was scheduled. Teachers who were trained in developing better schedules increased their students' instructional time by 23 to 34 minutes a day, giving their students 10 to 16 more days a year of learning time (Davidson and Holly, 1979). Further, with an increase of only 5 minutes a day in silent reading time, elementary students' reading skills grew by one month on grade-equivalent scores on standardized reading achievement tests (Guthrie, 1982).

How teachers schedule and pace activities, shift topics, decide when and how to change activities, signal correct behaviors, and make transitions are measurable differences in student learning. These distinguish between more effective and less effective teachers. Methods of developing each of these skills will be described in this chapter.

DAILY SCHEDULING SKILLS

The average secondary teacher is reported to work 39 hours at school and 10.5 hours at home or after school. This teacher will complete 37.1 activities per school day or 1 activity every 12.5 minutes (Cypher and Willower, 1984). Thus, without appropriate schedules (which will be discussed shortly), there appears to be a potential danger that, once every 12.5 minutes, the "best laid plans" can go astray.

There are 12 ways in which classroom time can be effectively managed on a daily basis. Developing a method of taking action in each area as soon as you read it appears to be the most successful way to make the commitment to use the scheduling technique on a regular basis.

Schedules Are Visible at All Times

Research suggests that teachers who keep their lesson books open and lesson plans before them throughout the day spend more time on task, take fewer bird walks, and report student standardized achievement test scores that are significantly above those of teachers who do not (Douglass and Douglass, 1980).

Methods of keeping the daily schedule in view that have been used by other teachers include

1. Keeping your desk clear except for opened lesson plan book and allowing (or not allowing) students to refer to the day's schedule.
2. Reproducing a copy of each week's plan and posting it in the classroom.
3. Placing your teachers' manuals and lesson plans for separate subjects in separate places in the room.

What will you do to keep your schedule before you each day?_____

_____

Opening Activities for the Day and Each Class

When we schedule before-school and beginning-of-school activities carefully, we set an uplifting tone for the day. By selecting a method of addressing each of the five procedures given in Figure 3-1 smoothly and consistently, lessons begin on time and are not rushed. As you read Figure 3-1, circle the numeral that corresponds to the method of scheduling that would work for you.

Enhancement of the Time on Task During a Lesson

Good seatwork procedures and guided practice sessions greatly reduce interruptions. For example, more effective math teachers schedule their lessons so well that students are engaged in teacher-led discussions and structured learning activities for more than one-half of all classroom periods. These teachers also allow less time for seatwork and procedural duties than less effective colleagues (Evertson, et al, 1984).

Students in these rooms also know what to do with materials, how to "officially," leave the room, when to give attention, when to talk to others, how to obtain help, and what to do when seatwork is complete. Their teachers have explained and modeled each procedure. I recommend that as you select the methods you will use in your classroom from the following list, you add these to the methods selected in Figure 3-1. As you read the follwoing discussion, you will increase your ability to schedule time on task for your students by listing each of your methods on an overhead transparency and presenting them to the students.

Methods of scheduling in-class time and movement include the following:

1. Allow students to leave the room. Hang hall pass near the door so student can go out if no one else is gone; students sign out and in on their own; set a school policy; allow students to go to locker but give no credit for work not brought to class; students can go to locker but a slight penalty is awarded (e.g., students are then counted tardy if they have to return to their locker); or students without materials must look on with another student. Your selection: _____

Figure 3-1

OPENING CLASS PROCEDURES

Attendance Check Methods

1. Check orally from grade book.
2. Check silently from seating chart.
3. Have classroom officer or adult volunteer aide check the attendance.
4. Give each student a number and have each call out his or her number or raise his or her hand as you or classroom officer calls out the number.

    Your procedure: _____

Administrative Duties

1. Have a standard procedure in place so students know what they are expected to do while you have administrative duties; they should not sit idle.
2. Have a timer and as soon as students walk in, set it and then tell them that they have 3 (or 5, etc.) minutes to finish _____ . When time is up, you could have finished the administrative duties, and you will grade the student papers, forming a 100 percent club or other incentive program for perfect or 80 percent plus work.
3. Have students write in a daily log, diary type format, for a six-week reward that class values.
4. Display brief assignments on overhead projector screen or blackboard before students arrive and let them work the minilessons as soon as they walk in; these lessons could be reviews of yesterday's work, introductions to the lesson of the day, brainteasers, crossword puzzles for vocabulary development, or logic problems.

    Your procedure: _____

Students Who Are Tardy

1. Initiate a schoolwide policy and encourage all teachers to never make exceptions as if one deviation occurs, for example, letting a few students slip in late at the beginning of the policy period, the procedures will break down.
2. Assign detention unless reason is excused.
3. Place a "t" in the grade book (or classroom officer places "t") each time a student is tardy and the tardiness results in some type of action on the student's part.
4. Put clipboard by the door and students who are tardy sign in when they arrive each period and at the end of the day; you or your classroom monitor changes the absences to tardies in the grade book.

    Your procedure: _____

Students Who Are Absent

1. Post weekly assignment lists on bulletin board.
2. Each time a handout is given, place five extra copies in an ongoing folder for Absentees, put the date on each handout (or have classroom officer responsible for handing out papers stamp dates and file handouts); absentees know where to get handouts and can check lesson plan book to complete work missed prior to the period for completing makeup work has ended.
3. Decide how much time will be allowed for makeup work and stick to it, for example, students have the number of days after their

continued

Figure 3-1 continued

return to school to complete assignments as equals the number of days absent—one day means all missed work is done day after student returns to school.

4. Decide if there will be a penalty and how much it will be for missed work and/or any paper turned in late.

5. Set a place where the students can turn in makeup work and where they can pick it up after it's been graded (e.g., trays/folders labeled "absent in"/"absent out" and allow slower learners to grade and write explanations on each incorrect answer as to why it is wrong to assist the slower-learning grader in increasing his or her learning. If anyone aside from yourself grades makeup papers or if you decide to grade once each week, you will need to have a system to verify that the papers were turned in within the time period allowed.

6. Set a time before or after where you, volunteer older students, or class officer will be available to help students with makeup work.

7. Establish a procedure whereby class officers or monitors can use your teacher's edition to help classmates with makeup.

Your procedure: _____

_____

Giving Clear Directions for Assignments

1. Give oral explanations of mental set, rationale, objective, as described in Chapter 1, but also give visual outline of key points on board, handout, or overhead.

2. Specify standards of form and level of neatness for each assignment, or give a blanket standard that students are expected to use always; tell students which system you are using. Include what heading you prefer, whether students are to write on back of paper, use pen or pencil, erase or draw lines through and/or how to number and due dates; and remind students of policy if work is late (e.g., points subtracted, staying after school, turning in assignments on time even if incomplete).

3. Post a sample heading and remind students several times in the early weeks of school to refer to it and use it.

Your procedure: _____

_____

_____

2. Be sure students give complete attention to the presenter. Use same word or phrase to designate the need for complete attention and tell the students that the phrase is the signal for "complete attention," for example, "Class," "May I have your attention," and/or usually stand at the same location when you start a lesson and do not begin speaking until class is attentive.
   Your method: _____
   _____

3. Specify that class discussion will or will not require raised hands and when helping each other is and is not allowed. Can students ask you for help at anytime; or only when no one is at your desk; or only when they've tried to work the first one on their own?
   Your procedure: _____
   _____

4. Are students allowed to get out of their seats freely and move to any spot, when the movement is purposeful, and how do you define purposeful and nonpurposeful completely? Are students clear that they are not to get out of their seat (even for a tissue?) until independent practice begins or are they clear that only one person is to be up at a time and, if so, what is the signal you use to change that rule during small-group projects?
   Your procedure: _____
   _____

5. What do you do with completed seatwork: in and out boxes have separate containers for separate subjects or classes; have monitor collect at end of period; you collect at door as students leave? This procedure must be built upon what would work best in a typical day yet be simple enough that it can easily adapt to days when special lessons are completed.
   Your procedure: _____
   _____

Closing a Lesson and a Day

When you consistently tell students when it is time to end the class, they will depend on you to do so, and they won't as often be tempted to stop their work early. In addition, when you are conscientious about giving students sufficient time to complete all clean-up procedures, students sense the respect you give to them and their next teacher in doing so, and they return the respect by working harder and doing a more thorough job. Methods of accomplishing these clean-up tasks include

1. Use a consistent signal that it is time to begin the closing of class, for example, "It's time to stop work now," "Let's review and prepare for the next day."
   Your signal: _____

2. A good closing procedure has the class restate the objective for that day's lesson, ask for any questions or pieces of information they'd like to continue tomorrow, remind students of items needed for the next day, or ask if anyone has an issue or concern about which he or she would like to receive other students and your viewpoints.
   Your closing comments might include: _____

3. Be consistent in the procedure you use to signal dismissal: Will you or the bell tell them when it's time to leave? If a few students get up to leave early, on the following day, allow all students to leave except those who got up to leave early on the previous day.
   Your procedure: _____

Monitoring Small and Large Groups

While Chapter 7 will center upon the special management decisions needed for good group work, there are two daily procedures that enhance learning. First, group monitors can be allowed to come to class early and be responsible for setting up supplies and writing assignments on the board. Second, if you feel you waste too much time having to select someone to call upon (such as who will read next, so as to avoid going down the row, or who will answer the next question, so as to avoid handwaving), students can write their names on slips of paper and place these in a small can. You then draw a slip out of the can and call upon the student named. Then, you place the slip in a second can. Sometimes you will draw the name from the second can of names (those who have already been called upon) so all students must continue to participate and attend to the lesson after having been called upon once. This technique also increases the probability that all students will be asked to contribute equally.

Schedules for the First Week of School

Evertson et al. (1984) suggest that everything be done as one large group during this week. This procedure keeps activities uncomplicated and helps students feel successful. They also suggest that the class build rules together, writing each as a positive sentence (for example, instead of "No talking" say, "We can talk freely at designated times"). On a chart, each rule is followed by a consequence that (1) will help students learn to follow the rule and (2) can be monitored without providing negative reinforcement to the child or disrupt the lesson in any way. For example, students have a class officer, or they monitor their own rule enforcement; consequence for chewing gum in class (Rule 7) is for student or student officer (at your signal) to write the number on board beside your name and remain in at lunch period to clean top and underside of all desks. Evertson et al. (1984) go on to suggest that teachers not enter students' names in their grade book until the end of the second week when most class changes are complete.

Some teachers are required to stand near the door during passing periods, and they use this time to note ways in which they will address problems in lessons or with individual students. Others find that by telling students about their interests/hobbies/family, why they enjoy teaching, the goals they have set for the year, and what they wish to accomplish together, rapport builds more rapidly. Special scheduling needs for the first week of school you will address include _____

_____

Detecting and Correcting Student Management Problems

Don't worry if a few students have trouble following rules or handing in papers on time or if a few bad behaviors or lessons cause you concern. Only when two or more management procedures or class rules are being disobeyed by several students should you adjust your daily schedule.

One of the most valuable daily scheduling skills appears to be the ability of knowing the most appropriate time to detect and correct misbehaviors. The following short test helps to asses your present skill in detecting student misbehavior. Put the letter that indicates the correct answer in the blank that precedes the question:

_____ 1. When do you *most often* label a classroom incidence as one involving misbehavior?
   a. When a student "tries" a rule that the student understands and that has been in effect.
   b. When several students break a rule.
   c. When it takes more than a count of three to settle a class.

_____ 2. When you work with a group of students or you work individually with a student at your desk,
   a. you don't feel a need to monitor the remainder of the class.
   b. you feel the noise, disruptions, and work avoidance is higher than when you are giving a class lecture.
   c. you correct student misbehaviors that are outside your major center of attention.

_____ 3. When you feel the students are misbehaving to gain your attention,
   a. you don't feel this occurs in your class.
   b. you give it your attention and you hold an individual conference with the child.
   c. you gently discourage these actions with courteous but negative responses.

_____ 4. How many times in the course of a day should a teacher ignore inappropriate behavior?
   a. Rarely.
   b. Only when more than one rule is broken at a time, and in such cases you only focus on correcting one of them.
   c. As often as possible.

_____ 5. If students frequently seem confused about their work assignments, first,
   a. the teacher should change oral and visual presentation of material.
   b. the teacher should change the difficulty of his or her objectives or place students in smaller groups.
   c. the teacher should identify if a peer group leader is starting the discussions for reasons other than to clarify procedures.

The correct answer on each item is "a." Some teachers may lack skills in detecting misbehavior because they are overly absorbed in their immediate goals, overlooking incidents in the periphery of the class. Others may be overly aware of negative behaviors and use overreactions as a response to each.

If you feel you have a problem in any of these areas, you may wish to add five daily schedule changes:

1. Shorten the length of each activity during a class lesson and change to using more than one activity in each class period.

2. Increase student participation in planning and during the lessons.

3. Schedule a periodic review of your management plans and make changes in procedures without being abrupt or unnatural.

4. Implement a new daily behavior management system at the end of a reporting period as classes are more accepting of change in these periods.

5. Increase students' good behavior by rewarding their efforts by providing variety in the incentives you offer. To assist in creating this variety, these incentives seem to be most appreciated by secondary students:

a. Attractive award certification designed by the teacher and signed by teacher and principal; these can be given for effort, improvement, or acomplishment and awarded privately or publicly, based on individual students' personal needs; *It's Positively Fun! Techniques for Managing Learning Environments*, by Phyllis Kaplan, Joyce Kohfeldt, and Kim Sturla (published in 1974, by Love Publishing Company in Denver, Colorado 80222), contains a wide variety of such awards, contracts, and communications for students and parents.

b. Modern psychedelic stickers for effort, improvement, or accomplishment that students stick on their notebooks.

c. Systems similar to honor rolls.

d. Long-range incentives such as schoolwide, city, regional, and statewide competitions initiated by you or an agency that you can contact and apply for your class to join.

e. Within class rewards, special prizes, or treats to reward the group with highest average grade on spelling at end of month.

f. Between-class competitions for class that does not have good rapport or has cliques or bullies.

g. If class is having trouble turning in assignments, you can encourage improvement by allowing students to redo their work. Post a chart where a gold star is displayed for each "A" received on a paper turned in, silver for "B" and blue for "C." If a student redoes his other paper, a new star is placed over the previous star. The chart saves the teacher time in recording grades and in averaging at the end of each grading period, and by displaying the chart in a prominent place students are encouraged to turn in and improve their work.

h. Extra-credit assignments are popular with some students, for example, posting extra-credit logic problems on a bulletin board, changing them weekly. These extra-credit problems can be stored in notebooks, with completion of each increasing the notebook grade by one point. Teachers can also post a list of extra-credit projects (their deadlines, points to be earned, and requirements) that can be completed individually or in groups. Books on topics studied can be completed on a standardized written or oral report form.

i. Gamelike competitions. For example, a math teacher made a bulletin board shaped like a mountain (with varied plateaus) with math problems of increasing difficulty at each elevation. Each elevation had a space for ten names. The names of the first ten students (from all classes) who completed the problems at each level were posted. When the tenth name was posted, a coupon, good for one free hamburger was posted for each student to discover and remove.

j. Giving special privileges to students, based on attitude, behavior, grades, and attendance each week, for example, 15 to 20 minutes of free reading discussion time or class competition on Fridays or posting pictures (obtained from parents) for "Student of the Week" who had grown the most during the week.

k. Weekly point systems—this gives students responsibility for keeping track of their own work.

Analyzing Your Scheduling Skills

Continually analyze your scheduling skills by comparing them to the original plan. All teachers should develop a system whereby they can mark off the things that actually occurred each day and what they intended to occur. The most important part of this directive is the comparison. You may begin by determining if there is a part of the lesson plan that is consistently cut short, a particular subject or time of day, or particular type of student neglected. Second, either place a note in a prominent place to build your ability to strengthen this area of weakness or make a significant reorganization of your daily schedule at the end of the six-week period. Begin by completing a one-week analysis of your daily classroom procedures. Once completed, you will be able to list two specific improvements that could be made.

Limiting the Number of Samples or Models Used

Limit the number of times you make more than the first sample or model of individual, written, or art projects for students. In a study of the National Education Association's Teacher of the Year Award recipients (Tschudin, 1978), a scheduling principle they followed was to never use time making a lot of the same thing. Whenever there was a need to make several copies of an item, students, volunteers, or "adopted grandparents" from nursing homes were asked to do them. In return, these people became honored guests at special class presentations or last day of school activities. Teachers who used this scheduling strategy made contacts at the beginning of (or preceding) the school year and planned well enough in advance so that the volunteers (or early finishers in class) had at least a week to complete the drill cards, report card forms, art designs, or bulletin board ornaments before the time needed.

What repetitious tasks can you schedule for motivated assistants to complete?

_____

_____

Schedule for Variety

Provide variety in the weekly schedule so monotony will not influence your expectations and time use. Monotony decreases the intensity and endurance of student effort toward learning and increases the amount of time needed to learn facts. It can be eliminated by scheduling the use of "variety" on a daily/weekly basis. To call your attention to this scheduling need, make a symbol in the lesson plan book that marks the spot where you plan to schedule a change or weekly "surprise" in teaching. Some special "surprises" that have been used by other teachers are listed later in this chapter, under the subheading of "Reusing the Best of the Past." In addition to scheduling special activities, you could

1. Decrease the amount of time spent in one aspect of the lesson plan so as to vary the habitual way one structures the class (e.g., do independent practice orally instead of as seatwork). Make this change in the subject area you least enjoy teaching.
2. Schedule a regular break each week so students have a sense of anticipation for this day and simultaneously increase their attention during the normal schedule.
3. Start one subject later on Fridays.

Keep a Check on Your Attitude Toward Scheduling

Several research studies discovered that a teacher's perception of classroom time is not "that it is a scarce resource to be allocated with care" (Arlin, 1979; and Wiley and Harnischfeger, 1974). Rather, many teachers schedule "just to be sure all the time is used; to kill time in the easiest, fastest way, ensuring students have none to kill."

In other studies, teachers did not know the criteria upon which they made their decisions concerning schedules (Barr, 1974, 1975). Most effective teachers were able to explain that they used a specific "steering, criterion group" of students. That is, these teachers would watch the body language of a specific group of students to determine when enough time had been spent on a particular activity. This is when they would leave one item and then move to the next item in the schedule.

A separate "criterion group" was used to determine when these teachers needed to add more variety to the schedule, using students' affective responses as the stimulus for change (Kounin and Gump, 1974). These data may also suggest how a teacher's "pets" emerge. Perhaps these students are the ones who are in each of the criterion "steering groups" the teacher uses. These "pets" would be very valuable to the teacher if this were true.

The greatest difficulty in changing activities seems to be that we do not consciously pay attention to the criterion group or we do not select the appropriate criterion group. A college professor found it very valuable to pause and identify the students who influenced her most in each of her classes. By so doing, she was able to monitor if the impact they had upon changes in her instruction were appropriate for the majority of students she taught. This strategy not only increased her objectivity but kept her from responding best to those students she most liked. Further, as Good, Grouws, and Beckerman (1978) discovered, teachers who used an appropriate criterion group covered 34 more pages of text in a year than did teachers who did not monitor their schedules.

Reduce the Amount of Time Spent in Transition

You may fail to schedule time and means by which students and materials will be moved from one activity to another. Because of this, you may *expect* transitions between activities to be loud and difficult. By providing security through monitoring transitions as a scheduled activity, students learn to move into them easily and efficiently. This learning comes because they sense that you have planned and set aside time for the change, so you must still be in "charge" of this time and the change must be important.

While monitoring need be only a signal at the secondary level, lower grades need to begin a transition monitoring early in the independent practice session of a lesson. At both levels, students need to know the pattern and the same pattern of actions on your part needs to be used as frequently as possible. Ways to reduce the amount of time spent in transitions follow.

1. You monitor independent written work at the end of the class. You walk from one side of the room to the other, observing each child's work. Students know that you have planned enough time so you will be able to stop at each desk and that as soon as you have reached the last student you will give directions for the transition to the next subject. On the other hand, if you were to not plan time for the monitoring and transition, you might move from one student to the next as individual students raised their hands. Students begin to feel insecure and as if they are to structure themselves. In so doing, they begin to go off task, looking at the clock, looking to see what other students are doing, and asking for your attention. Since many do not yet have the skills or desire to monitor their own transition into a new subject, noise will increase.

2. You could end your directions for independent practice and allow students to work till they finish. You will have already established a routine

procedure that they perform individually to prepare for the next subject. For example, you modeled at the beginning of the year that as students finish their algebra problems, they will always be placed in the box on the file cabinet and then the students may work the extra credit problems on the charts or read a book. You will call each to the front as you grade the work or need to talk to each.

3. You have a phrase you say to end work. You then read one page from *Winnie-the-Pooh*, as a middle school math teacher did (or any book that students want). The book sharing, or a few moments of talk on an issue, is valuable. For as a student in the "Winnie-the-Pooh class" explained, "We're not only learning math but philosophy and Latin as well. Our teacher cares about us and treats us as people." For you see, the *Winnie-the-Pooh* book she read was in Latin/English and summarized each page with a moral for the 1980s. The student felt the importance this teacher placed upon efficient transition periods and translated the reason for the teacher's concern to be one of caring for and protecting her students.

To conclude the discussion about daily scheduling skills, you might wish to use the following standard to assess how well your skills are developing. Your class will be pleasant. It will appear orderly and inviting to passersby. People will tend to look in your room often. You will not frequently remind students of the rules or procedures once the first few weeks of school have passed. Your students will also be more tolerant of others and make more group decisions. Your students will not continue to test limits.

THE BENEFITS OF YEARLY SCHEDULING SKILLS

Blocking out time for special events is easy and saves you time. By blocking out sections of time at the beginning of the year for special projects you wish to complete during the year, you will receive several benefits. You will provide lead time so you can ask for volunteer assistance on projects. As mentioned in Chapter 1, scheduling small, consecutive blocks of time to celebrate seasonal events properly will help you to sustain the biological, rhythmic harmony of your class. Without scheduling lead time for projects in your lesson plan book, tension and hurried conditions lessens an activity's learning potential and enjoyment. You might avoid these situations by taking your lesson plan book and blocking out 30 minutes a week one month in advance of a special event to complete the project. You will also be demonstrating to your students how they can better prepare for special events in their lives.

A third benefit was reported in a research study conducted by Van Loozen (1982). When school board members were asked to log special periods of time for their major areas of responsibility on their calendars, they were (1) significantly more satisfied with their job, (2) used more time to enlist aid and resources from colleagues and subordinates, and (3) were caught off guard, having to use only their own time as a resource, less frequently than untrained school board members.

Fourth, let's consider the research of Karwiet (1985), Rossmiller (1983), Halasz and Desy (1984), Harnishchfeger and Wiley (1978), and Frederick, Walberg, and Rasher (1979). The average teacher will be absent or dealing with student absenteeism for an equivalent of 18 days of the school year. This "average teacher" will also spend 8 days out of work due to strikes, inclement weather, and/or inservice days. Each day of the week this teacher will also use 40 percent of the day in noninstructional activities such as hall monitoring, lunch duties, and distributing papers. He or she will discipline students for 1 hour and 12 minutes daily and will interact with students who are inattentive or who are not staying on task for 1 hour and 15 minutes. The average teacher will have only 2 hours and 18 minutes to devote to productive learning. In these conditions only the most foresightful schedules enable a commitment of time to any additional curricular and extracurricular activity. These facts may also help you better appreciate why you feel so tired and pressured when you try to do something special over and above your regular schedule. You have less than 2½ hours a day to get it all done!

Scheduling annual events early and blocking out lead time also develops the skill of selectivity (see Chapter 1). That is, this scheduling skill enhances your ability to recognize the parts of your work that are beginning to become obsolete, as soon as their effectiveness begins to diminish. By dispensing with less effective products, methods, and procedures early, you continuously make time in your schedule.

Last, yearly planning can prepare for those days that will hold special stress. Early in the year you can write in potentially "hurried" days, such as noting that in the last week of school in your eighth grade classes, "I will be signing autograph books for my students." Then when May arrives and you are too busy for everything you have to do, this note reappears, as a reminder. You can automatically modify the week's daily activities to make them less "hurried."

Similarly, a high school English teacher used this skill to circle the last boxes in red for each of the Monday–Friday periods prior to the end of each reporting period. She was then able to remind herself to require written homework to be due prior to this week so she could spread out the work needed to be done in grading make up work and averaging grades. By so doing she often even had time to write each student a special progress note.

Other methods that can be used to make a yearly schedule are:

1. Select a special color for holidays; special colors for school reports, deadlines, and inservices; and special colors for elementary student birthdays or secondary schoolwide award days. Mark the day the exact event is to occur as many hours of the school day prior to that day as you feel you want to use to prepare for it in the color that designates that event.
2. Make notes in the margin of your lesson plan book. These remind you to change the regular schedule, during a particular week, to a unit format of student, self-monitored work so you are freed of your instructional at-school time to work with small groups of students. Without yearly scheduling, you may have to rely on less efficient, unrelated "dittos" to fill students' time because you've been caught off guard by special projects.

3. Schedule meetings with students and other resource people the week preceding the special block of time to divide labor, increase student ownership over projects during the planning stages, and add quality to ideas while reducing the work load for all.

4. Schedule special types of tasks outside of instructional tasks as well; for example, block out two hours each year to clean out cabinets and to distribute outdated and unused teaching aids to others. Knowing this is to occur you can keep your mind alert to an opportunity when someone else needs some teaching aids (e.g., a colleague's son is beginning his teaching career) and invite the interested party to come to help sift through your things. They take what you don't want and the task as well as the task completion time is cut in half. It becomes more fun as well.

5. Schedule small blocks of time for several days before a larger, predetermined goal is to occur. As Cypher and Willower (1984) noted, without such scheduling skill a typical day will proceed at a fast and "unrelenting pace with many varied, brief fragmented segments . . .. Activities that have immediate payoff, liveliness, and verbal exchanges are preferred to those that require more time to prepare and execute, leaving teachers without time to work on larger-payoff activities unless these are scheduled in smaller sections."

HOW TO USE THE BEST FROM THE PAST

Avoid feeling rushed all the time: "Too busied with the crowded hour to fear to live or die," said Ralph Waldo Emerson, in *Nature*. If you identify with this condition, the next time the world seems to cave in upon you, it may help to pause and reflect: Am I confusing motion with progress? Am I constantly busy without gaining results? Am I working harder and not smarter? Am I acting before I take 5 minutes of quiet time to plan a better method?

To overcome the "busyness" pressure you may feel, start thinking about and outlining a task as soon as it is assigned. Gather materials and ideas as you are doing other things. As soon as you have an idea, write it on a separate sheet of paper and file it or stack it with materials that will be used with it. For example, a sixth grade art teacher wanted to make papier-mâché animals in class the next day. As he completed the present day's activity, he jotted a note to get the model out of the school storage bin and placed the note in the pans, near the paste, that he was just putting together to prepare for the activity tomorrow. He also asked the student who had just finished putting her supplies away to go next door and get the filmstrip that he would use to begin the lesson. He then placed the filmstrip in the pan as well.

As he thought over his plan, students finished cleaning up the activity of the day. He remembered that Robert, a former student, volunteered to bring his robot, which he had made last year, to show to this year's classes. Robert would give tips on how to best use papier-mâché. So, this teacher jotted a note to remind Robert to come.

Consequently, by outlining the task as soon as it comes, you can often be prepared for the next day's activity in the amount of time students spend ending the activity in progress.

A third rule is to reuse the best sections of past activities again and again, with new improvements each time. Mark sections of lesson plan books in a special way (e.g., highlight in yellow/circle it) as soon as you file it away or begin to plan for the upcoming week. Refer to these ideas as you begin to make your yearly schedule. Note "see file on bacteria" in plan book to remind you of different kinds of special reusable items. Then, improve upon the last time the idea was used each successive time.

In this way, you will increase your skills in scheduling time to activities as you will be better able to estimate time needed. The activity will likely be more successful as well. The past, reinforced experiences will become a guide to provide insight about the significance of different environmental factors and cautions of point in which you could commit errors.

In summary, using the best of the past is akin to using a idea from one of the great "giants" in our educational past. By using this idea, you climb upon the shoulders of this genius, and being there, you see much more, can dream and accomplish much more easily. Many successes can occur if the fruits of your previous successes are used as the foundation. Figure 3-2 is a summary of many ideas teachers have shared as to how they have used this skill in their classes.

DEALING WITH
WHAT YOU MOST DISLIKE DOING

Of all the skills and methods you'll develop, the ability to schedule and complete those professional tasks that are difficult will be the hardest to acquire. Time management theory suggests that a means of accomplishing difficult tasks is to make it a habit (see Chapter 5), schedule it as the first activity in the day, or reward yourself for doing it.

People who have learned to schedule difficult professional tasks outside their areas of expertise/talent at the earliest point in the day enjoy the day more and feel more productive (Collins, 1981). As noted in Chapter 2, because these people do not consciously/unconsciously have to give their attention to the tasks they dread, throughout the day, they can use their full potential and attending behaviors on other tasks. If you have never used this method, I have found that many teachers have to make a conscious commitment to do it. Also, you should not work on a difficult task first in the day if it is not the first priority of the day or if it doesn't call upon your highest capabilities. An extended reward system is a better method for these types of tasks and will help you to complete them faster. Examples of these systems are in Chapter 8.

You can also use a method of counteracting the externals that interrupt your schedule. When an interference occurs, you follow it by immediately setting an uncancellable appointment with yourself to do your job for the amount of time interrupted. Then, you will keep this appointment even though it may be difficult at first to do so. But, by pressing "on 1 minute more" (see Chapter 2), your gains of self-worth and your results will be bountifully rewarded.

Figure 3-2

OTHER TEACHERS' BEST-OF-THE-PAST ACTIVITIES THAT HAVE BEEN USED AND REUSED SUCCESSFULLY

_____ Paired reading groups whereby two students on the same level worked together silently to complete their basal reading books and workbooks with teacher's two-week goals established with the two-person teams.

_____ Individualized contracts for three-week periods with self-selected awards if proper diagnosis of individual need is made by the student.

_____ Poorer readers tutoring students who are two grades younger.

_____ "Reading Is Fundamental" book fairs.

_____ Listening centers when readers hear their story read to them by teacher or aide as they followed along with the tape, pausing at points to ask questions or single-work responses that students wrote down.

_____ Individualized criterion-referenced skill tests making skills lessons over the skill needs by groups twice a week, with group composition changing to fit the individual skill needs of students.

_____ Multiple copies of a paperback book are available so that all members of the class and the teacher can read the same book simultaneously for several consecutive days, experiencing and sharing the same involvement in plot.

_____ To add variety to the instruction of vocabulary words, write one new word on a card to give, one each, to every child in a reading circle. Before the reading lesson begins, each child has learned his or her word's meaning and can pronounce the word. Then, at any time during the course of an oral reading circle, if any child does not know another's word, that child will tell his or her classmates the word and its meaning, if necessary.

_____ Have children make a dessert by reading the recipe.

_____ Fill lunch boxes with various types of flashcards or word cards with the words given in sentences. Children can take the boxes to their desks for practice [used by Ms. Sue Bolandi, Breckenridge, Texas].

_____ Have a folder for each child in a pocket on each child's desk. The folder can be used to place all notes that go home to parents and all homework papers you wish parents to see. The folders help to keep the room clean and children organized. The cloth pockets on the chairs can also be used to store glue, scissors, and crayolas for primary students [idea developed by Ms. JoAnn Phillips, Fort Worth, Texas].

_____ Dr. I.Q.—Each student researches the same topic individually, writing a question to ask his fellow classmates. He becomes a "Dr. I.Q." if no one knows the answer. All students get a chance to ask one or more question(s). The lesson can also be adapted to involve two teams competing against each other.

_____ World Series Baseball or Football Super Bowl review—either baseball or football is played with the ball being advanced or withdrawn as a result of correct and incorrect answers to questions that you ask in reviewing a unit.

_____ Hit Parade of _____ —Students select and vote upon the topic and issues within a unit that they most want to learn. You arrange the unit plan so that their first choice receives most time, second choice receives secondmost time, and so on.

_____ Use typewriter to teach vocabulary by writing stories with ten newly learned words each two weeks.

_____ Make individual student blackboards on cardboards so students can all answer at the same time.

Figure 3-2 continued

_____ Television units—use the TV as a unit of study or watch special programs on TV.

_____ Video-taped presentation.

_____ Audio-taped lessons.

_____ Overhead projector and transparency lessons.

_____ Slides.

_____ Travel pamphlets and maps.

_____ Charts.

_____ Round Table or Town Hall discussions—everyone picks a subject of interest or one aspect of a selected subject.

_____ Outside speaker(s) on a panel and students prepare questions in advance.

_____ "What is a_____" introductory plan for independent student self-selected study of a topic.

_____ "Sword drill" review—you or a student leader asks a question; first team or person to find the correct answer is the winner.

_____ Have a field trip debate or panel to discuss a topic. Then have a critique of the event as a William F. Buckley, Dick Cavett, or Meet the Press—type program.

_____ Game Show lesson—Students select their favorite game show. They spend one week getting ready for the one-week showing of the next week. In art classes, they make the stage settings; in language arts classes, they write the scripts. On the following week, the TV show is given.

_____ Excuse-type program—When a problem arises, a decision needs to be made, or an alternative action or program is needed in our country, in your school or classroom, or in the content areas of study—Spend over three classroom periods in "brainstorming sessions" where on one is allowed to critique anyone else's idea until a specified amount of time has elapsed or until all ideas have been presented. Then all "excuses" for not doing the actions are given. The end result is the design and enthusiastic implementation of a new plan/policy or simulation or a solution to a natural problem.

_____ Exchange program—Invite another class or another age group to share ideas, plans, and/or projects about a common goal or subject.

_____ Projects program—Each member of a group or of the class shares history, purposes, and future of separate projects that have been undertaken.

_____ Candle Light program—Students honor someone of past or present prominence by designing an honors program for the person. Research will have been done as a cooperative group effort concerning all aspects of the honoree's life and contributions to the school and/or society.

_____ Campaign drives—Real or simulated campaigns for newspaper collection, conservation, energy, social reforms, politics, cancer research (to name a few) will be advertised and conducted as classroom lessons.

_____ Appreciation programs—Special events are created, such as Homecoming, Circus Parades, Your Town's Day, World Hunger Day, Mexican Fiesta, Boston Tea Party Celebration. Students include activities typifying the events and the activities of the period of time in which the event occurred in the Appreciation Day activities. Parents, community members, and other classes of students are encouraged to participate in the "celebration."

_____ "Man-on-the-Street" program—Students either conduct a true public opinion survey or reenact a series of man-on-the-street interviews concerning a new topic of study.

_____ Skits or playlets.

continued

Figure 3-2 continued

_____ Outdoor programs—Normal activities are held outside for variety of settings, or special lessons are created around the special events, nature and happenings of the spring, fall, and winter seasons.

_____ Every child writes, cooks, and brings his or her favorite recipe to class; food is eaten and recipes compiled into books for gifts to adults.

_____ Guest lecturers who gave testimonials of how they benefited from reading for work and pleasure.

_____ Music—reading favorite songs of students and then singing along with record.

_____ Charts of progress that students keep records on.

_____ Weekly magazines such as _Weekly Readers._

_____ Dictionary "sword drills"—Contest for learning use of dictionaries.

_____ Creative writing and pair readings of classmates' stories once a week in English classes.

_____ Read a chapter of a book or a small book to students each day.

_____ Listening centers.

_____ Filmstrips and records with read-along scripts.

_____ Plays—both prewritten and student-authored.

_____ TV scripts.

_____ Student group leaders.

_____ Bringing animals from the zoo to class to be held after using library periods once a week for one month to study scientific books.

_____ Contests of who could read 1,000 pages of Newberry and Caldecott award-winning books so they can go to a grand opening of a book store, on a field trip, to meet William Armstrong, and so on.

_____ Puppet shows with paper-sack faces and sock faces.

_____ Name that _____ —To review or introduce famous names/characters or facts.

_____ Excursion programs—Visit to government offices, U.S. public health centers, blood banks, county jail, school board meetings, or other common societal offices and agencies as a large group, pairs of students, or individuals to learn about general areas of concern and to find resources and facts to answer specific concerns and issues.

_____ Workshop programs—Sessions that have been created by fellow students on a workshop-type format. These sessions will center on developing the students' skills in a particular area, e.g.; having a workshop of activities on "How to study better," "How to use a dictionary for more personal advantages," "How to save more money as a consumer," "How to become a _____ ," "How to become a better football player", "How to enjoy watching football games more," "How to become better liked by my peers."

_____ Having to take the responsibility for younger students could help an older student with problem behaviors to learn the importance of cooperation.

Best-of-the-Past Activities You Want to Use Again:

1. _____
2. _____
3. _____
4. _____
5. _____
6. _____
7. _____

As you are well aware, certain types of teaching tasks are impossible to reschedule later in the day. To release your attention to other priorities if you can't keep an appointment you make with yourself, record the amount of time missed. You will then make up this time as soon as possible. For example, to write this book, I made an appointment with myself each day. The appointment was for the first two hours after I awoke. On days when I had to disrupt this schedule, I'd block out my lunch. When both of these times were interrupted, I noted the debt of time I owed myself. Having recorded these hours I could more easily concentrate on the task before myself and repay myself as soon as I was in greater control of my schedule.

This method works so well that even when long stretches of appointments can't be kept, you can catch back up within days. This system of measuring a specific amount of time to allocate regularly has been successful in helping regulate new activities and bringing new subjects into a single class.

Finally, I have found that if on one day, I have several tasks I dislike doing, I complete more of them if I schedule all the distasteful ones consecutively in ordered ranking and don't intersperse them with less distasteful tasks.

Before I ask you to commit to a plan of action, you might be more successful if you experiment with each of the above and combinations of them for every item you have difficulty building into your daily or yearly schedule. When the right method of scheduling is identified, it will seem natural.

Remember the professional or personal task you most dislike doing. As soon as you read the following question, pause to answer it: What plan would you like to apply to include this task in your schedule tomorrow?_____

_____

Think of a reward that would be equal to having met the plan you devised, and plan the time you can give it to yourself.

Having now laid your plans, you have only to do them tomorrow. Tomorrow, as soon as they're finished, jot down the task you accomplished, the method you used, and the date in the margin of this book, for your future reference. In the future, when you open this book and see this jotted note, a new discovery about yourself will await, I promise. I'll not tell you what you'll realize, but it will occur. This will be a reward to you for daring to improve your skills.

A second reward is in the next paragraph. If you haven't yet scheduled your disliked task for tomorrow, do that now, before you read on. Now, for the second reward and the idea. Whenever you receive an evaluation, a written note, or a critique, a note that contains a message you didn't expect, a complex set of written directions, or a difficult assignment, force yourself to reread the paper. That is, just as soon as you finish reading the difficult message, remind yourself of what you read today. If you go back and reread it again, immediately before you lay it down, this second reading will clarify the points, lessen the hurt you have already experienced, provide a more accurate interpretation of the points in the note, and afford time for you to reestablish your objectivity. You can then return to more positive thoughts so you can begin to plan your best action to remedy the situation. In essence, this second reading provides the time to transform your shock and negative thoughts to positive stands and small, accomplishable steps you can take to respond productively. Without it, you may be tempted to never try in that area again or to postpone indefinitely your reply, limiting opportunities to respond to new responsibilities.

MINIMIZING CLASSROOM SPACE FOR MAXIMUM TIME USE

There are very few studies of the type of schoolwide organizational system that produces greatest learning. There are few studies that identify the type of desk arrangements that are best for each teaching style. Until we know more about environmental influences on learning we can better use space and materials.

The following actions, which have been taken in other schools, may be appropriate for your building or system. Even though some of these alternatives may be too extravagant to implement fully, check off those ideas that you can picture, in modified form, using your own setting:

_____ Extend the school day or week by inviting fathers and/or grandfathers to open and staff the school from 8:00 A.M. to 4:00 P.M.

_____ Open the library 30 minutes before school and remain open 30 minutes after school closes.

_____ Place television sets on school buses to give foreign language lessons for credit.

_____ Decorate halls and use foldout tables for small group work in corridors.

_____ Position old car, stove, repairable appliances to be taken apart and learned how to restore them.

_____ Have supervision at lunch. Provide parents or older elementary or high school students.

_____ Use color as a way of functionally separating learning areas.

_____ Use an empty classroom for all audiovisual displays with full-time volunteers on duty so film, filmstrip, or other teaching aids can be ready for students as soon as they arrive so teachers can stay in their classrooms.

_____ Plan minicourses one afternoon a week where pupils teach each other and choose which session they want to attend (e.g., cooking, chess, tennis, typing).

_____ Plan miniweeks where regular curriculum is set aside and school focuses upon a problem such as hunger, war, and the like, staffed by adults from the community and culminating in a contribution to the community.

_____ Place listening centers in corridors.

_____ Divide space on auditorium stage with portable boards or draperies.

_____ Use the cafeteria for study or individual work before or after lunch.

_____ Buy stackable chairs and tables.

_____ Use courtyards and areas near the building for art, music, reading, and special projects by installing picnic tables.

_____ Plant a garden on school grounds.

_____ Place pegboards on the wall below the chalkboards for additional displays and/or storage areas.

_____ Convert an empty classroom to a student lounge that students earn the privilege to visit and take a soda break when their work has been completed, or it can be used for enrichment activities.

_____ Encourage students to bring books to school that they no longer read and exchange them with students in other classes.

_____ Use telephone cable spools and milk crates for tables and storage, cutting the spools in half make them sit-down tables.

_____ Place masking or duct tape on tile floors to mark off areas for special activities.

_____ Use hot plates (often donated by parents) for cooking.

_____ Trade old textbooks and library books with a nearby school [the first seven ideas were originally suggested in an article by Drummond, 1983].

_____ Early in the morning survey the bulletin boards and wall and floor space arrangements of student/teacher's desk, small-group areas, book cases, centers, pets and plants, textbooks, teacher's supplies, and seasonal items for wasted space and clutter.

_____ Let students decide on the movement arrangements they would like in their room and any changes they would like in their schools.

_____ Develop a display and/or an exhibit in the room so the room has a special identity, for example, an old bathtub for students to read in [this and the next three suggestions were those identified as important to the National Education Association's Teachers of the Year].

_____ Rearrange desks in a circle each time a class discussion is scheduled so as to promote discussion and warmth.

_____ Use phonograph to reinforce learning and encourage creativity, for example, role play the emotions felt by music heard.

_____ Use common materials in uncommon ways such as using the tape recorder for a touring tape "through Athens."

_____ Before students use materials in the room, explain which ones can and cannot be used and why.

_____ Eliminate the problem of students not having pencils with them by (a) enforcing a rule that all pencils must be sharpened before the tardy bell rings or (b) storing a set of sharpened pencils in a container in the room and having students take one and put an unsharpened one in a matching container beside it and the pencil monitor sharpens all at the end of the day.

_____ All students will then remember to bring the correct notebook to class more easily. Have all students buy the same color notebook for the same subject, for example, all social studies materials belong in the red notebook.

_____ Explain why you don't want students to take liberties with your materials and give the rationale or list the specific instructions and post the list where the materials and equipment will be used.

_____ Tell students the standards of form, neatness, and due dates you expect. For example, can they use pen/pencil and what types of paper; can they write on the back of their paper; how stringent you will be in legibility and what consequences can they expect if they don't do it.

_____ Instead of saving bits of leftovers from projects to use next year, putting all leftovers in an art collage box would be more efficient.

_____ During lectures put a magnet on papers you will be referring to and put them on the chalkboard so your hands are free to talk and give directions.

Remember, one sign of a professional is his or her use of proper tools. Your own new idea of how you will improve your room tomorrow is

_____

_____

Orderly storage is significantly related to more effective time management. Walker and Parkhurst (1982) found that the best managers of time tend to be middle-aged adults, with a strong family cohesion, who have a sense of the importance of time usage and who keep orderly storage areas. Do only a little bit each week to become better organized and get the students to help, if you wish.

USING YOUR PLANNING PERIODS MORE EFFECTIVELY

To overcome the feeling of being rushed all the time, select one of the following three methods of scheduling your planning periods. Creative use of one's 30 to 45 minutes per day of unscheduled time can become the most important oasis of the day. This is especially true when your goals are not being accomplished as rapidly as you desire. Your planning periods will be less productive if you spend them getting ready to implement the next period's lesson. That is, instead of using your unscheduled personal time to mix paint, grade papers, put up bulletin boards, or hold parent conferences, use your time to accomplish a larger goal.

To do so, be certain that your "daily teaching" tasks contain a time during your class where students can clean up the activities in which they are engaged, turn in work at its proper location, and rearrange the furniture. Classes should begin with students or class officers getting their materials together for lessons. In this way, as the students leave in the period preceding your planning period, your room is clean, organized, and free for your use.

The first method of enhancing the benefits of your planning period is to perform a majority of activities that we'll set in Chapter 8. For example, during the week's planning periods, your professional needs can be addressed. Beneficial activities to do during a planning period could include the following:

Monday. During the weekend you discovered a community project for your students. Early this morning you scheduled a conference with your principal. During your planning period, you met with her to make arrangements for the students' participation.

Tuesday. You meet with the three other people on your committee to work on the schoolwide improvement that all three of you have set for this semester. You always look forward to this meeting.

Wednesday. Today you meet with your parent volunteers (or your student class officers). During the volunteer meetings you plan how they can be more effectively used in next month's activities. In officers meetings, you also make plans for improving the class routine and using officers' new ideas for projects.

Thursday. In planning the special activities you will do in the coming week, you have found that it is more fun to get ready for these activities on Thursday instead of Friday. You have also learned to keep a list all week and use Thursday as your "shopping day." During your shopping day planning period, you get the extra things that you need for the next weeks lesson, for example, spending 15 minutes in the library locating that special book you want to read, digging in the back of the old storage closet for the textured globe, calling to confirm that the guest speaker is coming, borrowing hot plate from the kitchen, and scheduling parents for next week's panel discussion. By challenging yourself to schedule only one day for enriching the curriculum you will create resourceful ways to maximize the available time as opposed to increasing the number of days you spend getting your weekly plans in place.

Friday. "My Day"—Rest, Revive, and Reorganize. Sit back, think for about 20 minutes about your professional/development goals. Reflect about ways to improve your teaching skills and content.

A secondary teacher colleague of mine shared how she is changing her planning periods and how much more time she is having for important activities:

Monday. Meet with committee and other committee members to discuss ways to help beautify our school environment.

Tuesday. Write a new unit test that employs matching and higher level thinking skills but that can be graded as soon as students finish taking it.

Wednesday. Use the "assembly—line method" and grade the papers just turned in, read the next chapter in the book that will be covered in class, and think about how the students can make their own folders for the parent conferences that I want to hold next week.

Thursday. Clean out file cabinets and discard obsolete materials.

Friday. Three or four times a year teachers from neighboring schools spend an hour together learning from each other and planning cooperatively.

In summary, one method of overcoming that rushed feeling is to use the majority of your planning periods accomplishing new, advanced goals for better lessons and for your own professional growth.

A second method is to divide the planning period between activities that aid student learning and activities that benefit your professional development. This method is a modification of the 7—11 method in Chapter 2. Set a routine 20 minutes a day on lesson planning and a coffee break and a routine 20 minutes taking care of professional development tasks.

A third method is to work diligently a set number of days on student-related tasks and other days on tasks beyond the classroom level.

With each of these methods, the following pointers will add to your productivity:

1. Plan a few moments each day for thinking and renewal.
2. Make yourself unavailable for just a few moments a day.
3. Move your desk out of view of the hall so social visits will be discouraged, or close your door at times to create a feeling of being out of the flow of traffic and its demands of "do this and do that."
4. Be aware of impulses you feel to engage in activities you didn't schedule.
5. Remember that if you develop the habit of jumping from one thing to another, you will develop a "low-level comfort zone" and may begin to feel that getting only one or two small things done in a planning period is O.K.

So often we don't plan our planning period. Because of the void this creates, the planning period becomes instantly saturated with low-priority and menial tasks that are beneath your professional level of competence. When you don't set a goal for each planning period that is a large goal, others will tend to use your planning time to accomplish their goals or talk about a problem they face.

When you have a goal for these precious solitary minutes of your day, you can exercise your choice to help someone else or complete your goal. Without a goal you could misuse your time and subsequently underestimate the time needed to meet your own needs. You could then become less conscientious or more pressured.

THERE ARE 5 MINUTES LEFT! WHAT DO I DO?

Keeping students on task for the most time possible means beginning classes when the bell rings and designing a thorough signal system. Halasz (1984) discovered that teachers who begin their classes when the bell rings, even if all the students haven't arrived, create higher rates of students' time on task. She also determined that if 10 students in a class of 15 wait only 10 minutes a day for at least 5 other students in their class to arrive, so all can receive the directions to begin, 30 hours of class time during a year will be wasted.

Arlin (1979) noted that creating a thorough signal system appears to be a function of continuity, that is, teachers frequently repeated procedures during a lesson and prodded between lessons. Arlin also found that the most effective teachers had two or three consistent methods of opening the class before the bell rang (e.g., offering an opportunity to begin problems early because they were on the board or overhead as the students entered; class officers began to distribute papers that were to be returned to the class) and continued class up to the last few minutes of class. These teachers also spent parts of the first two days of classes each year training their students to conform to the signal system they would be using to begin, sustain, and end activities:

> Often the continuity inherent in an activity has been created by the teacher. For example, one class seemed to make transitions with little if any external monitoring from the teacher. This one class seemed to be more orderly than other classes in the school, even during trips to the gym, etc. I asked the cooperating teacher if she did anything specifically to attain this. The teacher was somewhat embarrassed to admit that during the first part of the year she would drill children on putting books back on the side shelves, going to the gym, etc., even to the extent of having children put their hands over their mouths as they did so. The teacher apparently "tracked" pupils into the desired behavior patterns by "walking them through" the desired activities. Each activity triggered the next. (Arlin, 1979, p. 217)

Effective teachers consistently monitor students during lessons, as introduced in the discussion of transitions. Also, several minutes before the lesson's end, these teachers prepared the class, for example, "In 5 minutes we're going to start our math game. Finish as much as you can on your art work because I'll signal you to begin to clean up in 1 minute" (Arlin, 1979). In this way, teachers sustain the momentum of work and minimize pupil disruptions.

The term "sponge activities" has been used for lessons designed to last from 5 to 17 minutes and occur during the periods of transition, as students prepare to learn, and as the teacher waits for the entire class to return to begin a lesson. These activities are to use those few moments of class time that normally find students sitting idly. They "sponge up" these wasted moments to put them to use for student learning. Several of the following activities were developed at the University of California at Los Angeles and at the University of Texas at Austin. All are based on the discouraging data from the Center for Teacher Education at Austin that 3 to 17 minutes are wasted at the begining of each class period. That is, from the time the first student enters the classroom until instruction actual begins can range from 9 percent to 32 percent of total class time (Hord, 1984). The following activities should eliminate this loss in your classes.

1. When the problems or assignment to be completed in class is on the board before students enter, and students begin work on the assignment as soon as they enter, instructional time increases. These teachers have also prepared a motivational device and the device not only is so strong

that students are anxious to begin as soon as they enter the room, but the device requires higher-level thinking or activities outside the classroom environment where students can creatively structure the learning.

2. Have a class officer write the first few problems to be worked on the board and all students who can finish the problems before the class work begins can be allowed special privileges. Class officers are also responsible for (a) having done the problem ahead of time, (b) having the teacher grade them, and (c) checking each classmate's paper.

3. If the first few problems that will compose the next day's activities are given at the end of the lesson, students can begin to work the problems as soon as they get to class and avoid homework that day.

4. Project a page for students to read as they enter. Students are then to write questions from the reading to ask classmates as soon as class begins.

5. Allow students who arrive early to begin work on the homework assignment for the day by working in pairs.

6. Give the first question orally to the class and ask them to be thinking about the answer; after class begins or after the papers are distributed, ask them to be thinking about the answer and after class begins or after the papers are distributed you ask for their thoughts.

To avoid wasted moments at the end of class, you or a student can give oral review questions over material covered during the day, as students prepare to leave the class. Additional sponge activities can be found in *Mind-Stretchers*, by Pitman Learning, Fearnon Teacher's Aides, 6 Davis Drive, Belmont, Calif. 94002 (415-592-7810).

SUMMING UP

In conclusion, improving your scheduling skills, as you are already beginning to do, will not only increase student learning but your own sense of self-esteem and job satisfaction. Your competence and organization will model your goals, commitment, and work habits for your students as well.

To help crystallize what you have learned in this chapter, what was the most important skill on which you will want to improve?_____

REFERENCES

Arlin, M. "Teacher Transitions Can Disrupt Time Flow in Classrooms." *American Educational Research Journal*, Vol. 16, No. 4, 1979, p. 369-403.

Arlin, M. "Teacher Transitions Can Disrupt Time Flow in Classrooms." *American Educational Research Journal*, Vol. 16, No. 4, 1979, p. 369-403.

Barr, R. "School, Class, Group, and Pace Effects on Learning." Paper presented at the annual meeting of the American Educational Research Association in Boston, 1980.

Barr, R. C. "How Children Are Taught to Read: Grouping and Pacing." *School Review*, Vol. 83, 1975, 479-498.

Barr, R. C. "Instructional Pace Differences and Their Effect on Reading Acquisition." *Reading Research Quarterly*, Vol. 9, 1974, 526-554.

Collins, Cathy. "Time Management in the Classroom: Preservice Teacher Survey." Unpublished paper. Fort Worth: Texas Christian University, 1981.

Cypher, Thomas W., and Donald J. Willower. "The Work Behavior of Secondary School Teachers." *Journal of Research and Development in Education*, Vol. 18, no. 1, 1984.

Davidson, Jack L., and Freda M. Holly. "Your Students Might Be Spending Only Half of the School Day Receiving Instruction." *The American School Board Journal*, 1979.

Douglass, Merrill, and Donna Douglass. *Manage Your Time, Manage Your Work, Manage Yourself*. New York: Amacon, 1980.

Drummond, Harold D. "Using Time, Space, and Things Creatively." *National Elementary Principal*, 1983.

Evertson, Carolyn M., Edmund Emmer, Julie P. Sanford, Barbara S. Clements, and Murray E. Worsham. *Classroom Management for Secondary Teachers*. Englewood Cliffs, N.J.: Prentice-Hall, 1984.

Frederick, W. C., H. J. Walberg, and S. P. Rasher. "Time, Teacher Comments, and Achievement in Urban High Schools." *Journal of Educational Research*, Vol. 73, no. 2, November-December 1979, 63-65.

Good, T. L., D. A. Grouws, and T. M. Beckerman "Curriculum Pacing: Some Empirical Data in Mathematics." *Journal of Curriculum Studies*. 1978.

Guthrie, John. "Research Views: Effective Teaching Practices." *The Reading Teacher*, Vol. 36, no. 3, 1982, 319-321.

Halasz, Ida M., and Jeanne Desy. *Guidelines for Improved Use of Time in Vocational-Technical Classes*. Columbus, Ohio: National Center for Research in Vocational Education, 1984.

Harnischfeger, A., and D. Wiley. "Classroom Control: Room and Time for Improvement." *Educational Technology*, Vol. 18, May 1978, 27-29.

Hord, Shirley M. *The Teacher Change Program*, Technical Report. Austin, Tex.: Research and Development Center for Teacher Education, 1984.

Karwiet, Nancy. "Should We Lengthen the School Term?" *Educational Researcher*, Vol. 14, no. 6, June-July 1985, 9-14.

Kounin, J. S., and P. V. Gump. "Signal Systems of Lesson Settings and the Task-Related Behavior of Preschool Children." *Journal of Educational Psychology*, no. 66, 1974, 554-562.

Rossmiller, R. A. "Time on Task: A Look at What Erodes Time for Instruction." *NASSP Bulletin*, Vol. 67, October 1983, 45-49.

Sanford, Julie P. "Time Use and Activities in Junior High Classes." *Journal of Educational Research*, Vol. 76, no. 3, January-February 1983, 140–147.

Tschudin, Ruth. "Secrets of A+ Teaching." *Instructor*, Vol. 88, September 1978, 65-74.

Van Loozen, Luann. "Ten Tips for Better Time Management." *The American School Board Journal*, Vol. 10, no. 7, 1982, 107-110.

Walker, F., and A. Parkhurst. "Identifying Differences in Time Managers." *Home Economics Research Journal*, Vol. 11, no. 1, September 1982, 57-66.

Wiley, D. E., and A. Harnischfeger "Explosion of a Myth: Quantity of Schooling and Exposure to Instruction, Major Educational Vehicles." *Educational Researcher*, Vol. 3, no. 1, 1974, 13-19.

ADDITIONAL SCHEDULING IDEAS FOR MATH TEACHERS

Johnson, David R. *Every Minute Counts: Making Your Math Class Work*. Palo Alto, California: Dale Seymour, 1982. (a)

Johnson, David R. *Making Minutes Count Even More: A Sequel to Every Minute Counts*. Palo Alto, California: Dale Seymour, 1982. (b)

four

Identifying and Eliminating Time Wasters

A Teacher Comments on Chapter 4

As teachers, we have many responsibilities, some of which can become frustrating and stressful if we are unable to manage our time wisely.

In Chapter 4, Dr. Collins introduces many concepts and activities that have the potential to decrease greatly the frustration and stress and increase greatly one's time management. Each of these concepts and activities is supported by many sources and by personal experiences.

While reading through the sections, I found myself stopping and thinking about how I really felt at the end of each working day. Was I energetic because I accomplished something or was I worrisome and frustrated because I once again did not achieve what I set out to accomplish?

In doing each activity, I was able to gain a greater insight on how I was wasting my time and what I could do to eliminate these time wasters. In addition, I am better in touch with my feelings about different activities I have and have not done as a teacher.

In summary, this chapter aided me in understanding my attitude and improving my effectiveness as a teacher. If you are a teacher with time management problems, I encourage you to read and participate in all of the activities. You will leave Chapter 4 with an uplifted attitude about yourself and your work.

Ms. Krista Winzurk
Secondary Teacher
Marietta, Georgia

*Experts say that people waste two hours or more
every day. . . . The first key to effective time
management is bringing the time wasters that
interrupt your effectiveness under firm control.*

—*James L. Hayes*
Past President and CEO
of the American
Management Association

Time wasters are things we do without getting a return or payoff; doing something that could have been done better by someone else; something that keeps me from a more appropriate, higher-payoff activity; something that causes us to have negative feelings. Van Loozen (1982) made a 12-item test for school board members to help them determine if they are time wasters. If you'd like to take this test, it follows. In the space preceding each statement, place a "plus" if it describes you, a "minus" if it doesn't:

____ I have a messy desk and cluttered (or no) files.
____ I never can find anything I need.
____ I frequently make appointments, miss them, and then reschedule them.
____ I'm often late to meetings.
____ I often fail to read backup materials before attending board meetings.
____ I volunteer for tasks someone else could (or should) do.
____ I'm often tired and unable to concentrate.
____ I have problems getting people to understand me.
____ I tend to ramble during conversations.
____ I oversell issues even when there's already support for them.
____ I politic at board meetings.
____ I put off dealing with irate people as long as possible.

TIME WASTERS YOU MAY NOT HAVE KNOWN YOU HAD

Through observation of our educational system and the works of Hogarth (1980), Douglass and Douglass (1980), Rutherford (1981), Fisher and Berliner (1985), Lakein (1972), Hohenstein (1981), and Fenner (1980), we can compose a list of possible causes for wasting time at work. Of the total of 47, 10 to 15 are experienced by most teachers. By comparing the number of causes you feel in your present position, to this average, you may understand reasons for some of your superior or inferior performances and attitudes toward your work.

Whether you are experiencing more or less pressure than most teachers is not as important as is knowing what is causing pressure in your present situation and setting goals for further professional growth. What is important is to know that we can minimize the time wasted and feelings of being constantly busy in our work. While you may feel that being busy is good or that you seem to work best under pressure, unless you purposely create this pressure and it is noncontinuous, being under pressure is not the most productive state in quality time use.

Each of the activities in this chapter will teach new ways of overcoming time pressures. You will also learn to invest your time and talents in activities that increase the purpose and goals in your life.

As you read the list of most common time wasters in Figure 4-1, place a check in the blank nearest the number that describes a time waster you have. For example, if you feel frustrated at times because your desk is cluttered, place a check in the blank immediately preceding each item, as shown in this example:

_____ _____ _____ _✓_ A. Having a cluttered desk.

There are four spaces to mark your future growth. In subsequent months, you can write the date above the blank and reassess how many time wasters you still have. By the time you've made your fourth assessment, you will have permanently eliminated many time wasters.

Reread the items you checked in Figure 4-1 and make notes on another sheet of paper of the similarities and dissimilarities among your items.

We will return to these notes in Chapter 6. Ask yourself, "What is the most important thing I have learned about myself?" "What two things have I already realized that I can begin to do to minimize wasted time?" and "Is my wasted time caused by me or external sources?"

Douglass (1980) suggests that good time management is attained only when systematic plans and positive actions are used to overcome time wasters. Tyler (1962) suggests that we isolate time wasters by dividing one day into 15-minute segments and then write or reflect upon how much was accomplished in each block of time:

_____

_____

_____

_____

_____

_____

_____

_____

_____

_____

_____

_____

Figure 4-1

MOST COMMON TIME WASTERS

___ ___ ___	1. Being bothered and frustrated by the clutter on your desk.
___ ___ ___	2. Having to overcome an obstacle course each time you have to find a piece of paper in your files.
___ ___ ___	3. Not being skilled in the art of "wastebasketry" (Douglass, 1980, p. 153).
___ ___ ___	4. Being excessively motivated.
___ ___ ___	5. Attempting to do too much at the time or overcommitting.
___ ___ ___	6. Acting on biases.
___ ___ ___	7. Being unable to overcome *betriebsblind* ("company blindness"), one is so familiar with one's surroundings that the waste and unproductive movements are not noticed.
___ ___ ___	8. Participating in ineffective or too many meetings of limited value.
___ ___ ___	9. Being unable to say "no."
___ ___ ___	10. Having to contend with a lot of "red tape."
___ ___ ___	11. Spending too much time on the telephone.
___ ___ ___	12. Entertaining too many drop-in visitors.
___ ___ ___	13. Doing too much paperwork.
___ ___ ___	14. Making agreements with others about your time that result in negative payoffs for you or allowing others to set your priorities for you.
___ ___ ___	15. Being unable to discipline yourself as well as you would like.
___ ___ ___	16. Being unable to take responsibility for your time.
___ ___ ___	17. Being unaware or unable to distinguish what is truly important and most valuable in a situation.
___ ___ ___	18. Wishing to be well liked.
___ ___ ___	19. Enjoying the feeling of being busy.
___ ___ ___	20. Having bad habits in your working style.
___ ___ ___	21. Exhibiting disorganized behavior.
___ ___ ___	22. Making tasks too complex or big unnecessarily or "making mountains out of molehills."
___ ___ ___	23. Being unable to make decisions as well as you would like.
___ ___ ___	24. Using procrastination.
___ ___ ___	25. Lacking the strength or skills to select key activities, projects, and people with whom you want to spend time.
___ ___ ___	26. Socializing and/or participating in idle conversation.
___ ___ ___	27. Lacking good planning skills.
___ ___ ___	28. Communicating ineffectively or receiving poor/infrequent communications.
___ ___ ___	29. Being unable to listen actively or to receive as much as you would like from the time you spend listening.
___ ___ ___	30. Having ineffective delegation skills, or assigning to others less frequently than you say "I will do it myself."

continued

Figure 4-1 continued

——— ——— ——— 31. Leaving tasks unfinished or jumping from one task to another; constantly switching priorities.
——— ——— ——— 32. Attending to too many details or being a perfectionist.
——— ——— ——— 33. Waiting.
——— ——— ——— 34. Traveling.
——— ——— ——— 35. Commuting.
——— ——— ——— 36. Inability to establish self-imposed deadlines.
——— ——— ——— 37. Having confused chains of command or multiple sources of immediate authority/responsibility.
——— ——— ——— 38. Inability to maximize changes and to capitalize upon the opportunity of the moment.
——— ——— ——— 39. Making frequent mistakes or giving ineffective performances.
——— ——— ——— 40. Having no standards or standards that do not maximize your capabilities and capacity.
——— ——— ——— 41. Being unable to detect progress or to maintain achievement records.
——— ——— ——— 42. Experiencing mind wanderings.
——— ——— ——— 43. Exhibiting poor handwriting.
——— ——— ——— 44. Misplacing items.
——— ——— ——— 45. Failing to listen.
——— ——— ——— 46. Overdoing routine tasks.
——— ——— ——— 47. Brooding over a difficult assignment.

HOW TO ELIMINATE TIME WASTERS

These principles will guide us as we begin to eliminate time wasters:

1. All time wasters can be replaced by something productive and positive for you (Rutherford, 1981).
2. A problem well defined is half solved.
3. You can ask others, "What am I doing that wastes their time?"
4. You can be mindful that what might have been a good use of your time in the past may not be an appropriate use now.
5. An important distinction must be made between a time waster (inappropriate use of your time) and an obligation that you may not enjoy doing but is a part of your job.
6. You may lead a cluttered life because you try to do too many things that don't matter.

Do Not Be Frustrated by the Clutter on Your Desk

By clearing your desk after each task, you can control the amount of time you spend sorting, shuffling, stacking, and compiling. As one teacher reports, "During the first ten years of my career I maintained an 'average-cluttered' desk— my desk looked like most teacher's desks. Sometimes during the day I would organize my papers into small stacks; at other times, I would just place papers randomly. I was careful not to allow my desk to become too disorganized because I became too frustrated trying to find specific things. Yet, to clear my desk completely would have been a sign to me that I was not working hard enough, or worse yet, that I was trying to show off how 'superorganized' and efficient I really was.

"During these past seven years I have given more attention to my desk. As I did, the amount of time it took to complete tasks decreased." This is true because of the following points:

1. If your desk is clear as you enter each day, you will probably have two thoughts:
   a. You have a clear place to begin work, making a project seem fresher and more exciting.
   b. You don't dread working on it as much.
2. If your desk is not clear or a table is covered with one or more stacks of paper, different responses are elicited:
   a. "Where can I put the stuff I am holding to make room for the thing that I need to finish," an unproductive thought that not only builds fatigue but adds to the time needed before you can begin.
   b. "I have so much to do, I guess I'd better do this," selecting the top piece of paper on the stack regardless of the priority level of that paper and mindlessly plunging through the task.

 c. "I feel so guilty that I haven't had time to get these things done. What's wrong with me? Boy I'm so stupid (lazy, unorganized, pressured, etc.)," a negative thought that depresses your energies, attitude, and often the outlook you have upon the entire day. This response also reaffirms the fact that you should feel guilty or are truly stupid, lazy, unorganized, pressured, and so on, "because here is my desk, another evidence to it" and "Oh, well, that's just the way it is and I can't do anything to change it because I'm so stupid, lazy, unorganized, pressured."

3. A cluttered desk takes away many rewards you can receive from your job. Using a desk as one large "in" basket allows you to accomplish only one big goal:

 a. To someday *not* have any demands from others or yourself that you will not have solved before the end of the day.

 b. To set smaller goals and smaller goals (and no more new goals) until you get all these old things off your desk.

Evidence or proof of achieving these goals would be to have a cleaned desk, or is it the other way around: I will set this small goal so I can get my desk cleared.

4. An uncluttered desk allows you to direct all your attention toward the task at hand and to leave a large task in place before you for several days without the wasted time of picking up, stacking in order, putting in briefcase, or moving of stacks to left or right of center and respreading upon the onset of a new day or moving to a new location. Thus an uncluttered desk, by being free of distraction, will shorten the time needed for completion of both large and small tasks. Furthermore, with every completed task, you will feel the reward and rejuvenation that accompanies well-earned, quality-controlled accomplishments.

An uncluttered desk could spark new ideas from visitors in your room. Remember the last time you met with a colleague, and, when you arrived you sat at a clean desk to discuss your concerns? Do you recall if you began to feel less tense, somehow, because you knew that this colleague and you were going to be able to give undivided attention to the issue at hand? Did you feel as if your colleague had everything else off his or her mind? (In actuality, all you may have used to make this deduction was that everything else was off the desk.)

A second feeling could have been that you felt freer to talk more personally or more deeply with this person (there were no "barriers" of paper between you). You and your colleague may have even felt moved to rest your arm on the desk, relieving the physical tension of sitting straight and upright in the "hands-in-lap position," and this communicated receptive attitudes and openness. A third feeling may have developed: this colleague is one I can trust and seek out in times when I need guidance and help in addressing problems or new ideas. (This feeling of trust has often been spurred by the absence of any visible evidence on his desk that this colleague has a lot of demands being placed upon him by others and that he or she is not constantly in touch with so many people that his or her trustworthiness will be attacked often, more likely to ensure that he or she will be with someone else when you need leadership, or your problem or new idea will be discussed with others before you would have discussed it yourself.)

All these feelings arose from the simple fact that a clean desk was in the room? "Oh, come on!" You may be saying that this couldn't make that much difference, could it? Think about it. Think about the last time you felt one or more of these feelings during the meeting that you had with a colleague. Was a clean desk a part of this meeting, or did your colleague overcome the negative psychological responses of his cluttered desk by performing other actions that elicited these feelings from you?

If you choose to clear you desk in a moment—when I ask you to—you will be forcing yourself to

1. Develop the habit of finishing tasks and of keeping the runway clear.

2. Face a clean spot each morning that "encourages" you to begin important tasks first.

3. Complete a greater number of tasks and to focus on only one task at a time.

4. Give up feelings of guilt and negative accusations about your character.

5. No longer use delays in beginning to work, delays created because you have to clear a place so you can begin.

6. Face new ideas openly without "walls" of defenses before you to be used as excuses for not accepting new ideas.

7. Engage in meetings with colleagues who will frequently expect you to be more open-minded, more eager to become engrossed in their words, more personable, more informal, less tense, more trustworthy, as well as more powerful in times of problem-solving abilities and new idea development.

Before you make a decision to clear your desk, think about how difficult it will be for you to do each of these seven things. If it will be easy for you to adjust to all these items, I challenge you to leave this book now, go to your desk and find places to store the items there conveniently, clean the top, and then, as you sit down in front on your clean new work environment, plan how you will keep your desk clean.

If one or more of the items listed will be difficult for you to adjust to, eliminate parts of the clutter on your desk, in a step-by-step timetable fashion, until all clutter permanently disappears, allowing yourself ample time to adjust to the increased management capacity that a clean desk affords. It may help you to stay uncluttered if you begin to

1. Devise a personal filing system for notes and ideas.

2. Visualize an ideal working space and work to make it a reality.

3. Acquire appropriate reference tools for personal use and have them handy.

4. Develop the habit of deciding which papers to file and which to throw away.

5. Maintain an action file on the current projects or some other appropriate system.

Do Not Waste Time by Being Overly Motivated

Being excessively motivated tends to encourage you to channel your energy into excessively narrow thought patterns. On the other hand, limited motivation will not stimulate the persistence that will be vital to complete a task.

Many people have tried to determine the methods that most effectively motivate people (e.g., Chatton, 1979; Fonard, 1980; Henderson, 1974; and Hunter, 1973). While they have uncovered numerous effective motivational techniques, oddly enough none motivates all people. Rather, each has a negative effect upon some types of people.

You will discover that when many internally controlled or external motivational pressures are placed upon some people, the following conditions may occur:

1. The goal set cannot be attained in either the level of quality desired or within the established time limits.

2. The work associated with the goal is very satisfying to the person, or approval from the person who has assigned the task is sought and the person really desires the reward that the work will deliver.

3. An area in your life, involving external conditions unrelated to the area in which you are motivated is unsettled and you need extensive motivation to concentrate on the task.

4. The work being attempted is new, and you feel insecure or incompetent.

5. Competition is the technique being used to motivate; an attempt is being made to change something that has been done the same way for a long period of time, or an attempt is being made to change a person who is not ready to change as quickly.

Alternatively, if a person seems to be undermotivated to do a task,

1. The individual has not consented to the goal, or the goal is not valued or believed to be possible.

2. The reward received from the work is having less value than rewards from other activities.

3. The standards used to reach the goal or final products are too low or too easily accomplished.

4. The previous past performance was not as good as expected.

5. Personal fatigue, apathy, or illness prohibit a normal level of enthusiasm.

6. An inability to respond to competition or other motivational devices exists and one withdraws.

7. One standard of excellence has been set and the person's capabilities are either significantly above or below this standard.

As will be described in Chapter 9, when setting group goals, it is very important to consult with the group and obtain a consensus of how the group feels about what they can achieve and how.

There are four things you can do to avoid both excessive and limited motivation:

1. "Know thyself and to thine own self be true." Be aware of the speed, level of proficiency, and duration at which you best function. Every time a task faces you, map it out carefully, seeking to set the limits that are best for you. For example, how many minutes can you attend to a task, normally? Have you ever increased your attention span?

2. How well you react to stress or how devastating the stress will be to you will depend markedly on whether you were able to prepare for it and whether you think you have a way to cope. When stress begins to develop, remove yourself from the task so you can expand your thought patterns. By doing something as simple as getting up and stepping outside for a moment, you can create a mental break.

3. If you become bored, you can set a higher standard or develop a new, more efficient method of performing the task.

4. "Setting a specific, attainable goal will raise your morale, increase your energy and add purpose to living" (American philosopher William A. Ward). When your goals are more specific, your energy is guaranteed to increase.

Write down a goal that you want to achieve by the end of the month that will better train yourself to work within the most productive level of motivation:

_____

What date do you expect to have attained your goal?_____

Overcome Negative Aspects of Bias

It is important to know that two types of thinking can create wasted time. These errors are biases, which are systematic and predictable, and worries, which are temporal and result from inconsistencies in human conditions. Because biases are predictable, it is easy to determine how our biases toward certain conditions and people affect our time management. First, your biases create a tunnel vision, diminishing your ability to apply new ideas.

It is difficult to see how biases we have limits time effectiveness. It is even more difficult to guard against preconceived notions about other people's capabilities. By knowing your biases and improving your ability to focus upon people's potentials in each new situation, new time is created.

The following method eliminates wasted time because they invalidate the biases that influence your teaching. In new situations, you can borrow experiences and thinking of others by asking how they would approach the situation, and carefully removing what you detect as their biases from their answers.

Overcome *Betriesblind*

Betriesblind is a German word that means an inability to see distinctions clearly because you are so familiar with the object, condition, or decision you are about to interact with or to make. Business educators refer to *betriesblind* as "company blind," being so intertwined in your surroundings that you cannot see each aspect's unique characteristics.

Betriesblind is believed to be caused by stimulation of your senses through "wishful remembering." While the activity of wishful remembering is a sign of good mental health, it causes teachers to be unable to identify many reasons for their dissatisfaction at work. Wishful remembering is the term used to describe remembering what you most want to remember and forgetting what makes you feel uncomfortable.

Another aspect of wishful remembering is that you will often be most reluctant to do those things that you must need to do. You feel guilty about these unattended chores and force yourself to "forget them" so as to avoid guilt. *Betriesblind* results.

The first way to see and overcome time-wasting dissatisfaction is to identify why you are afraid to see the bad in teaching. Sometimes by ignoring "these enemies," we are not admitting that they are irritating us because subconsciously we fear that if we didn't have this thing to "fight," life would be emptier.

Angell (1979) has a second approach to conquering *betriesblind*. Your energy can be dissipated because you try to tackle a problem with insufficient knowledge or skill. By gaining knowledge, skill, and experiences (real or simulated) before you face a problem alone, you reduce the possibility that *betriesblind* will occur. For example, if you could visit another school site, you could observe the effects of *betriesblind* in that building while learning techniques that could solve your problems.

The third method is that by simply changing the time of day an activity is performed, *betriesblind* can be eliminated. As Meerloo (1970, p. 73) vividly illustrates,

> Among the Yogi, a number of whom try through regular rites and mental exercises to achieve identification with animals, sacred or otherwise, there have been instances where a change in time schedule disrupted the entire mental effort. One such individual who through use of his concentration and meditations identified with the yak did it so well and grew his imaginary horns so large that finally he was "unable" to pass through a narrow doorway. This extraordinary exercise in identification regularly took place in the afternoon. A fellow Yogi persuaded him to take his exercises in the morning instead. This broke the conditioned rhythm of identification and imagination, and he ceased to "be" a yak. Not until his inner clock became conditioned to the morning discipline was he again able to sprout imaginary horns.

If you would like to check yourself, identify the activities that dissatisfy you. Pinpoint four parts of the activity you've not seen clearly or from more valid perspectives:

1. _____
2. _____
3. _____
4. _____

In the next week if you begin to feel dissatisfied with a routine, remember that you may be preparing for wishful forgetting, which may lead to *betriesblind*.

Cut the Red Tape

"Red tape" can be avoided by following this three-step process. First, studies have indicated that correspondence will sit on a desk, in a hierarchy of importance, for an average of two weeks before decisions are made. Multiply the number in the chain of command by 2 (weeks) to estimate how long it may be before your plan can be actualized.

Second, heed the words of T. S. Eliot: "It is not wise to violate rules until you know how to observe them." Cutting through the red tape does not mean violating protocol, but it does mean creating a precedence, within the rules, that reaches the end result efficiently. Therefore, the second step in the process is to ask superiors if they can allow you to do anything that could help move your idea ahead more rapidly, for example, to hand carry and wait for signatures. These types of activities will often require your professional judgments and can thus become wasted moments or less than maximally beneficial use of your time. Because of this, it may be helpful to discuss your proposal with those who must approve the idea, and seek their suggestions, before the written document arrives on their desk. Each of these actions will use protocol to accelerate your proposal without pressuring others or alienating future support for your ideas.

Third, you can be aware of signals that your proposal has fallen behind in "log jam." That is, another issue may take precedence over your concern, and you may need to point out the urgency of your request. The passage of time is one of the most destructive forces against a written proposal. As time passes, timeliness diminishes. Frequently revisions will be necessary. Signals of log jamming are (1) person responsible for the delay avoids you; (2) person reviewing the matter mentions it to you frequently without mentioning the progress being made; (3) person signals that your proposal is not receiving the attention needed when you hear that your idea, proposal, or _____ is "in the process" (the person making the statement may not even know who has your proposal); (4) person says, "We will look into it," which means that "by the time the wheel makes a full turn, you will have forgotten about it, too, or we hope you will have"; (5) someone says, "I won't be able to get to it right away," which may indicate that your proposal may not be viewed as a timely matter—it may also be placed at the bottom of the work priorities.

Phrases you can use to counter log jams are

1. "Could we place the item on the faculty meeting agenda for a vote?" If this question produces an affirmative response, you can begin to develop rationale for each of your points that will be used in answering questions. If the answer is no, you can follow with a request by asking when a better date would be.

2. "Would you share your positive and negative reaction to this proposal/ project with me?"

3. "Could I come to see you tomorrow, for approximately 30 minutes, to discuss the proposal?" In this way the person will refresh himself or herself on issues concerning your request and put it as a top priority.

Set Availability Hours

Setting availability hours is one of the most effective methods of decreasing the number of unannounced student, colleague, and parent drop-in visits. The best time to make yourself available is from 11:00–12:00 or from 3:30 to the end of the day. To be most effective you will announce to all your constituents and colleagues, orally (and in writing, if needed) that you can usually be reached in your room for personal visits or phone calls during one of these times. *Encourage* these people to contact you during this time, remembering that each issue you address during this "availability hour" will eliminate a drop-in visitor, phone call, and/or interruption during another block of time.

Those who have used the availability hour concept depend on it as a time management tool, this hour being their most consistently productive hour of the day. By scheduling when *you are* "available," you set aside time for the concerns of others, and you purposefully clear you mind of personal priorities and give your visitors more complete attention, direction, and assistance than would be possible, on a drop-in basis, at any other time of the day.

Second, with an availability hour, colleagues can depend on your availability at that time and they call then because answers can be gained quickly and their concerns are addressed with undivided attention. The hour may be filled by more than one person's visit, enabling (1) students, teachers, and parents to interact with each other while waiting, often improving their ideas or generating their own solution to problems before they get to you, and (2) teachers who set the availability hours often praise the quality of work of the students, teachers, or parent before others who are there.

If you have established availability hours, you may want to draft a memo to thank your colleagues/parents for the work they are doing to make your conference time so valuable. You may wish to cite specific instances of where these people helped one another during the time they waited to see you or how you were able to reach a complex decision rapidly because of their thorough preparation prior to the meeeting. Also, you may want to commend parents for electing to telephone during the availability hours.

Because you will be handling telephone conversations during the availability hour, a brief note concerning time-effective phone calls may help you. The following techniques reduce the time you'll spend in unnecessary conversation:

1. Ask the people you call regularly for the times when they are not busy. Give them the same information about yourself.

2. Screen the calls you make and group these so that all calls made concerning the same topic are made consecutively.

3. Before you make a call, list the key points and leave spaces on the same paper for the answers.

4. Very good times of the day to make phone calls are right before you go to lunch or go home for the end of the day as you are slightly (or severely) fatigued and you should do a less demanding, lower-level task such as this at these times. Similarly, the person you call will probably feel the same and will welcome the break and purposefully contribute to the call without undue extraneous talk.

5. Initiate the callback system so you can call at a time of your choosing and terminate the conversation at your choice.

6. Early-morning calls should be avoided as they can easily distract your thoughts and interrupt the important big tasks of the day. Early-morning incoming calls can be screened by the secretary, and she can tell them you will return the call before noon or at 3:30 to 4:00 in the afternoon.

7. When you have difficulties getting to the point or reaching the main point of your conversation, you may want to say
   "Here's what I called about."
   "What I really wanted to know is . . ."
   "What do you think?"
   "Can we do that?"
   "What do you think about . . ."

8. When an impending appointment awaits, tell the person, "I've got an appointment waiting;" "I have only a few minutes and I'm going to have to get to the point quickly;" "Someone is waiting for me but I could reach a decision (or present the issues you wished) at this time (specifying a time ____) better than any other point in my day," or "In consideration of my waiting guest, I'll be brief. Please tell me if I'm not clear."

9. Keep a mental note of phone calls; consciously reduce the number of times you call those who depress your energies by their telephone habits.

10. Meet with as many people, in stand-up meetings, as possible, on the way to other stops and priorities.

11. Observe the mannerisms of others who speak to you. Keep a written record of the good phrases or methods on increasing the effectiveness

of telephone conversations that these people use. By writing these points below, you can use this activity as an ongoing reference for yourself in the future. Think about the person you most enjoy talking to professionally on the phone. What does this person do that helps you enjoy your talk so much. Use this answer as the first item on your own list for improvement:

1. _____
2. _____
3. _____
4. _____
5. _____
6. _____
7. _____
8. _____
9. _____
10. _____
11. _____
12. _____
13. _____

Develop Self-discipline

Self-discipline, as defined by Fagen and Long (1979), is the capacity to flexibly and realistically direct and regulate personal action and/or behavior so as to cope effectively with a situation. They add that self-discipline can be seen when someone demonstrates appropriate behavior in conflicting situations. Fagen and Long also discovered that self-discipline can be developed by working on a difficult task in sequential, continuous steps.

Lakein (1973) found that the most successful means of attaining time discipline is to (1) maintain a positive attitude in spite of previous failures, (2) do something each day to advance your time efficiency, (3) attend to fears about things you can't control as soon as they arise, and (4) resist doing easy, unimportant tasks that come before you. Lakein also developed his own will power by training himself to be less compulsive. That is, he controlled his time by interpreting each action in light of the criterion of whether or not the action was the thing that he wanted to do. Your self-discipline can also be improved if you change your environment so as to reward the new behavior you attempt.

Surprisingly, such external rewards are not always the best for developing self-discipline; as Fenner (1980) discovered, how long something will take seems to depend more upon the degree of excitement, hope, or despair the person associates with the task. Thus, external rewards are less effective because the conditions surrounding the behavior in which you are seeking more discipline compete with the reward being offered. That is, when you depend on others to develop your self-discipline, you will only improve in your ability to respond to that person or reward and will not develop control in similar future situations (Polsgrove, 1979).

Your self-discipline can improve only through the process of self-monitoring and self-reward. As Piersel and Kratchwill (1979) demonstrated, self-discipline is a function of basic enabling skills and systematic enabling skills. *Basic enabling skills* are the range of behaviors that are subject to personal direction and regulation. The wider the range of these skills, the more self-discipline a person demonstrates. *Systematic enabling skills* increase desirable behaviors that are incompatible with previous undisciplined actions. These skills are *selection, storage, sequencing, ordering, anticipating consequences, appreciating feelings, managing frustrations, selective inhibition,* and *delaying relaxation.*

Thus, *to increase your ability to discipline yourself, you need to strengthen both sets of these skills.* Figure 4-2 will help.

To close our discussion, let's look at four points that help to develop self-discipline with less work:

1. Self-discipline is so closely related to how alert and sensitive you are that as you develop better ability to be alert and not be as preoccupied to what's going on around and within, you will automatically increase your self-discipline.

2. Self-discipline often requires renunciation and delaying of instinctual fulfillments. Such ability is developed either by a wise parent at a very early age, with unconscious programming, or through a mature adult's developing increased patience and tolerance.

3. Setting arbitrary deadlines and limits on yourself will enhance your self-discipline by decreasing your tendency to be a perfectionist.

4. Self-discipline will be aided by the confidence you have in the growth-producing properties of time, the trust you have in the regenerative forces that are constantly at work during the waiting period. Such confidence is more easily developed when there are numerous positive reinforcements in other aspects of your life.

Select the Most Important Job

If you are not able to distinguish what is more valuable in a situation or to select the activities, projects, and people with which or whom you most want to spend time, you may be routinely wasting time.

When the most important aspect of a project is not selected first, work has to be redone or discarded. There appear to be two reasons why teachers are unable to select central points or key people. Teaching creates a conflict between your values and the many different levels of need you continuously address. Moreover, you may not care enough. That is, you may not be motivated enough to care which aspect of a task or situation is most valuable.

Curing these two states requires (1) a decision to change and (2) a process that increases confidence in yourself built upon the successes you had in the past. Creating a need for increased quality of action can occur through changes in

Figure 4-2

PROCESS FOR DEVELOPING SELF-DISCIPLINE

1. Write down the behavior, thought, situation, or task over which you wish to have better control:

   _____

2. Describe your positivism, faith, or optimistic attitude concerning this behavior, even if you have failed in self-discipline in its regard in the past. _____

   _____

3. What can you do each day, beginning today, that will strengthen enabling skills (see the following list for suggestions):

   a. _____
   b. _____
   c. _____
   d. _____

   Do you need to increase, decrease, or change the self-reward you receive?

   Do you need to become more selective about your environment, noting which aspects of the circumstances associated with an uncontrolled object (behavior) that most contribute to your lessened discipline?

   Do you need to reflect more upon the goal you have or the successful mental associations you know about your goal?

   Can you sequence your life or the uncontrolled goal better?

   How might you best learn to anticipate in advance the consequences that will result from controlling your undesirable behavior? How can you anticipate a step that you can take to reach your goal sooner?

   How can you better appreciate and identify the negative feelings associated with a lessened self-discipline and the positive feelings associated with increased discipline?

   What basic enabling skills can you use to manage frustration?

   What is the best method for you to use, right now, to delay your desire to relax and not work on your desired change?

4. At what point will you set a new self-discipline goal? That is, write down the behaviors you will expect to witness when you have succeeded. Write this statement as a goal, stating exactly what you picture as success.

---

attitude, exposure to competition, lessening one's value of the end products of others who have already completed the task, and adding an aspect to the task that will advance one of your high-priority goals without detracting from the most important aspect of the situation that your are going to begin.

For example, let's pretend you really would like to make your room, or help another teacher make that room more attractive, but you believe it takes too much of your time away from your students. Using the points just given you plan a way to build rewards, and satisfy your goal of individualizing instruction. For example, you might get together with three other teachers and hold a contest between classes. Each classroom will be able to spend one art period a week for three weeks designing the most attractive room. The following rules could be established: (1) students will select judges, (2) all decor must be designed to increase the system by which continuous progress can be recorded and stored, (3) all work must be planned and implemented by students, after teacher approval, and (4) at the end the winning class will be treated to a party planned by students who did not win.

This example points out how low-level needs and value conflicts can be resolved through combining two different values or goals in creative ways.

Recognize the Negative Aspects of Being Excessively Busy

Does this sound familiar?

No matter how hard I apply myself and reallocate my time, I can't escape a nagging feeling that I have more work to do and more people to see than I can satisfactorily handle.

There are several reasons why "being busy" is viewed as a positive aspect of the American culture. Grossin and Clement (1979) argue that "the program" in a contemporary, industrial society has so constrained and controlled people that they cannot organize their leisure time so it expresses their "being" as well as their time at work can. That is, many teachers try to enjoy their work more to enhance their life; in this way their identity becomes more closely tied to their level of success in work-related performances. Evidence of this phenomenon was found in other professions as well by Timor and Guthrie (1980). They reported that compressed four-day workweeks produce no greater stress than do less compressed weeks because the people in both groups do not use leisure periods to overcome the negative aspects of work.

Second, the increased production and competition that has resulted in our industrial society has increased the amount of time most people need to reach the success in achievement they expect and desire.

Third, our society's interpretation of time is very clear: There is nonworking time and working time. Nonworking time is valued only because it serves as a break from "work-related" hours (e.g., coffee breaks, weekends, and lunch hours are valued only because they can release stress that could occur if one worked without them).

Last, many educators seek to be constantly busy because society has prescribed so few acceptable ways of "not being busy." "Society" sets precise standards; builds sterile waiting areas; contracts with people to uphold traditional procedures when they accept a job; creates a need for reservation, a feeling of obligation, the sense that one is constantly influenced by persuasion and coercion. "Society's" only acceptable "nonwork-related activities" for a teacher are calling in sick, personal business leaves, and the establishment of *limited* commitments outside the profession.

The negative effects of this constant state of "busyness" are high blood pressure, sleep deprivation, hypertension, and fatigue. In turn, high blood pressure, for example, stimulates baroreceptors, neural receptors that are sensitive to pressure, which numb the brain's response to unpleasant stimuli (Campbell and Hinsie, 1970). This failure to respond to and, hence stop the unwanted unpleasant conditions ironically causes us to keep on being "busy". We tend to stay "busy" because we don't know how to take action to eliminate these negative aspects of our life. Spending so much of our time in work-related activities can also lead to (1) an inability to function effectively in retirement, (2) a shortened life span, (3) fragile self-concepts, (4) irritability, (5) depression, and (6) psychoses. In 1974, the Newspaper Advertising Bureau found that the quality and quantity of Americans' leisure time is based upon a person's psychological and sociological inclinations toward passivity or activity. For teachers, this means that until teachers have time for new hobbies, they cannot claim to be managing their time well (Angell, 1979). The books listed below contain suggestions that will increase your skill and enjoyment in using your leisure time.

Allen, Joseph, *The Leisure Alternatives Catalog: Food for Mind and Body.* Del Mar, Calif. Whole Earth Publisher's, 1979.

Brightbill, Charles Kestmer. *The Challenge of Leisure.* Englewood Cliffs, N. J.: Prentice-Hall, 1960.

Cheek, Neil H. *Leisure and Recreation Places.* Ann Arbor, Mich.: Ann Arbor Science Publications, 1976.

Clayre, Alasdair. *Work and Play: Ideas and Experiences of Work and Leisure.* New York: Harper & Row, 1974.

Ellis, Michael J. *Why People Play.* Englewood Cliffs, N.J.: Prentice-Hall, 1973.

Flesch, Rudolf, and A. H. Lass. *A New Guide to Better Writing.* New York: Warner Books, 1977.

Graves, Donald, and Virginia Stuart. *Write from the Start.* New York: E. P. Dutton, 1977.

Harlirn, E. O. (revised by Bob Sessoms). *The New Fun Encyclopedia.* New York: Abingdon Press, 1983.

Kando, Thomas M. *Leisure and Popular Culture in Transition.* St. Louis: C. V. Mosby, 1975.

Lobsenz, Norman M. *Is Anybody Happy?* Garden City, N.Y.: Doubleday, 1962.

Manchester, Richard B. *The Second Mammoth Book of Fun and Games.* New York: A and W, 1980.

Ross, Marilyn Heimberg. *Creative Loafing.* New York: Communications Inc., 1984.

You may prefer to set a period of time for relaxation and leisure everyday. If only for 15 minutes, allow yourself time to do some thing(s) you love to do. You can develop a new skill, a new aspect of yourself that you can be proud of —yoga, racquetball, karate, wood carving, skiing, cabinetwork, sewing. You can also plan a program for self-improvement—one that will increase an area of strength. You can talk to people whom you admire and find out how they use their leisure time to strengthen their happiness and lives.

Take the Mountains Out of the Molehills

Before anyone begins a new program or faces a difficult problem, we have already discussed that developing alternatives is an excellent process for reaching solutions (see Chapter 2). If, however, after doing so, you worry about the outcome, Douglass and Douglass (1980) suggest that you make a "worry list." The first time I read this procedure, I was skeptical. I thought, "Why should I list every possible thing that could go wrong; listing all the horrible things that might happen seems like a waste of time! Wouldn't this create a self-fulfilling prophecy?" Then, I tried it, listed everything I was worried about and was amazed! As I completed the list, my mind was relieved of worry completely. Somehow, the list made my worries more specific, more concrete. In the process, I realized that I could overcome the difficulties associated with the problems, and I grew more determined to create positive, valuable outcomes for the problem.

For smaller concerns, you can adapt another technique that was created by professional counselors. Whenever I begin to gripe or worry, I ask someone to ask me to "tell them the worst thing that could happen." As soon as I do, my worry vanishes.

Now, you can practice both these techniques. Pause for a minute and think of a professionally related concern you have. What's the worst thing that could happen in that situation? What else? What person would you like to help you overcome your time-consuming habit of worrying? Would you feel comfortable asking that person to help you face the worst outcome as a means of overcoming worries?

Then, think about the biggest problem you face. List all the things that could go wrong, all the horrible things that might happen. Think hard. When all worries have been listed, reread your list about them. Then write how you feel. Use this technique any time you begin to worry. It works. It saves time and pain.

Overcome Indecisiveness

Hogarth (1980) outlines six factors to consider in making a good decision:

1. What boundaries exist? What is the most good that can be accomplished and the worst that could result from the decision one has to make?

2. Identify reliable inputs you can use. Can some of the undependable resources be utilized in a productive manner?

3. What effect will human regression to comfort zones have? People will gravitate toward the level of performance that produces less stress, and less risk, and decisions must be made in light of this fact. After people are stimulated to grow and to change, they will identify a range within the domain of possible actions with which they desire to operate.

4. "Every time a person begins to think, she or he places some portion of the world in jeopardy" (Anonymous). As a warning, one should announce the actions, changes, and strategies that are likely to affect people before a decsion is made so the ineffectiveness and inefficient use of time, during the implementation stages, will be reduced.

5. When creativity is used to generate a solution, motivation to complete the task is increased. Use of creativity should be limited, however, in situations where the cues and circumstances are not familiar, as decisions in these situations are often based upon chance observations of irrelevant cues.

6. Good decisions need not be prefaced by an intensive sales pitch to be successful. Because more commitment comes from involvement in the decision-making process than from having been a recipient of a motivational exchange, a wise teacher will spend a larger proportion of time in lessons and classroom decision-making processes, including students in the lessons and decision making rather than developing a plan of how to motivate them to work or implement a decision that the teacher has already made.

Decision making has been described as the "process of thought and action that culminates in choice of behavior" (Taylor, 1980, p. 41). McCoy (1959) also found that when people can't find an answer, they often need to stop and restate the problem. How will you take the first step to become decisive? _____

Eliminate Disorganization

Being disorganized creates a sense of being overwhelmed, decreasing our desire and energy. Organization not only prepares a path in which we may begin our work, but it also clears our consciousness, helping us to focus more energy and mental activity on the work ahead. Becoming organized takes two things: (1) block of time whereby the most convenient schedule of time and location for materials can be found and (2) a few seconds to return materials to their proper location after each use.

The best times for me to organize and/or reorganize something is during the last hour of a workday in my teaching and the first hour of the day for my personal priorities. This is because my fatigue and stress at the end of the day are released when I spend my last minutes organizing for the next day. Also, I feel a sense of "painless accomplishment" because I have not tried to pursue a task that is too demanding. By stopping when I am overly fatigued and organize for the next day, I also do something that will allow a fresher beginning for the next day. Similarly, when I begin the evening and weekends by organizing my personal hours, my energy is generated. When are the best times for you to do your daily organizational duties?

What parts of your life and your environment need to be more organized?

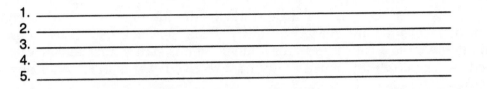

1. _____
2. _____
3. _____
4. _____
5. _____

On the line following each number, put a realistic time in which you can spend a block of time doing the organization. For example, I need to reorganize my file cabinets. It's October 17 as I write this, but I will not be able to do it until December 15, so I wrote December 15 in the blank following the item, and I write this down in my Professional Development Column of my lesson plan book for December. I recommend you develop this habit also; then allow yourself ample time for the tasks, and concentrate only on that task during the planning period on the day you have planned to do it.

If you have trouble putting things back where you got them, know it is a skill that is easy to learn. Through practice it rapidly develops. Focus attention today upon returning each item in your hand to its proper place. Notice how you feel and the results. Everyone you see who is highly organized *learned* to be so; ask these people their secrets. I am always surprised when I hear them. People have created ingenious ways of persuading themselves to be organized. I believe you will really enjoy such conversation. Even more, you will enjoy trying your friends' ideas yourself. Further, since "imitation" has been labled as the highest form of flattery one can bestow, you will be complimenting your friends' wisdom as you do.

In closing, it's important that we understand why we tend to become disorganized. Fear of failure is the main reason. We disorient ourselves and our work so that even small tasks seem complex, thus creating "a reason" for failure if it was to occur as we greatly fear it might.

Use Socialization to Increase Your Time-Use Skills

Socializing and the "pursuit of happiness" are two aspects of our society that have become almost synonymous. Oddly enough, however, those who oversocialize are often those who are most unhappy. When two unhappy people socialize, perceived or desired goals of the socialization may not be met, creating a new need for more social activity. On the other hand, teachers who avoid socialization are often guilty of "wasting" as much time as those who oversocialize while on the job. Their limited interactions diminish their ability to understand diverse perspectives instantly, and they waste time creating work that is not as appropriate as it would have been otherwise.

"Wasting" is defined as "the action of devastating; gradual consumption; wearing away" (*Webster's Third New International Dictionary*, unabridged). Therefore, if socializing is devastating, wearing away, or gradually consuming your time, you will benefit from one of the two exercises that follow.

People who socialize a lot (while on the job) tend to have few valuable relationships outside the office. The need for interpersonal contact either takes precedence over the value of their work, or the job does not provide enough intrinsic motivation and reward to satisfy them. On the other hand, the person who rarely takes a coffee break, or seldom attends staff parties, either values or needs work for self-fulfillment or does not receive rewards from socializing with colleagues.

Neither of these conditions is a problem unless the "wanting to socialize" in case 1 or "having to socialize" in case 2 are perceived, by you, to waste the time you would rather spend on other activities.

For "Case 1" People. Oversocialization is causing problems. Analyze what types of situations and which people give you the most pleasure. On the job, why do you socialize? If you reduce the frequency and/or length of time at each socialization, what effects would this have upon you? Upon your work? Your colleagues? What would you most like to be doing that socialization may be intruding upon? Could you do this activity in conjunction with one or more of your colleagues? What would you do more efficiently to enable you to socialize and to complete the other tasks that you value? Jot notes on another sheet of paper to answer these questions and date them so as to be able to record future changes in your behavior.

For "Case 2" People. You rarely wish to socialize. When placed in a socialization situation, talk about every nonwork-related task you do that makes you happy. Show yourself (and help others to know) who you really are and not merely what you are capable of doing professionally. For the first three times you do it, these discussions can be viewed as experiments. *You* will be discovering how exciting *you really are*. Then, during the fourth encounter, you will begin to expand your personality by setting goals that will increase the efficiency of your socialization skills. By becoming good at socializing, you will be able to add the expertise of many other colleagues in new goals set, goals that would be impossible to achieve alone. Also, by the time of the second socialization meeting, you will probably display a more positive and optimistic view of the experience.

Use the 80/20 Principle

As you begin to decide the priorities for each day, you will accomplish more during that day by using the discovery of the nineteenth-century Italian economist and sociologist, Viefredo Pareto. [Joseph Juran (1964) brought Pareto's work to the attention of American businesspeople and educators.] The principle states that the significant items in one's work normally constitute a relatively small portion of the total work one does. Juran labeled the concept as the *vital few and the trivial many*. This phenomenon explains why

80% of your joys in teaching come from 20% of your students.
80% of the learnings you create are taken from only one-fifth of the work you do in a daily schedule of responsibilities.
80% of the used sick leave time and student absentees are the result of 20% of all teachers and students.

80% of the dirt in your room and floor can be found in the 20% that is most frequently used.
80% of the time you spend reading the Sunday paper is spent on the 20% of the pages you most enjoy.
80% of all discussion in large group meetings or in a new classroom grouping will come from 20% of the students.
80% of the time you spend teaching to your whole class, as one large group, you will use 20% of the teaching methods you know.
80% of the parent phone calls you receive at home come from 20% of the parents.

To use this principle to avoid wasting time, you can choose to give your best to the vital issue or student of the moment without feeling guilty that this same issue demands a disproportionate amount of your time. You can also accept that if only 20 percent of your day is *truly* productive, that's good! You can also relax by remembering that all things will not be equally valuable and doing your best on the highest priority of the day will be better than giving equal time to the "trivial many." Possibly, by understanding the natural tendencies of human nature recorded in this principle, you can increase your patience when you seem to be giving and giving and giving (the 80 percent and you don't yet see the reward (the 20 percent).

As an aside, Edward Bliss, (1976), a prominent corporate employee developer, trained business men and women to work on their two highest priorities as frequently as possible each day. These business people increased their productivity and found that they also were able to accomplish their third, fourth, and fifth priorities many days. Prior to using this 80/20 principle, these people reported to have ended most days not having accomplished a single priority.

This principle affords educators three major benefits. It can help you make daily tasks produce greater gains. As Bliss discovered, you can enjoy teaching more when you schedule and complete at least 20 percent or 2 hours of work that reached the goals you believe are most important in the day, for example, spending more than one class period this Friday finishing the newspaper and not trying to do it in conjuction with the regularly scheduled assignment but making up the latter by "doing it better" next week.

Second, you can accept that you will never be the sole determiner of which proportion of your actions will fall into the camp of 20 percent of the "productivity" and which will contribute to the 80 percent of work where gain is not visible. You must, therefore, do everything possible to decide to work on the activities that hold greatest possibility for gain.

The third benefit is that when you are engaged in an activity that you (1) value, (2) are performing to the best of your ability, (3) have worked on for many hours, and (4) do not yet see the fruits of your labor, you must remember Pareto and press on. Since you will never be able to determine when you have reached the top of the 80 percent of invested groundwork or, when suddenly and almost magically, the next step you take becomes the first in the 20 percent of visible productivity, you must never lose faith that your goal is in view. Patience in every day, every way, every student, every assignment, and every thought is the key in those things you most want to accomplish.

In closing this section, you may want to test yourself informally. Are you spending approximately 1 1/2 to 2 hours every day on those tasks, lessons, and interactions that are most important to your students? Are you now more understanding of the need for patience during the implementation stages of projects? Do you sustain when a task requires it? Do you need to schedule more time for your productive priorities?

Avoid Wanderings

When you find yourself jumping from one task or activity to another, constantly switching priorities, or spending time daydreaming, time may be slipping through your fingers.

To minimize daydreaming, remove yourself from view of other priorities or turn your back on windows or other distracting views. If you cannot do so, don't give up the first priority either. Instead, refocus your attention back to that student who needs your individual help or any other priority you have for that single moment when you are being distracted. One of the best means of refocusing attention is to break the task down into smaller dimensions. You can use this same technique to assist students to refocus upon their work as well. For example, Mary Gail Henning, a teacher of the emotionally disturbed adolescent, used this skill to build her students' ability to work independently. No sooner had she completed a description of how to work a set of problems, than students began to come to her and say, "I don't know what to do." Instead of restating all she had just taught, she began to focus these students' minds by asking the question: "Where are the directions printed on this page?" When the students answered, she broke down the next task with a second question: "What is the first sentence in the directions?" As students read the first sentence, she stopped after key words and asked the students to point to that item as it appeared on the page, such as, "Point to what you think is the list they are asking you to use." In this way, her students decreased their mindwandering. They quickly learned that they needed to pay attention. Their teacher would not repeat everything to them.

It is important to note that some mindwandering is positive. It creates desire by stimulating earlier pleasant experiences that are lived out again in the mind, which in turn strengthens the idea that future attempts will be fulfilled. Therefore, when you learn to and teach your students how to use mindwanderings productively, imagination, fantasy, and creativity can combine freely to form new ideas and wedge old/present/future successes together. As a matter of fact, work to induce daydreaming experiences have fostered cognitive reorganization, increased awareness of inner experiences, and a solidification of emotional and intellectual elements in bringing unconscious content into consciousness (Kilinger, 1978; Brill and Allen, 1978; and Wittmer and Loesch, 1978).

Angell (1979) discovered, however, that many people waste too much time in preoccupation—a form of daydreaming. You may have many methods to overcome preoccupation. The most productive seem to be to stop whatever work you were trying to do and engage in a physical activity, talk to someone about the topic with which you are preoccupied, or tell yourself that, at the end of a specified amount of time, you will allow yourself all the time necessary to solve the issue causing preoccupation. In addition, you can take your work to another area, another teacher's room where there are people, or ask a friend or student to come to your room and work on one of their tasks while you complete yours. Working in the presence of other people will keep you from being tempted to stop and become preoccupied.

Improve Your Oral and Written Communications

Learning to communicate effectively makes life fuller and saves time. To identify your present level of skill, complete the rating analysis in Figure 4-3.

After you circle the number that best represents your skill level concerning each item, compute the sum of your responses as follows:

0–30	You may need to receive intensive training in the areas of communication skill.
31–45	You are below average in your ability to communicate with others. You should identify your lowest areas of skill and select one that has most value to you. Either talk with someone you admire who possesses this skill or find the sections in the references listed below that will best meet your needs and digest and implement the guidelines given.
46–60	You are on the road to becoming an excellent communicator. Incorporate one communication skill weakness per month into your goals for professional development. Select methods for the coming year. Retake this analysis one year from today. You are in for a big treat then and throughout this coming year as you increase the amount you are able to get done through the closer working relationship you will establish with your colleagues.
61–75	Fantastic! You are an excellent communicator. You are now in a position to help others develop this ability and to add items to the checklist that represent other skills you use in communication.

Here are two lists of references you can use to receive training in the areas of communication skill:

How to Improve Speaking Ability

Baker, Virgil L., and Ralph T. Eubanks. *Speech in Personal and Public Affairs*. New York: David McKay, 1965.

Borden, George A. *Speech Behavior and Human Interaction*. Englewood Cliffs, N.J.: Prentice-Hall, 1969.

Chase, Stuart. *Power of Words*. New York: Harcourt Brace Jovanovich, 1954.

Diehman, John. R. *Get Your Message Across*. Englewood Cliffs, N.J. Prentice-Hall, 1979.

Fleming, Alice M. *What to Say When You Don't Know What to Say*. New York: Scribners, 1982.

Hellman, Hal. *Communications in the World of the Future*. Philadelphia, Penn.: J. B. Lippincott, 1975.

Hoffman Gloria. *Speak the Language of Success*. New York: G. P. Putnam, 1983.

Taylor, Anita. *Speaking in Public*. Englewood Cliffs, N. J.: Prentice-Hall, 1979.

How to Improve Writing Skills

Anderson, Sherwood. *The Writers Book*. New York: Scarecrow Press, 1975.

Bloomenthal, Howard. *Promoting Your Cause*. New York: Funk & Wagnalls, 1971.

Figure 4-3

ANALYSIS OF ORAL COMMUNICATION ABILITY AND ORAL COMMUNICATION EFFECTIVENESS

	Very limited activity	Can do it, but only occasionally	Do it 50% of the time	Do it very often, but takes conscious attention to remember to do it	Do it always, automatically almost out of habit
1. Rehearse important oral communications in my mind before I speak.	1	2	3	4	5
2. Sense when I have incomplete or inaccurate data concerning an issue and I search for a need of clarification before going to a new point.	1	2	3	4	5
3. Arrange information that I wish to present into a logical order, using structure words such as "first," "for example," and "in addition" to aid my listener.	1	2	3	4	5
4. I try to limit my sentences to nine words or less.	1	2	3	4	5
5. I use the simplest words that will clearly communicate my message.	1	2	3	4	5
6. I pause effectively when I deliver important messages to allow the audience to become familiar with the concepts.	1	2	3	4	5
7. I am aware that people feel well informed on the topics	1	2	3	4	5

Figure 4-3 continued

	1	2	3	4	5
9. I am an active listener, consciously forcing myself to use all my faculties to listen to and think only about the message being given by the speaker; that is, look at the person, listen closely, and keep in mind what is being said.	1	2	3	4	5
10. I know that I listen to the meaning that people are conveying and not just to the words they say.	1	2	3	4	5
11. I refrain from passing judgment on what is being said until the speaker is finished and then only if asked to do so or if I feel a strong obligation to redirect the thoughts.	1	2	3	4	5
12. I restate an idea in a variety of ways very effectively, ensuring that people truly receive my message.	1	2	3	4	5
13. I value the need to praise people during a conversation so that a positive atmosphere can be created and productive thinking can be stimulated.	1	2	3	4	5
14. I encourage others to tell me exactly how they feel about an issue so I can more clearly understand the points of concern that are most important to them and to increase my sensitivity/ knowledge concerning the specific facts in an issue.	1	2	3	4	5

Buckley, Earle. *How to Write Business Letters.* New York: McGraw-Hill, 1985.

Butterfield, William. *Common Sense in Letter Writing.* Englewood Cliffs, N. J.: Prentice-Hall, 1963.

Carr, Jess. *How a Book Is Born.* New York: Moore, 1978.

Fruehling, Rosemary T. *The Art of Writing Effective Letters.* New York: McGraw-Hill, 1972.

Gunther, Max. *Writing the Modern Magazine Article.* New York: Writer, 1982.

Mack, Karen. *Overcoming Writing Blocks.* Los Angeles: J. P. Tarcher, 1979.

Roman, Kenneth. *Writing that Works.* New York: Harper & Row, 1981.

Ross-Larson, B. C. *Edit Yourself: A Manual for Everyone Who Works with Words.* New York: W. W. Norton, 1982.

Skillin, Marjorie E. *Words into Type.* Englewood Cliffs, N. J.: Prentice-Hall, 1974.

Writing and Selling Fillers, Light Verse and Short Humor. New York: Writer, 1982.

Written communication can be improved by following several simple principles. Before we discuss these, however, I would like to give you the opportunity of identifying causes for poor written communication. Read the following memorandum (Figure 4-4), forwarded to me from the author who wrote this in his first year as a principal in a fairly large school district. As you try to answer the questions that follow, write down the reasons why you have difficulty.

1. When does each department begin emergency operation?_____

2. How many cycles (programs) will the ADP Center process for each department? _____

3. What is the main purpose of the emergency operations? _____

4. How will the updated charts be used? _____

5. Describe balanced policy flexibility. _____

You may have had difficulty understanding this memorandum because

1. Information was not given.

2. While it is not specifically stated, you may have assumed that an infinite number of programs will be processed, and, if this is so, you may have wondered how the system could be successful. This skepticism could have decreased your support of the procedures.

3. The paragraph lacked organization so you did not know what the main points were.

4. "Program X-5" is a term that was self-explanatory to the author but had no meaning to you.

5. Many vague concepts and jargon were used.

Building on this example, let's compose a list of points to use when you must communicate in writing:

1. I will not use sentences longer than 17 words, with 11 to 14 words being the easiest for others to read.

Figure 4-4

WAYS OF IMPROVING WRITTEN COMMUNICATION

MEMORANDUM

SUBJECT: Emergency Procedures

TO: Department Heads

All departments must complete their emergency plans NO LATER THAN 18 Jan. A copy of each emergency plan, and subsequent revisions, will be forwarded to the Executive Office for reference. In case of an emergency, Region XII must retain balanced policy flexibility at all times. Responsive logistical timephasing will begin within one hour of alert signal. The ADP Center will remain open 24 hours per day to process your compatible transitional concepts. Printouts of your data will be delivered by runner within 5 minutes of completion of the ADP cycle. The ADP Center runner will return for your updated charts on synchronized incremental mobility within 45 minutes from the time the original printouts were delivered to the department. Department charts will be processed and merged with Program X-5 data. When the last chart has been processed, the Executive Office will ring the alarm buzzer three (3) times. This will be the signal for all departments to begin functional monitored programming immediately. At this time, parallel digital projections may be processed on Priority 1-A-1. When the "all-clear" is sounded, all emergency operations will cease. Critiques of the emergency operations will be sent to the Executive Office within 7 days of the "all-clear."

---

2. I will use exact dates, numbers, and descriptions on each communication, regardless of the informality of the note.

3. I will tell people exactly what the correspondence is intended to do, describe long bodies of information step-by-step when possible, and close with information about when they might expect the next piece of information about the topic.

Change Bad Habits to Good Ones

As MacKenzie (1975) stated, "We are all just walking bundles of habits." Psychologists have identified five steps that change bad habits to good ones. You can change by having

1. A desire to change.
2. Knowledge of how to change.
3. A picture of what the change will look like.
4. A plan to begin the change.
5. An action-oriented decision during each step of the change process.

While all five steps must occur to change ineffective teaching actions to better behaviors, the emphasis will be on the actions you take—after you determine what triggers your less effective habits.

Once this triggering event has been isolated, you can (1) change or avoid the event, (2) change your response to it by investing the time and energy the very next time the trigger exists, and/or (3) change both the triggering event or the method you use to avoid the trigger and then change your response to the event itself through changes in attitude and actions.

William James, one of our earliest educational leaders, is credited with the following strategy to eliminate less productive behavior (as cited in Harnischfeger and Wiley, 1978):

1. Launch the new behavior you desire as strongly as possible, making no exceptions to performing the new segment, gradually but continuously adding actions relating to this behavior. A lapse into an old habit is like trying to manage a car through a skid; it is much harder to regain control than it is to maintain control so as to avoid the skid entirely.

2. Once the behavior is decided upon, seize the first and every subsequent opportunity to practice the new behavior.

3. Recognize when spontaneous recovery has occurred (you unconsciously are slipping into the old habit without having planned to do so), label the slip as a normal, human tendency, and restate your goal and actions against it. Soon the benefits you receive from the new, more effective habit will be so superior to those received from the old that it will be easier to continue the new habit.

In summary, as you begin to change bad habits, you must determine the extent to which you or any individual must be modified and the extent to which the environment has to change. Determine the appropriate method to induce the desired changes in the environment for you or another individual. Explain exact areas of inadequacy of the problem and the situation that it handicaps. Engage seriously and persistently in the practice to eliminate the habit.

Habit training is an involved process whereby an individual learns inconspicuous competing responses. *Relaxation therapy*—preventative training where you practice a competing reaction for the habit—is another new method being used by many educators. *Habit interruption*—segmenting parts of the action to replace the part with a competing response—is the method introduced here. Many researchers have studied the process of habit changing and have concluded that success depends upon one's motivation to change (Azrin, Nunn, and Frantz, 1980; Baker, 1978; Cohen, Monty, and Williams, 1980; Cordle and Long, 1980; Horne and Wilkinson, 1980; and Rahaim, Lefebure, and Jenkins, 1980). Habit training is an involved process. An individual learns inconspicuous responses that complete and conquer less valuable responses. Relaxation therapy, preventative training, or the practice of creating a new action that competes with a bad habit are methods that can best prevent a bad habit from being triggered. Habit interruption is a third method being applied in clinical settings, and this method was already described, namely, segmenting parts of an action to replace the part with a competing response. Some educators prefer to gain knowledge of how to change through use of the self-recording clinical method; that is, educators document the frequency, conditions, surroundings, and duration of each incident of the bad habit. The researchers cited agree that social support during the last part of the change process is a valuable tool to increase motivation as well as to help identify the immediate sources of reinforcement necessary for controlling the habit. I have also found it helpful to reinforce myself by recalling the ancient proverb from the Jabo tribe in Liberia: "The fruit must have a stem before it will grow just as it is only the full-grown forest that yields the buffalo."

Take an Optimistic Approach to Life Changes

To have a positive approach to life changes, you must have a positive attitude, good health, and a general well-being. Hope, confidence, optimism, and the illusion of a desirable future and the ability to think things through (and to think ahead) are the major contributors to one's ability to approach a change optimistically.

Unfortunately, many people resist change. In doing so, they miss positive effects, the renewal and salvation qualities that change adds to life. Before any of us can receive the benefits, we must accept that each change must be experienced alone—no one else can change for us. This fact is so simple yet difficult to view positively.

Hassett (1978) has found that the key to beneficial change is in a person's ability to change the point of view they hold when confronting changes. This change of point of view will be one of solitary courage, positive projection, and an ability to be confident with success. Once you increase your acceptance of these attitudes, you can expect your actions to follow the projects you created. You will find yourself receiving changes as a matter of good course, if indeed you are not doing this already. Merely understanding this knowledge can be enough to change you toward welcoming growths.

To create changes most rapidly in your positive response to changes, you can work toward improving your own mental and physical health. Taking more efforts toward forming cooperative, honest relationships with others and adding rest, aerobic activity, recreation, and relaxation are key elements in the recipe. Learning to care for yourself reinforces your recognition that you alone are responsible for your own mental health.

In addition, because of the positive physical changes that will occur in your body, you will have happier thoughts in general. These thoughts will help you feel good. They will enable you to impart a sense of well-being to others.

Very personally, what things do you know that can help you face change better? After you have jotted down five things, describe exactly what each will contribute to your ability and date the list. You will refer to it in the future and see the different teacher you are by then. You are beginning to lay a stronger foundation for increased joy and fulfillment in the near future.

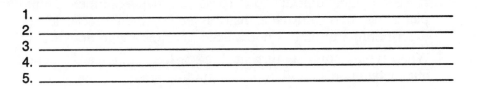

1. _____
2. _____
3. _____
4. _____
5. _____

One last step: look back at your list. Cross out each item you listed that increased your fears concerning change or decreased your confidence. In one paragraph, write three sentences that describe what you will do in the future when you have a change to make. According to Dr. Harry Broudy from the National Society for the Study of Education, one of the most important changes we must make is a change in the traditional school climate. As he stated in his speech at the American Educational Research Association Annual Conference (Chicago, 1985),

> We must give attention to school climate. Teachers must no longer be led to think, "Oh, it's just school. I'm just a teacher." We must give attention to the quality of life with which teachers are associated. We must increase the quality of the institution of education and say the names of teachers and all students often; we must build ways that "the school" makes teachers feel that what they do is very important before teachers will begin to feel that the institution is a quality institution. Such a change will begin when interactions between all people associated with the institution are based on mutual trust and respect.

Become a Time-Saver Tips Scavenger

Time management is not time mastery. You can compare learning to manage time to learning to be a good person, in my opinion. That is, there is the possibility that you may become frustrated when you get one "time waster" under control and suddenly realize that another is begging for your attention. Maybe by knowing that each time you make better ways to use your time you are making better ways to contribute more to others and to yourself. You are constantly increasing your awareness of your skills.

This skill is ongoing. By reading this chapter you may have already eliminated several ways you previously wasted time. This increased awareness also increases your alertness to the ingenious and unique strategies your colleagues are using. In the last few inservice training sessions I have conducted, I asked teachers to note strategies they've used to help them make more time for teaching in the classroom. I've listed 48 of these as my intent in collecting them was to assist you in beginning to collect ideas from others. I wish you the success of collecting as many as two new exciting, time-making ideas each month for the rest of your life. Place a check before the ideas in the following list that you've already had yourself. I bet you have already begun to use ten.

1. Have eighth grade student helpers set up science labs.
2. Put tabs on grade book to turn to specific period class roll quickly.
3. Write a "number" for each child on popsicle stick and keep in a jar on your desk. Whenever you need to assign groups, have extra jobs done, and so on, "draw" a number or numbers from the jar.
4. Have enough "official" jobs (pass out papers, lunch count, water plants, etc.) so *every* child has his or her own special job (and job description) and time is not wasted deciding "who does what."
5. When typing students turn in three or four papers a day, check only one or two items on each. Use a grading scale.

6. Have materials prepared and organized in advance.

7. Make a list of no more than five at a time to accomplish.

8. Put grades in grade books in minus points (-2 for 98) to save time in averaging grades.

9. Put grades on computer so teacher will have list and average for unscheduled as well as scheduled conferences.

10. Primary reading—have folder for each story in the reading text. In folder, keep all materials that are specifically related to that story. Store folders in boxes in order they are presented in book.

11. Involve a parent to help with running off materials, grade objective-type papers, and make games.

12. Learning centers cover work previously covered in class. These centers are self-checking and have a reward for completion (stickers, book marks, etc.).

13. When grading English essays, read the critique into a tape. Have student provide tape, circle mistakes on the paper, and give criticism orally.

14. When grading homework, have students supply answers. The correct answer isn't what is necessary—correct answers can be supplied by teacher during the class discussion—the object is to get the students to do homework and think about the subject, when you reach the third student who has not done the homework or even attempted, the papers will be taken up and graded. The grade is given for the percentage of questions attempted, not the percentage of answers correct. Result: quick, easy grading, peer pressure to do homework, and the realization that to do the work and learn is as important as to get the correct answer.

15. Use student tutors to remediate skill areas.

16. Allow students to do initial filing and alphabetizing and check them rather than your doing it all yourself.

17. Lunch count graph—students have clothespin with their names on them; clip on one side for buying and other side for lunches brought.

18. Have a seating chart so you don't have to call out everybody's name when checking roll.

19. Put lesson plans on computer and use word processor.

20. Print daily grades in pencil, test grades in ink (failing grades in *red*). Daily grades are on one page and test grades on another, so that averaging the two becomes easier. It is easy to spot a child having trouble because of the red grade.

21. Keep a list of all assignments in a notebook, and if a student has been absent, he or she only needs to get the notebook and not bother the teacher until the end of class for any needed clarification.

22. In math, use different color chalk for different parts of a problem. (yellow, dividend; red, divisor; or orange, quotient).

23. Use a parent helper in the classroom each day to work with (two of five groups) on reinforcement skills (50 minutes a day).

24. Carry a pocket notebook to make to-do lists.

25. To increase efficiency without decreasing effectiveness,

   a. Standardize everything possible: schedules, notes (e.g., "This week we are working on _____, I made _____ on test. Hurray! Not up to level. Please return this practice sheet." etc.), reports.

   b. Inform callers and ask secretary to inform callers of callback time so if the caller will not be available at that time you won't waste time (Travers, 1983).

   c. Keep pad and paper and carbon in your mailbox so you can answer notes on the spot and directly on original and xeroxing or carbon copying one for yourself (McGee-Cooper, 1985).

26. Place a tape recorder in the car so you can tape listening center activities as you are driving to work. You could also put in a separate tape on the way home. This tape would become a day-by-day record or the work completed that day in each class so that by inserting the tape, students who were absent during that day could make notes of assignments missed and get caught up without missing any class.

27. Keep a notepad by your bed at night; if an idea comes, it won't be lost.

28. A stitch in time truly saves nine. I find I take stitches by trying to give my full attention and make the best decisions with each task before me. To illustrate, read this case study cited by Rudolf Dreikurs, in his book, *Psychology in the Classroom* (1968, p. 89):

   A discouraged-looking boy in my second-grade class was dragging his feet past me on his way for lunch.
   "Miss P," he said, "I don't think I'll ever learn to read." "What makes you think you'll never learn to read?" I replied. "Oh, I'm just too dumb, I guess."
   I reached into my filing drawer and pulled out a large folder. I said, "You know, Johnny, I know for sure that you aren't dumb. When you first came to this school, a teacher had you answer a lot of questions. You did such a good job on these questions that we know that you are not dumb."

   Had this teacher not taken the time at the beginning of the year to select and file positive samples of test performances, it would have taken at least nine times as long to help this student overcome his feelings of inadequacy.

29. When you write down appointments in your planning or date book, establish the habit of writing what, when, why, and personal responsibilities and materials needed at the meeting. By writing all these specifics in your appointment planning book you can dispose of unnecessary invitations, notices, pamphlets, and letters that clutter your

desk. Then, set aside a space where you can put items that you will need to take to the meeting. As you come across something that you need or think of something that you will need, begin to collect the materials and leave them in that spot. Continuously file or place necessary items in your designated space so that time is not wasted in "finding what you need" or "finding the memo that tells the room number where the meeting will be held." Do this activity now by updating your appointment planning book and finding spots for meeting materials.

30. What is most important is not to be able to read rapidly, but to be able to decide what not to read (McCoy, 1959, p. 14).

31. In the past year, I have developed a method of further limiting wasted preparation time. I have begun to store objects of like uses in the same location. That is, on a tabletop or a shelf on my bookcase, as well as in the drawer of my desk and in the cabinets, you would find several different types and sizes of materials stored in the same category of use. People tend to store two objects in the same space because the objects have the same size, not because they can be easily obtained when needed.

32. Make prepared tapes without making them boring.

33. Have students get rid of their gum and bring class to order.

34. Make lists and *scratch* off what is done.

35. Between classes, have student pass papers out to students as soon as bell rings. Use an assignment board as students can start work as soon as they walk in—No wasted time.

36. Write assignments on the board before class begins.

37. In physical education, limit the time to 10 minutes for dressing out.

38. Write down everything you have to do—in order of importance.

39. Keep teacher morale high.

40. Give students an outline of the subject for the whole year.

41. Students learn more when they read, write, and listen!

42. Use humor to get the point across or when giving examples.

43. Use positive reinforcement as a means of student evaluation. Examples: Use posters with the students' names and stars next to each essential element they accomplish. Display the students' highest graded papers.

44. Try to get everything done before it's scheduled. This allows some free time.

45. Use praise for individual and team accomplishments in class, which develops same behavior in students as a model.

46. Use yourself as a motivation model to get students to do work in class.

47. When lecturing or presenting something, to keep the students' attention, use their names in the lecture or lesson. Example: "*Juan*, today we are going to multiply fractions. Now, to multiply fractions, *Rosie*, we

first check to see if we can reduce within the problem. After we've done that, *Robert*, we multiply the two numerators and the two denominators. When you get your answer, *David*, check to see if you can reduce it further."

48. Set restricted areas in the classroom for yourself and students.

SUMMING UP

You have probably already started to overcome time wasters. We will reassess your skills in eliminating time wasters later in the book, and I hope you will be surprised to see how much you have improved.

REFERENCES

Angell, Frank J. "How to Get the Most Out of Your Time." *National Underwriter* (Life Edition), Vol. 83, January 6, 11–12, and January 13, 1979, 11–12.

Azrin, N. H., R. G. Nunn, and S. E. Frantz. "Treatment of Hairpulling (Trickotillomania): A Comparative Study of Habit Reversal and Negative Practice Behavior." *Behavior Therapy and Experimental Psychiatry*, Vol. 11, 1980, 13–20.

Baker, Roger G. *Habitats, Environments, and Human Behavior*. San Francisco: Jossey-Bass, 1978.

Bliss, Edward C. *Getting Things Done: The ABC's of Time Management*. New York: Scribners, 1976.

Brill, Arthur, and Diana Allen. "Productive Daydreaming." *Viewpoints in Teaching and Learning*, July 1978, 79–81.

Broudy, Harry. Speech given at the American Educational Research Association's annual conference in Chicago, 1985.

Campbell, Robert, M.D., and Leland Hinsie. *Psychiatric Dictionary*. New York: Oxford University Press, 1970, p. 178.

Chatton, H. B. "Support and Motivation in the Young Child." *Child Development*. October 1979, 503–510.

Cohen Richard, Hope Monty, and Deborah Williams. "Management of Thumbsucking Using Self-recording with Parent as Observer and Experimenter." *Perceptual and Motor Skills*, Vol. 50, 1980, 136.

Cordle, Christine, J., and Clive G. Long. "The Use of Operant Self-control Procedures in the Treatment of Compulsive Hair-Pulling." *Behavior Therapy and Experimental Psychiatry*, Vol. II, 1980, 127–130.

Douglass, Merrill. *Successful Time Management for Hospital Administrators*. New York: Amacon, 1980.

Douglass, Merrill, and Donna Douglass. *Manage Your Time, Manage Your Work, Manage Yourself*. New York: Amacon, 1980.

Dreikurs, Rudolph. *Psychology in the Classroom*. New York: Evanston, 1968.

Fagen, Stanley A., and Nicholas J. Long. "A Psychoeducational Curriculum Approach to Teaching Self-control." *Behavioral Disorders*, Vol. 4, no. 2, February 1979, 68–82.

Fenner, Jack D. Successful Time Management. New York: John Wiley, 1980.

Fisher, Charles W., and David C. Berliner. *Perspectives on Instructional Time*. New York: Longman, 1985.

Fonard, J. "Group Achievement Motivation and Individual Motive to Achieve Success and to Avoid Failure." *Journal of Personality*, 1980, 297–311.

Grossin, W., and A. Clement. "Les sociétés industrielle et les Temps programme." *Revue Francaises des Affaires Sociales*, January–March 1979.

Harnischfeger, A., and D. Wiley. "Classroom Control: Room and Time for Improvement." *Educational Technology*, Vol. 18, May 1978, 27–29.

Hassett, James. "Teaching Yourself to Relax." *Psychology Today*, Vol. 12, no. 3, August 1978, 28–40.

Henderson, L. "Sensitive Periods and Motivation." *Oxford Educational Review*, 1974, 173–183.

Hogarth, Robin. *Judgment and Choice*. New York: Wiley Interscience, 1980.

Hohenstein, C. Louis. "Time Management for Managers." *Sky*, February 1981, 64–67.

Horne, David J., and Janet Wilkinson. "Habit Reversal Treatment for Fingernail Biting." *Behavioral Research and Therapy*, Vol 18, 1980, 287–291.

Hunter, Madeline. "Make Each Five Minutes Count." *Instructor*, November 1973, 172–173.

Juran, Joseph. *Managerial Breakthrough*. New York: McGraw-Hill, 1964.

Kilinger, Eric. "The Nature of Fantasy and Its Clinical Uses." *Psychotherapy: Theory and Practice*, 1978, 223–231.

Lakein, Alan. *How to Get Control of Your Time and Your Life*. New York: New American Library, 1973.

MacKenzie, Alec. *The Time Trap*. New York: McGraw-Hill, 1975.

McCoy, James T. *Management of Time*. Englewood Cliffs, N. J.: Prentice-Hall, 1959.

McGee-Cooper, Ann. *Time Management for Unmanageable People*. Dallas: McGee-Cooper, 1985.

Meerloo, Joost A. M. *Along the Fourth Dimension: Man's Sense of Time and History*. New York: John Day, 1970.

Piersel, Wayne C., and Thomas R. Kratochwill. "Self-observation and Behavior Change: Application to Academic and Adjustment Problems Through Behavioral Consultation." *Journal of School Psychology*, Vol. 17, no. 2, Summer 1979, 151–161.

Polsgrove, Lewis. "Self-control: Methods for Child Training." *Behavioral Disorders*, Vol. 4, no. 2, February 1979, 116–130.

Rahaim, Sara, Craig Lefebure, and Jack O. Jenkins. "The Effects of Social Skills Training on Behavioral and Cognitive Components of Anger Management." *Behavior Therapy and Experimental Psychiatry*, Vol. 11, no. 3, 1980, p. 3.

Rutherford, Robert. *Just in Time: Immediate Help for the Time-Pressured*. New York: Wiley-Interscience, 1981.

Taylor, William A. "A Psychology of Decision Delay and Decision Avoidance." *Psychology*, Vol. 16, no. 4, 1980, 41–46.

Timor, T. B., and J. W. Guthrie. "Public Values and Public Policy in 1980." *Educational Leadership*, Vol. 38, November 1980, 112.

Travers, Barbara W. "Improving Speech and Language Services Through Effective Time Management," *Language, Speech and Hearing Services in Schools*, Vol. 20, No. 3, 1983, p. 86–93.

Tyler, Chaplin. "Steps in Becoming a Better Manager." *Chemical Engineering*, April 30, 1962.

Van Loozen, Luann. "Ten Tips for Better Time Management." *The American School Board Journal*, Vol. 10, no. 7, 1982, 107–110.

Wittmer, Joe, and Larry Loesch. "The Use of Fantasy and Imagery in the Classroom." *Humanist Educator*, December 1978, 71–80.

five

Avoiding Overcommitment: the First Step to Making More Time

A Teacher Comments on Chapter 5

The best teachers I know have become skillful at the art of sharing responsibilities with others. They see a new class of thirty-seven youngsters . . . as thirty-seven potential teachers. I haven't gotten as good at this as I hope to become . . . but I have had enough experience to know that much of what I teach quarter after quarter, from use of equipment to printing photos and transcribing tapes to recognizing and dealing with comma splices and misspellings, can be shifted onto the shoulders of students who can teach such skills at least as competently as I.

Eliot Wigginton
Taken from Sometimes a Shining Moment:
The Foxfire Experience

*Published by Anchor Books/Doubleday, 1985.

The truest definition of time management, as I see it, is the art of chasing your tail when you've bitten off more than you can chew.

—*Angela O'Donnell*
Graduate Student
Texas Christian University

Being overcommitted does not mean that you have too many different types and sources of obligation. Some people have a variety of talents and, to feel actualized, have to be involved in many different activities. Other teachers place a high value in using most of their resources in single causes. For this reason, only you can detect and learn to avoid what you judge to be an overcommitment for yourself.

IDENTIFYING AREAS IN WHICH YOU HAVE OVERCOMMITTED

There are two negative developments that will help you identify if either the intensity or number of commitments you have limit your ability to make time. First, ironically, you will notice that you begin to feel insignificant. Your self-esteem and estimate of self-worth will drop. As Shakespeare's Henry V said,

Glory [commitment] is like a circle in the water
Which never ceaseth to enlarge itself.
Till by broad spreading it disperses to nought.

Second, you may feel as if the past decisions limit your freedom to say yes to new ones. You reach the point Bliss (1976, p. 10) described as "When over-whelmed, I put every 'must do' on paper and then I forget everything, and I mean everything else."

It appears that these negatives result from several sources. Often the activities, organizations, and responsibilities in your life, do not fulfill your basic human needs. Therefore, you continually reach out for something new to fill the void.

Sometimes the people with whom we make a commitment may not be as loyal, talented, or devoted as we had first judged. We tend then to overcommit to the cause ourselves "to compensate." Third, it may become clear that the amount of time needed to meet a commitment will not warrant the reward you will receive, or the amount of time you intended to commit has been completely depleted and the return is not visible. You continue to invest time, anyway.

128

Last, there are times when overcommitment results from not beginning work on prior commitments soon enough. Not only will beginning work on a commitment as close to the time you make it improve the estimate of the amount of time needed to complete the task (see Chapter 2), but the satisfaction you gain from doing a job may feel so good that you will begin to not seek a new commitment until a previous one has been completed.

If you need to eliminate one or more activities but are not sure where to begin, the following activities will help. First, look at your watch right now. For the next 2 minutes, list all the activities, organizations, and duties you have right now, in the first column of Figure 5-1. Stop at the end of 2 minutes. Do this now.

Next, number each item in order of the amount of enjoyment and importance it holds for you, beginning with number 1 as most important. To the right of your list is a "time" column. In this column check whether the activity takes "very little" or "much" time to complete the way you would like. Describe the true amount and the ideal amount of time you'd like to commit. Now decide the activities in which you would like to limit your involvement.

Begin with those ranked lowest in importance/enjoyment and highest in time requirement. You may want to draw a line through one activity that you do not want to do any longer. Each time during the next three weeks that you find yourself in situations that might call you to do one of your "overcommitted" tasks, think of this list, say "no" to yourself, and suggest the names of others who might do any of the tasks requested. If you feel that you will have trouble saying "no," turn to the third section of this chapter; it contains a discussion designed to strengthen this skill.

WHY IS IT SO DIFFICULT TO SAY "NO"?

We will discuss reasons why you may find it difficult to tell colleagues and students "no." We will learn methods of learning to say "yes" and "no" effectively.

To identify the major reason for your susceptibility, rank the following statements by placing a "1" beside the statement that most closely describes you, a "2" beside the statement that would best describe you if the first statement had not been given, and so on.

_____ A. The needs of others are more important than my own.

_____ B. When I say "no" to my friends, it is important that they understand the reason(s) why.

_____ C. I say "yes" to more than 50% of the requests made of me.

_____ D. The majority of the time I would rather work as a team than alone.

_____ E. When I have made a commitment that is more taxing than I had anticipated, I stick to it no matter what the cost.

Think of two situations in which you tend to always say "yes."

Figure 5-1

IDENTIFYING AREAS IN WHICH YOU HAVE OVERCOMMITTED YOURSELF

Activities, Organizations, and Responsibilities	Order of Importance to Me	Real Time Requirement (hours per week)	Time You Want to Give

Now, reread the statement you ranked as most closely describing you. Find the discussion below marked by the letter that corresponds to the statement you chose, and read the explanations and means of "overcoming overcommitment," that holds particular value for your teaching/personality style.

A. Often in our society, we are taught (or it is inferred) that it is more virtuous to give to others rather than to ourselves.

Whether our "learnings," "values," or "impressions" on this issue are valid is not of importance in learning to avoid overcommitment. What is important is for you honestly to assess if the values you have for the priorities you set for yourself are as high as the values you hold for priorities that others persuade you to value. Most of us need to be reminded that we should have as high a priority for actions and thoughts that contribute most to our own growth and happiness as the priority we give to helping others grow. One reason for setting one's own priorities is, in doing so, we better ourselves as well as the quality of thoughts and decisions we can share with others. Being able to give more to others, and to ourselves, centers on our learning to refrain from giving a little of ourselves to all needs and requests.

The moment you have a tendency to say "yes" to a need of others, ask yourself these questions: "Do I have the special resources and talents that can truly eliminate the specific cause for the need?" "Have I helped others or myself overcome this problem before?" "Is this person a 'significant other' so I also benefit from saying 'yes' because in strengthening this person I strengthen myself? Is it best for both of us if I help?" "Is the person asking me to do something for him or her that they should really be doing for themselves or we should do together?"

If the answer to any or all of these questions is "no," perhaps you should *refrain* from giving half-hearted assistance. Rather, use your time on your priority and give a suggestion as to how the other person might meet his or her need in a better way. This decision can aid the person more than had you met the original request.

By helping to identify a person who has greater skills and resources to help the person solve his or her problem, you may also help to eliminate a future frustration for the person. Specifically, the action you might have taken to ease some aspect of the problem could have been ineffective or designed merely to alleviate the person's anxiety. The resultant delay in solving the cause of the problem or the complications your naive actions could have caused may have increased the problem.

If you do choose to say "no," refer the person to someone else, or explain why you feel you are not the best person to call upon, you are in a position to direct your talents and capabilities to others with greater ease and more effectiveness in the future. And by systematically and consistently working within areas of talent, you increase your capacity to create new and better ways of giving to others.

There are several techniques you can use to develop the ability to say "no." You may select an action that feels natural from the suggestions that follow.

1. As soon as someone asks you to do something and just before saying "yes," think to yourself, "Others will determine priorities for me if I don't have my own." Each day, list (or have in mind) two important things you want to accomplish by the end of the day. Then, when requests are made of you, you can respond by telling the person(s) the priority on which you are working. The person(s) is then likely to respond by (a) apologizing and asking if there is a better time for you to meet the request, (b) offering to help you finish so you both can work on their request for help, or (c) noting that they were unaware of your interest or involvement in a project of that type and seeking information about how you got involved, how you find time to do it, or how they could become involved. With each of these responses you can help the person(s) increase their skills and resources, using this area personal talent and priority.

2. Tell the person that you have already committed yourself to one of your own prior commitments.

3. Don't feel guilty when you say "no," because anytime a person asks a "yes/no" question, he or she should have a 50% chance of receiving "no" as the answer. When someone asks "Can you do me a favor?" your response can be "I hope I can" and then you weigh the requests with equal value for an affirmative and a nonaffirmative response.

4. Many people overcommit because they try to solve someone else's problem for them. In reality there are two very important things a person can do for a friend or colleague when the friend faces difficulty: (a) You can sincerely and actively listen, always questioning to help that person better discover their own feelings and wisdom, and (b) You can offer advice—advice based on your own personality, circumstances, and knowledge; advice that must be given, without your ego involvement, so the person feels completely free to act upon or reject it. The moment you cross the line from listening and advising to acting, thinking, and deciding for the person, you have assumed too much responsibility. This step could diminish the other person's potential for growth and increase the time demands you place upon yourself.

B. When you say "yes" to another person's request, you do not need to give a reason; when you say "no" to another person's request, you do not need to give an extended explanation.

You may feel a need to give a reason to others when you say "no" because people sometimes interpret denials as a rejection of their personhood and not of their request. Sometimes you give your reasons because you don't want to look incompetent or incapable. Ironically, you can address both these concerns and communicate the other person's importance by not elaborating upon your explanations for saying "no." By not justifying your "no" answer, you (1) communicate that you (and they) can trust your decision that "no" is the correct response you should give; (2) do not enter into a conversation that will encourage your friend to argue, plead, or persuade you; (3) avoid a conversation and you and the other person can more rapidly select an alternate person or method of attaining the request; and (4) can turn your second sentence toward solving the potential problems you could have created by saying "no." Examples of sentences that effectively substitute for extended explanations for saying "no" follow:

1. "It sounds like a (wonderful opportunity, great fun, valuable experience) and I bet (another person's name) would like to go."
2. "You are such a good social director for us; I never have to worry that our next activity will be just (as much fun, as valuable) as this one. I am so glad that you always ask me to be included because some might not ask again if I had to decline in the past." or "You are such a special friend because you know my saying 'no' does not mean I don't consider the activity to be valuable or that I don't value you. I look forward to your next call."
3. "Could I suggest someone to take my place?"
4. "Could I do the task at a different time?"

As you begin to use one of these techniques to increase your time management skills remember that every "no" answer does not have to be justified and that an honest answer will not offend true friends and associates.

C. One important explanation for always saying "yes" is that you may not take initiatives easily and/or think long enough before you respond to another person's request.

Many people have developed two ways of avoiding requests. Either (1) they avoid the persons who most frequently make requests upon them or (2) they act as if they are deaf, ignoring requests where "no" would be the answer they prefer to give. Both these "skills" are unhealthy because they build guilt and a less than honest interaction with others.

The following skills will increase your ability to say "no" to less important requests in a positive way:

1. Place priority upon one or two important aspects of your life, and seek suggestions and assistance from friends and/or family in valuing the time your priorities will take. For example, study how other people make strong commitments to high-level priorities you value. Discuss why you say "yes" so often with those you trust. Let others tell you ways to make decisions about when to say "no."
2. If for some reason you can't say no when you really want to say no, just stop and say nothing. Count to ten before saying "yes." In so doing, others frequently realize that you are hesitant, and they will help you say "no" because they will think of someone else who would be even better for the job when they sense your reluctance as you pause to answer.

3. One of the best ways to lose what Douglass and Douglass (1980, p. 124) call the "rabbit habit" ("taking off in any direction that beckons you") is to identify why you attempt to handle all requests made of you. Many teachers find that they need approval and/or praise from others to satisfy ego needs. Others assume that generosity will buy respect. Ironically, they feel "used" instead. To deal with these concerns, you must check yourself and realize when your self-sacrificing, impulsiveness, or generosity is causing you to promise unrealistic performances. You may also be building so many responsibilities for yourself that you have to do less than your best. *This could lead to low-quality work and a loss of respect, the very reward you said "yes" to receive.* Also, if you say "yes" when you really can't do something or do it to the level expected, or when you really don't intend to do it when it really comes down to it, this "yes" is really a lie.

D. We know that group work is the best way for many task completions.

Many high-achieving people spend 50 percent or more of their time alone or with few people. If you truly enjoy being with a group of people all the time, you may become so much of a "groupie" that you could lose sight of what *you* are and what you believe. You could lose sight of the unique qualities you possess. Moreover "the group" may limit your ability to experience many, different aspects of life. You probably expect yourself to bring new things to your group, and you would like your group to bring new things to you. To experience the joys of working alone, you can set a goal to work by yourself or with one other person to develop a new idea, new object, project or activity to share with your group. You will probably experience a new type of growth. You will develop your ability to take a risk. Taking intelligent risks develops self-confidence more rapidly than any other single action. If you feel you are only a "yes-person" you can become a stronger "partner" in the enterprises you wish by spending time building unique contributions you want to make that others can't give as well as you.

One way to practice saying "no" if you are this type of teacher is to learn to identify when you should tactfully decline offers of work from those who are above you in rank. Such declines are justified when others may be taking advantage of your talents and goodwill. Phrases that people might use to signal that their problems or their work is about to be passed to you are "We have a big problem." "I think you would be interested in . . . ." "I told them I knew you'd be the person for the job." "I know you'll be excited to hear that we just received _____ and you'll be _____." "You are the only one I can depend on." "I knew I could count on you." "When I heard about it, you were the first person that came to my mind." "Have you ever . . .?" "So you know Mr. _____ or Mrs. _____? He/she will be here _____, and I want you to have the chance to talk with him/her."

When one of these or similar phrases has been stated, you can gently and sincerely ask, "Why are you telling me this?" "Why do you want me to be involved?" "What talent do I have that you feel would be valuable for this task?"

Based on the answer you receive, the personal prior commitments you have and the value that the work holds for you and your educational community, you can decide to accept or to refuse. If you decide to refuse, the next sentence could be: "Thank you for the compliment but I'll have to decline. Can I offer a suggestion?" or "I would have been very happy to help you or to accept, but I have . . .," letting others know that you are more than happy to help, if you are, when your time is not so tight. You will then be included in future situations.

One of the most important laws of time management is the "law of the path of least resistance." If you always say "yes," you'll be the first person called upon to do what others don't want to do. You must realize that when people seem to assume that you will say "yes" to their request, *you* are to blame for the time pressures and undesirable jobs you end up doing. You are responsible for the types of requests people make of you because you encourage them by projecting an image of one who had few prior commitments.

E. When we feel we make commitments that are more taxing than we had anticipated, we should not demean ourselves.

No one cannot perfectly judge the length of time all tasks will take. The truth you must accept is that, in our present understandings of time, there are no guarantees that the amount of time you wish to commit to a task will be sufficient for the task. While having had experience doing a task increases your ability to estimate how long it will take, we must learn how to handle situations that are more taxing than we originally hoped. Methods of addressing these types of commitment are to (1) ask others for help, (2) ask for an extension of time, (3) eliminate some of the frills that you hoped to include, (4) ask to add those parts not yet complete at a later time, or (5) share the completed portions with people to whom you gave your commitment and ask them to help you decide what to do to meet the deadline.

It will also help if, when you are asked to do a new task, you tell the person making the new request all things that you have already been obligated to do and ask which you should do first.

LEARNING TO SAY "NO"

Greater freedom to say "yes" will evolve from having developed your ability to avoid overcommitment. Now that you are more aware of the reason why saying "no" was so difficult for you in the past, you have taken the most important step to overcome the problem. The only thing you must do now is develop a procedure to encourage the habit of saying "no." You have already begun because you chose one of the phrases from the earlier discussion to begin to practice in responding to undesirable and unimportant requests.

I'd like to ask you to practice using this phrase now and to repeat that phrase three times out loud, right now, if you are alone. You will have to trust me that it will be of value to you because you will feel silly saying it orally right now. Say it now.

Having done this will make it easier for you to say it later. Now, picture yourself in one of the two situations identified in the previous discussion in which you tend to always say "yes." Visualize the setting and then say the name of the person and the phrase you just rehearsed. As you say it again, out loud, fill in all the details, making it as realistic a setting as possible.

Learning to say "no" means that you have practiced your new skill enough that it has become automatic. Soon, the skill of saying "no" will be as well developed as your present skill of saying "yes." You will have added a new skill to aid in objective decision making as well. You will begin to handle a wider variety of difficult situations.

Prior to developing the skill of saying "no," you may have said yes so frequently because you believed it was easier. You may have thought you wouldn't have to worry about what would happen next: you would simply do the actions you said you would. Now, you may better appreciate the difficulties that overcommitment creates. You may have confidence to face what saying "no" could mean. That is, when you say "no," you do not have control over the next thing that will happen. The more skilled you become and the more successes you have as a result of helping others by saying "no," the stronger teacher you will become. The next test is applying this new skill in the classroom, with students, who may have identified this previously weak area, as your Achilles' heel, and been capitalizing upon it to keep from learning as much as they can.

OVERCOMING THE EXCESSIVE DESIRE TO BE WELL LIKED OR TO PLEASE OTHERS

Ability to make more time is closely linked to a high level of self-esteem. This is true because each time you make time for something new, you demonstrate the strength to have (1) combined two familiar activities so as to do them in a new way in less time, (2) discarded an obsolete goal or activity, and/or (3) expanded your level of capability. Doing so also demands high, internal standards and an ability to judge, reward, and guide yourself. Because teachers most often enter their profession to serve others, an excessive drive to please can develop. This excessive desire can, in turn, diminish your potential. Before we learn more about making time, let me clarify what I intend as prerequisites:

1. A desire to be well liked is normal and is very good for people.

2. A desire to be well liked helps to develop one of the most important aspects of a well-rounded healthy personality. Can you name that aspect? (a) _____;

3. There are two ways to achieve "being well liked": you either win the approval of those whom you wish to please, or you avoid disapproval.

4. To become well liked, a person must invest considerable time in discerning the factors that will (b) _____ (Azrin, Nunn, and Frantz, 1980);

5. The skill with which a person can positively influence others determines how long it will take a person to become well liked, how rapidly that person will be able to use time wisely, and what response the person will have to his or her next excessive drive to be well liked, as documented by Baumeister, Cooper, and Skip (1979);

6. To develop a skill of sensing what others view to be the most positive aspects of your personality, you must learn to recognize (c) _____. People value this quality.

7. People will expect specific things from specific people, and you must be able to detect similarities or conditions that surround the (d) _____ others have of you to be able to deliver what is expected from you.

Answers: (a) the major cause for "nonself-centered" behaviors, (b) positively influence others, (c) why, and (d) expectations.

An excessive desire to be well liked is closely linked to one's ability to conform, which tends to decrease your level of self-esteem. Baumeister (1979) discovered that excessive conformists ensure that their performances will be inferior so as to protect their own low levels of self-esteem.

The ability to resist group or self-induced pressure to be less than your best can be developed. Allen and Wilder (1979) found that you first must identify the area in which you seek approval to an excess. Then you must select two or three people whose actions you would most like to emulate. Separately place each person in your situation and visualize the responses he or she would make. Now place yourself in that situation and perform actions similar to those exhibited by the person you respect. This method also works well when you feel you have temporarily lost some of the rapport you have with your students.

A second method is to increase your level of independence. You can do this by predicting, in a given situation, what the actions will be of the people you want to impress. By thinking about these possibilities in advance, you can select an action that will be pleasing to you both. If you have not yet discerned probable responses people could have, you can try to identify two or three that could occur and plan a beneficial response to each. This method works exceptionally well when you are to interact with an administrator you do not know well.

Third, you could discuss difficulties you have when you face certain pressures or expectancies. The person listening should respond by helping to confirm your decision or reduce your excessive need to be self-liked. If your listener does, you will learn more quickly to channel your time into other areas. If the person responds by saying, "Don't worry about it" or tries to ameliorate your anxiety and fear by denying that you are like that, you will need to select a different confidant—one who will talk of reasons why you will benefit from channeling some of your time into other areas will be of greater value, one who will help to develop a plan of action and point out ways that you gained respect in the past will also be helpful. Your discussions will lead to increased self-confidence and ability to think independently.

Finally, whenever possible, you can reduce other people's natural tendency to conform to you when you serve as a leader by asking people to express their thinking and decisions anonymously. This reduces the power of public expectancy.

To review, you can overcome an excessive desire to be well-liked by (1) simulating the actions of people you admire in situations you wish to master, (2) planning for probable responses others will have to you so you can satisfy both your needs in your interaction, (3) discussing your desire to be well liked with a confidant, and (4) building anonymity in difficult group decisions.

MAKING TIME BY NOT MAKING EXCUSES

Prior to beginning this study of time management you may have thought you had an excellent time management technique. You may have learned to use many different types of excuses to make time for yourself. However, while excuses appear to reduce pressures, they have numerous unproductive side effects. For example, sometimes the excuses you make become reality. Did you ever tell someone that you would "love to do _____ but you (excuse) are not feeling well. Subconsciously you may have worked on this self-suggestion and forced yourself to get tired or sick so as to not have lied to that person or to yourself.

Excuses tend to be negative statements or negative self-affirmations. Through their use, you demean yourself (e.g., "I can't because," "I didn't because"). This self-talk becomes a self-fulfilling prophesy for many teachers.

Second, excuses can become a habit. They block your ability to meet and create new responsibilities and face difficult challenges.

Last, when you give student and colleagues opportunities to learn more about you and the situation you face, by not using excuses, you become more consistent and dependable. Your students will also see a model for how more responsible decisions can be made. When you begin to eliminate excuses in your life, you will also begin to realize how much energy you were using to avoid judgments and the difficulties you were creating by spending time creating believable excuses.

One teacher shared this experience she had in learning to not use excuses:

My students asked me, "Do we have to take a comprehensive final?" In the past I would have replied by avoiding the real reason why I was giving a comprehensive final for fear they would not like me. I would have replied with an excuse: "Yes," I would have said, "I wish we didn't have to but it is required." "Being required" was only partly true, as the principal told the faculty that a final was required but the choice to make it comprehensive or not was ours to make. The major reason I elected to give a comprehensive final was that it was my best method of discriminating between the amounts my students had learned. By learning to not make excuses, I told my students the exact reason for my decision. I was so excited about what that response did! I taught them something about testing, about me as a person, and about my perceptions about the large amount they had learned. I showed how proud I was of them and this freed them to share this high evaluation of themselves as well.

If you are tempted to make excuses, as you read the list of excuses that can be used (see Figure 5-2), either think of the words or write the words you have heard yourself saying in the past as you made excuses to yourself or others. For example, as you read the first entry, you might have used this excuse by saying "I can't team teach because I've done it before and it didn't work." In the space to the right of the excuse you would write "team teaching" and note the date as which you last used that excuse. These dates will become a benchmark for your improvement and can be changed if you use the excuse in the future. Eventually, each excuse will be eliminated; some will take a few weeks to be replaced. As you progress through the list, place a checkmark before each excuse you have never used, as these will be signs of previous skill in selecting productive responses in these types of settings.

Now you may want to select a method of eliminating excuses. As you read the list in Figure 5-2, you may have analyzed what your excuses have in common. For example, many teachers have found that by making things that had been "excused" in the past (1) more comfortable to approach, (2) more interesting to do, or (3) more slowly paced, the excuse wasn't necessary. That is, if we assume that in the past you used the excuse "I can't _____ because I'm too busy," in the future whenever you are tempted to use this excuse, honestly ask yourself when you will make the time to do the activity. If you discover that you never intended to make the time, you can keep from promising a future time by rethinking the excuse as a positive statement; you then reply "I am more interested in completing _____. Thank you for asking if I wanted to be included."

You will also not be as tempted to use an excuse when you feel as if someone is asking you to play a "role." While being a teacher means that you are committed to play many roles and to enact the conditions of your contract, others can impact your time to the point that you feel "mortgaged," without any choices as to how you wish to manage your time. Future restrictions can be avoided. You offer alternatives as to how their and your role could be realized in more effective ways instead of trying to push their endless demands away with excuses. Your past strategy of seeking flexibility, giving excuses, only intensified the strength of other people's future requests; that is, they felt if they just made their pleas more urgent, you could "get over being tired," "squeeze it in," or "go ahead and do it *all by yourself.*"

Teachers have told me they experienced a new joy when they no longer needed to use excuses as a "crutch." They felt stronger and observed how they faced and conquered larger, more important, challenges in their lives. I wish you this joy.

Figure 5-2

Excuses	Conditions Of Use And Date At Which I Last Remember Using This Excuse
1. I can't _____ because I've done it before and it didn't work or it (I) wasn't good.	_____
2. I don't _____ because no one told me that it was OK to begin.	_____
3. I can't _____ because that isn't my job.	_____
4. I can't _____ because I'm too busy or tired, or if I had more time I'd _____ .	_____
5. I don't have time to _____ .	_____
6. I forgot to _____ .	_____
7. I didn't _____ because I didn't know it was so important.	_____
8. I didn't _____ because it was good enough for them so it should be good enough for me.	_____
9. I can't do _____ because I just can't seem to get started.	_____
10. I would _____ if I just didn't have so much to do right now.	_____
11. I don't because _____ isn't worth the time, energy, or effort.	_____
12. I don't _____ because it bores me.	_____
13. I'll _____ later.	_____
14. If I wasn't so fat, ugly, lazy, I'd __ .	_____
15. If I didn't have so many responsibilities at _____ I'd _____ .	_____
16. If I were in complete control of my time, I'd _____ .	_____
17. I don't want to _____ because it makes me feel uncomfortable.	_____
18. I don't _____ because I don't want to.	_____
19. I didn't _____ because it wasn't important.	_____
20. I don't _____ because I'm scared, ashamed, or mad.	_____
21. I can't find "it" _____ .	_____

GIVING RESPONSIBILITIES TO STUDENT AIDES AND CLASSROOM VOLUNTEERS

W. Michael Born (1979) wrote that delegation is one of the least understood and most abused of all management techniques. Teachers have misunderstood the task and needs of giving responsibilities to students in two major ways. First, they have not been taught that the emphasis and purpose of delegating is to develop students (or adults) or to initiate creativity. Second, it is assumed that the "lazy" teacher uses delegation of responsibilities to students as an "easy way out." Delegation has become synonymous with a lack of commitment to "hard work."

Delegation is a difficult skill to learn and a very difficult challenge for teachers. Delegation cannot begin unless students and teachers have a high level of trust for one another. Delegation cannot exist unless a strong positive classroom climate has been built. Delegation cannot exist unless skills in sharing and a sense of job unity have been established. Teachers must show students how each delegated responsibility adds to the total learning experience and how it enhances every other member of the class's learning. Such teachers must also be highly skilled in extending confidence to others as well as developing open, free-flowing communication between other teachers, aides, volunteers, administrators, students, and themselves.

To begin, you must realize that giving responsibilities to others will not "get rid of work" or necessarily give you more time. Rather it will increase the scope of your responsibility. It will expand your teaching effectiveness and potential for impacting the delegates as well as the profession. Proper delegation involves holding a meeting where all people agree to the specific standards and procedures of the task. Moreover, you must select the right person for each job, as people who lack confidence, fear criticism, or do not value the responsibility or opportunity to be involved in a shared goal are not yet ready for independently led delegations. The best types of tasks to delegate are ones that students or others enjoy doing more than you enjoy doing.

Teachers who have delegated classroom tasks in the past may have failed because they did not train the students/aides on how to do the task in advance. Some may have not supervised effectively to circumvent problems. Some may have not provided alternates for times when the student, aide, or volunteer was absent. Some overdelegated to only the same, few people. Such actions reduce, rather than increase, class unity. In essence, if a task does not require your professional expertise and someone else could strengthen his or her skills by doing the task, the task can be delegated effectively.

These points can guide you:

1. If giving up duties is difficult for you, you may wish to *delegate the task of delegating*. Select a key student to watch classroom routines and teaching methods to identify means by which both could be improved through disseminating more responsibility to students and other adults.

2. Give time schedules and points where periodic checks of progress will occur; give authority and resources as well as freedom for the student,

(aide or volunteer) to think, create, and develop resources, within the realm of responsibility.

3. Be certain that all students (aides or volunteers) measure and assess the quality of the work under their responsibility and turn their evaluations to you during and at the end of the project.

4. Remember that it takes courage, patience, trust, and often external motivation incentives for students for shared responsibility to be successful in a classroom. Teachers must be patient with and truly forgive and forget past mistakes, entering each new shared responsibility positively with an optimistic outlook and a clear, important goal in mind.

5. Perhaps the most difficult of all is to learn to delegate to each person good jobs, not just the jobs that are tiresome or the ones that you do not wish to do.

6. Discuss openly with the entire class all changes that have to be made with each new delegatee. You may want the person who has the delegated authority to make these announcements.

7. Plan realistically so delegation can occur gradually, in advance of the time at which the first action is scheduled to begin. Tell your people why you have chosen to delegate these "whole pieces" or "complete tasks" rather than do them yourself. Check back with the delegatee four days prior to the deadline so you can initiate any discussion of needs, saving the delegatee any possible embarrassment or avoidance-type behaviors toward you.

8. Be certain that you do not feel threatened that the student (volunteer or aide) will perform the task in a way that was better than the method you might have used or that they will begin to command a special rapport with the students.

9. Truly let go of the job and do not interfere in the work unless asked to give advice, and then give more than one suggestion so the student can make the decision concerning the course of action.

10. Evaluate if you have a desire for perfection, defining perfection as that which must be achieved in your own preset manner.

Many educators are amazed when they first begin to delegate because the amount of time they have is reduced instead of increased! To avoid this condition and to increase the amount of time you have for higher-priority items, you must increase the proportion of authority you delegate. If you overcontrol delegatees, checking too frequently on the individual decisions that they are making, you will essentially increase your own work load by 40% above the amount that would have existed had you done the job yourself. As stated previously, if a task takes more time to delegate than it takes to do it yourself, do it yourself. If a job has been delegated, adhere to the checklist on the previous page and spend your time pursuing a job that requires your skill, and your skill, alone, to be most successfully completed.

Two final notes. Be certain that every person knows who is to make decisions until (and after) the product is complete. And remember that it is very difficult to be an effective delegator, as Joseph Conrad expressed vividly in Chapter 42 of his book, *Lord Jim*:

> Some great men owe most of their greatness to the ability of detecting in those they destine for their tools the exact quality of strength that matters for their work.

In Chapter 9 we will have a ten-item postcheck to let you see how much your skill in giving increased responsibility to students has grown! In the meantime, complete Figure 5-3.

REFERENCES

Allen, Vernon I., and David A. Wilder. "Social Support in Absentia: The Effect of an Absentee Partner on Conformity." *Human Relations*, Vol. 32, 1979, 103–111.

Azrin, N. H., R. G. Nunn, and S. E. Frantz. "Treatment of Hairpulling (Trickotillomania): A Comparative Study of Habit Reversal and Negative Practice Behavior." *Behavior Therapy and Experimental Psychiatry*, Vol. 11, 1980, 13–20.

Baumeister, Roy F., Joel Cooper, and Bryan Skip. "Interior Performance as a Selective Response to Expectancy: Taking a Dive to Make a Point." *Journal of Personality and Social Psychology*, Vol. 37, 1979, 424–432.

Bliss, Edward C. *Getting Things Done: The ABC's of Time Management*. New York: Scribners, 1976.

Born, Michael W. "Time Management for the Harried Campus Administrator." *Educational Research*, June/July 1979, Vol. 8, No. 6, p 10-21.

Figure 5-3

DO I AVOID OVERCOMMITMENT?

Yes   **No**

_____ _____ Have you identified what "overcommitment" means in your life? Have you thought of a method to avoid overcommitting in the future?

_____ _____ Could you paraphrase in one sentence, the main reason why it was so difficult for you to say "no" in the past? If "yes," do so here: ___
_____

_____ _____ Can you recall a method you will use to appropriately respond "no" in the future? _____
_____

_____ _____ Did you have an excessive desire to be well liked or to please others that seemed to impact your teaching in negative ways?

_____ _____ Do you know which of the following were not recommended as a method of tempering a desire to be well liked: (1) discussing your desire to be well liked with a confidant, (2) limiting the number of people you seek to please, (3) visualizing probable responses people will make to you, or (4) placing a person you admire in your situation and replicating what they would do.

_____ _____ Have you noticed that you already use fewer excuses than you did before you read Chapter 5?

_____ _____ Are you looking forward to referring back to the list of excuses you wrote in this book because you are consciously working to developing the skill of not using excuses?

_____ _____ Are you eliminating excuses by rephrasing them in a positive way?

_____ _____ Are you eager to try to delegate some new responsibilities to your students?

_____ _____ Have you already delegated your first major instructional duty?

144

six

Creative Problem Solving: Making More Time for Teaching and Learning

A Teacher Comments on Chapter 6

I found Chapter 6 easy to read and interesting and the "fill in the blanks" excellent. I thought about how we, as teachers, by encouraging creative thinkers and problem solvers, help to develop minds that can make valuable decisions and create new, rewarding ideas. These new ideas may not agree with our own, however, but the students' enthusiasm gives us the patience to understand; therefore, we grow more receptive. Observing independent, free thinkers, wanting to try new things, experimenting with new ideas while forging ahead without fear is breath taking and rewarding. The students are our continuous link to the future and optimism. They must be taught techniques and procedures that stimulate and produce enthusiasm that will keep the ideas fluid. This is a part of what Chapter 6 is all about and what it helped me to be able to do.

Karen Trujillo
Secondary Teacher
Colorado Springs, Colorado

Recognize [that] most problems result from actions
[taken] without thought. Those who know what to
do succeed once. Those who know why [they
succeed] will succeed again and again.

—Alec MacKenzie, The Time Trap (1972)

The best classroom managers seem to change strategies and methods of handling classroom difficulties so as to engage the affective and cognitive domains effectively in their and their students' decisions. With each new difficulty, they build their flexibility in thinking and their tenacity. They use some of the six major approaches to classroom problem solving. They implement the following principle of creative problem solving.

The principle is that while you can "try and try again until you succeed," your first trial will not differ significantly from subsequent ones unless you obtain some extra information between trials. If new information is not used in subsequent trials, the problem is likely to increase.

While this principle of time management seems simple, it may prove difficult for you to implement. Too frequently you may have tried to do one of two things whenever you faced a classroom problem. First, you may have taken the same set of actions you first took to solve the problem and that led to the first failure. Second, you could have given up and stopped trying to solve the problem.

When we truly understand the underlying meaning of this principle, you will more frequently choose a third, more successful option. In the future when something fails, you will first locate the part of the plan that failed and save all parts of your actions that worked. Then, you will develop a better plan using these parts. For every goal and every individual trying to reach that goal, there is one best plan. The task is to use one of the following basic approaches to create that plan.

VARYING YOUR APPROACH TO CLASSROOM PROBLEMS AND SITUATIONS

There are nine basic approaches to solve classroom problems. As new problems arise, reference this discussion to select the approach that best meets the new problem situation. Then develop your unique action plan to address it. The nine approaches are described in a list format so they can be more easily referenced each time you face a new type of difficulty.

The "Laser Beam" Approach

The *laser-beam approach* refers to the use of insight to solve problems. When your goal is to uncover the core of a difficulty, the laser-beam approach uses past experiences to enable this to occur. This is the fastest problem-solving technique.

To use the laser-beam approach you must have had several experiences solving similar problems and a large amount of intuitive and perceptive abilities. This plan will not be successful when you are not sure what to do. You must know specific steps that are needed to solve a problem. You can predict the ramifications your actions will have.

The "Sectional" Approach

The *sectional* approach is followed to examine the most visible extension of a difficulty. By sectioning a difficulty into parts, you create opportunities to view various parts of the environment around the problem. This method is very successful when you want to "cut a problem" out of a larger operation. That is, by singling out individual variables, by cutting away all external aspects and influences upon that variable, a solution can be reached faster.

To illustrate, a high school biology teacher wanted to solve the problem of students' copying answers from peers during experiments. In this teacher's third-period class, a table of students was always finished with the experiments too quickly to have worked them and yet they always had the correct answers. This teacher reported that he tried the strategies of confronting the students, separating the students, and punishing the group as a whole. Nothing had worked. After reading this chapter, the teacher decided to take the "table" one section at a time. He decided to take four different days to isolate variables. He asked Bob, the student he most suspected as the leader of the group, to do a special assignment in the library during the biology class during the first day of this four-day plan. That day, the remaining three completed the experiment early and had all lessons right. The same situation occurred the next two times the teacher tried his plan, as he did not do it systematically, on subsequent days, so the students couldn't predict what was occurring. Only on the fourth day, when Tom was asked, impromptu, to go to the library at the beginning of the class, was the group at a loss. The teacher discovered that Tom had been copying answers from a person in the teacher's first-period class to gain the friendship of the three other students. Through this teacher's carefully implemented problem-solving plan, the student was helped in many ways. The teacher met with Tom separately on several occasions, and Tom developed a strong self-concept. All four students learned more about biology, and the rest of the class did not know that anything had happened, so no new seeds for future occurrences were planted.

The value of this approach is that the goal can be reached and the problem solved without distrupting other vital, environmental elements that will be needed for the eventual solution to flourish.

The "Top-Down" Approach

Using the *top-down approach*, you begin at the most visible extension of the problem or confront the people with greatest power. This approach is analogous to "starting at the top." When answers are not apparent, people of greater authority can provide insights that help. Another interpretation of this approach is that if the group in which you are working does not produce the results you expect, you can add members or take away members from the group, in either an ascending or descending order of authority to identify better solutions to group problems. For example, you divide the class into groups for a project. One student does not fit into a group and constantly complains and disrupts all groups. Rather than disbanning the project, this student becomes a group of one who is then given either an inflated or deflated role in the end product for the project.

The "Bottom-Up" Approach

The *bottom-up approach* is best used when you are not involved in the classroom problem personally and/or when the incidents causing the problem are so intertwined that the initiator is not clear. "Grass roots" politics is the most visible application of this approach in our society. When key issues or irritations in your room are not clear but mounting, planning a means of allowing each individual in the room to suggest his or her interpretation as to the source of irritation can be the best approach to solve the problem.

The "Divergent and Convergent Thinking" Approach

The *divergent and convergent thinking aproach* is an approach to problem solving whereby teachers look at several, distinct examples before generating a solution. You try to generate an ideal, to build examples and incidents to support this image and then implement one example at a time.

The "Committee" Approach

In the *committee approach*, you call together a group of students or colleagues to "develop a plan of action" to solve a problem. The difficulty in using this plan, as you may have experienced, is that in specific types of problem-solving situations, the committee can become sidetracked. Discussions tend to circumvent the real problem because each person has a different, uncompromising perspective that must be addressed. Gradually, the discussion centers on these separate perspectives rather than on the issue itself. Before the problem can be solved, many hours are spent in uniting all needs/perspectives and in agreeing upon what the problem really is rather than upon solving it.

These discussions can subsequently lead to an elaborate, highly specialized plan of action that is never enacted, as so much time has been spent in developing a plan that the enthusiasm of the first meetings of the committee has evaporated. Worse are the instances in which the time spent in meetings was long enough that the problem itself changed and the solution was no longer applicable.

When committee members are alerted to this difficulty, actions can be taken to guard against it. This method works well when each committee member is responsible for researching and presenting one dimension of a problem within a specified time period. The committee approach is also useful when all members agree to be on guard and modify each other's biases and when the committee is addressing plans for future advancements in the class or school, advancements where prior problems have not existed.

The "Call-in-the-Expert" Approach

The *call-in-the-expert approach* is the easiest to use. You identify the person or people who you wish to involve, based on their unique expertises. This expert can come to observe the problem or meet with you in private, as you may already be doing.

The "Diseased Tree" Approach

The *diseased-tree approach* attacks the easiest aspect of the problem first. This method uses the strategy employed by tree experts as they approach the problem of destroying a diseased tree. The expert does not step up to the tree and saw through the base of the trunk and be done with it. Instead, the expert clips the tiny uppermost branches; then, one by one, he or she saws the larger tree limbs. The expert ends by cutting the trunk apart section by section. Tree experts, it appears, are taught that problems should be addressed by tackling the easy parts first. When the problem is approached in this way the rest of the problem will become simpler and smaller as each stage of the work progresses. Such an approach is also valuable in overcoming the ramifications of a less than best decision you have made. That is, rather than scraping the entire lesson, you eliminate the easiest ineffective aspect of the decision or lesson first, leaving the most difficult parts engaged till the ramifications have been eliminated.

The "Creative Problem-Solving"Approaches

Creative problem-solving approaches involve creating a new idea to solve a problem. There are six ways to create these new ideas, all of which will be presented after the next discussion as they are learned skills. Six lesson plans to help students learn these problem-solving techniques are included in the discussion later in this chapter.

WHEN TO USE A SPECIFIC APPROACH

How do you know which of these approaches to use? As stated previously, if you use one of these approaches to solve a problem and it fails, instead of using the same approach a second time, you might either select a different approach or study which part of the first approach was ineffective. The next four paragraphs describe the characteristics of problems that are most amenable to each of these approaches to assist in your skills of selecting the best "first" problem-solving approach as frequently as possible.

Problems that involve a teacher and one other person, problems that do not arouse a teacher's negative emotions, problems that are within the teacher's talents and areas of expertise, and problems that have one clearly superior solution respond best to insight (using the laser-beam plan of action to stop the situation before it involves more people and time). If a problem involves a schoolwide policy, another teacher or a parent, to call upon higher authorities is the best plan. Never act on your own intuition in these type of problems. If you do, you may find that you are the one who is blamed for the problem. In essence, whenever a difficulty exists between anyone except the teacher and the teacher's students, the most effective approach is the top-down or bottom-up plan; delay any decision and even delay expressions of one's opinion in such situations until the principal or other appropriate authority are present to make a joint decision.

The sectional plan is best used when a problem has multiplied into several different problems. Most often, it is also the best approach to use in a second trial when one of the other five has failed. To illustrate, let's pretend that one of your students begins mumbling something under his breath as you are leading a class discussion. Several around this student began to mumble and giggle. You decide to use "insight" (the laser-beam approach) because this had occurred previously, and walk to the back of the room with the intent of continuing the discussion as you stand beside the desk of the student who first mumbled. As you begin down the aisle, however, you trip because several students had not picked up their notebooks and books from the floor as you had requested earlier. The class begins to laugh; then they grow concerned that you might have fallen and they become very quiet. As you try to regain your composure, the "ball is in your court" and you have a very difficult response to make and complex problem to solve. What would you do as you straighten upright?

A teacher who is knowledgeable in the field of classroom problem solving would think, "I can't use my insight now becuase this is a different type of class than I am used to and this is my first year to teach the seventh grade. I can't call the principal as the students have not broken a rule that involved more than our own classroom procedures. I can't use the committee approach because several different problems exist, and the problems are not affecting all members of the class equally. I can't use the diseased tree approach because if I focus on the smallest aspect (the books on the floor), it will not lead to the main problem (the trunk of the issue) because the problems have distinct, unconnected roots. I'll merely circumvent the bigger problem if I use the diseased tree approach. I should use the sectional plan as the problem has many complexities, and it is also the plan that works best as a second try. "My first plan of attack (my laser-beam walk to the back of the room) was certainly not successful today." Then this teacher enumerated to the class each of the three separate problems that interrupted the learning. The teacher then handled each separately with simple, sentence directives and no emotions were expressed as the thinking had helped the teacher become more objective in the response to the class and problems.

The committee approach is excellent for problems affecting an entire group equally or for problems that involve one section of students disrupting a second, where the teacher isn't involved. The diseased tree approach works well when you aren't really sure what the cause of the problem is or when so many problems or perspectives concerning an incident exist and the teacher is called upon to be the "expert" and solve the problem (e.g., when two groups of students are having a dispute over a score in a softball game that just occurred but the teacher called upon to resolve the dispute wasn't there at the time). By beginning with the simplest issues, the complexity of the problem diminishes quickly.

To help you retain what you've just read, fill in the name of the method in each of the following blanks that is being defined. We will check your responses on the next page. Good luck.

1. _____ = the approach to use when two groups of students are having a problem, you aren't involved, but you want to help them use this method as a means of resolving their difficulties. Both groups select members to represent their concerns in discussion of the solution.

2. _____ = the approach that allows you to solve a small piece of the problem so as to estimate its depth and how long it may take to solve; the approach to use when the problem extends beyond your jurisdiction and you call in experts or more people who are above, equal to, or below you in rank.

3. _____ = the method that is more successful for experienced than inexperienced teachers and requires great skill in the perception of problem elements and human frailties.

4. _____ = this approach is very effective in chaotic situations where you are not involved as a participant but are required to solve and in situations where one central issue or problem is surfacing in different ways (e.g., different behaviors students exhibit when they judge a teacher's decision to be wrong).

5. _____ = this approach is used when several different problems are in action at once and as the "most likely to succeed" plan when a first attempt to solve a problem has failed; each problem is solved separately.

You may want to check your answers now: 1. committee appproach, 2. top-down or bottom-up approaches, 3. laser-beam approach, 4. diseased-tree approach, 5. sectional approach.

AVOIDING CLASSROOM PROBLEMS BY INVESTING MORE TIME IN HIGHER-LEVEL THINKING ACTIVITIES

There appear to be two prerequisites that enhance our ability to avoid classroom problems. First, we must realize and accept that any change in and of itself requires energy and time. Thus, if you are willing to give time to learning to avoid classroom problems, you can be prepared for the pain that may occur in the growth. Second, as Cross (1980) discovered, classrooms that undergo the greatest decrease in problems are led by teachers who have performed "the most difficult of feats: they have changed their own habits."

If you set goals that are too small for your capabilities, you will inadvertently create problems in your classroom. As you know, teaching requires that time be spent in disciplining students, managing administrative duties, organizing papers, moving furniture, and cleaning the room. Activities such as these can be labeled "implementation duties." They do not involve many of your high-level thoughts or decisions. Thus, if you spend a considerable part of your day executing such duties, you will build frustration and discontentment for yourself and your students. These will often, in and of themselves, create student problems for a wide variety of reasons.

Before we proceed with our discussions, in pencil (so you can erase if you wish) and very honestly, for your own benefit and for use in the next discussion, write the five activities that consumed most of your time in the classroom yesterday:

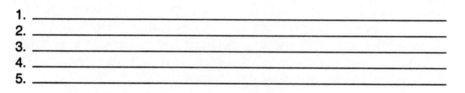

1. _____
2. _____
3. _____
4. _____
5. _____

Now compare your five duties to those that were most often cited by the most successful teachers in our country. (Tschudin, 1978):

1. Planning activities to teach.
2. Modifying a curriculum plan to match the level students attained in the activity just completed.
3. Testing students' learning.
4. Enhancing my professional skills.
5. Developing the character of my students.

If you presently center your goals and duties on any task or value that does not demand your professional judgment, take steps this week to delegate or expand your activities. If you begin to center more of your activities on the foregoing types of activities, you will begin to avoid classroom problems.

Beside each of the goals in the following list, write down one way in the next week you can increase the amount of time you spend performing each. We will refer back to this list at the end of the chapter.

1. Planning the activity.
2. Modifying a curriculum plan to match the level students attained in the activity just completed.
3. Testing students' learning.
4. Enhancing your professional skills.
5. Developing the character of your students.

Throughout the remainder of this year, continually remind yourself that, to be most productive and happy, you should strive to spend the greatest majority of your time in duties that require your professional judgment. By the end of the year, you will have achieved many successes that you may, at this point, feel are unlikely.

THE CREATIVE PROBLEM-SOLVING APPROACHES

Bruner (1960) defines a creative act as one that "produces effect surprise." . . . or a unique impactful impression upon the senses and memory that changes a person's thinking, emotions, or productivity level. Psychologists have identified three stages in the "creation act." You can set these in motion in the classroom to make time. The stages are *the preparation stage*, where materials are collected, read, and pondered; *the productive stage*, where ideas relevant to the problem are generated; and *the judgment stage*, where ideas are evaluated, selecting the best solution.

The activity in these stages involves (1) introspection, (2) combining unusual objects and ideas together, (3) emitting a series of thought trials blindly without foresight or hindsight until the unspecified criteria fit and something "clicks," (4) the creative genius that directs, the insight production, and (5) sometimes the ability to perform correct actions without understanding why the actions were correct. Roe (1951) first identified several factors that distinguish creative people from less creative counterparts. The more creative were harder working, and they engaged in greater numbers of higher-level thoughts. They also experimented more than less creative people.

Creative people are also now known to be more highly self-directed, showing preferences for intellectually challenging situations rather than socially challenging ones (Guilford, 1967; and Johnson, 1962). Psychologists have also agreed that creativity often requires freewheeling, irrational thought that can be applied to the logical structure that is in place in the rational world. Creativity appears to be initiated from the tension between spontaneity and limitations. The latter, like the banks of the river, force spontaneity into a form that can be seen in the completed work.

Further, it has been discovered that "originality" involves a special quality. That is, if colleagues often tell you that your ideas are "so original," your thinking ability has a special quality of being adaptative and flexible. You appear to be able to analyze the factors that make up each dimension of a problem in connection with the unusualness of responses one dimension makes upon each other dimension when each is combined.

You and your students can increase your creative capacity and creative problem-solving skills by using the lesson plans given in Figures 6-1 through 6-6. These plans can help students learn to identify wasted time in the class and reduce the amount of time used in solving classroom problems.

Students' problem-solving skills can also be developed by giving them important decision-making responsibilities in the classroom. These responsibilities simultaneously create more time for you to be engaged in the higher-level thought processes and professional judgments discussed previously in this chapter. Feel free to select from the list that follows or allow students to create their own jobs. Gifted students can write job descriptions for each position and then run for the offices they wish.

Figure 6-1

	LESSON 1
Mental set	Present the introduction to the students in a manner that you choose.
Rationale	Explain how creativity can enhance students' thinking. You then caution them that before they begin to apply creative thinking techniques, it is important to be aware of the internal and external obstacles that lie before creative problem solutions. Point out that the environment will not often be as supportive of creativity solutions, that they have emotional vulnerabilities that could be pulled upon, that they may have been programmed to rely more upon their logical analytical skills than upon the skills they will next learn, that they may have also agreed that they must be perfect, that they must be liked by everyone, and that they should not vary too much from the average accepted standards.
Objective	State that at the end of the lesson, the students should be able to apply the five factors of creative thinking and the four rules of creative problem-solving skill to a problem you give them. They will know they have been successful when they use the skills on the six-week test and unsolicited in their own problem-solving situations.
Input	Preselect a content subject that is partly designed to strengthen students' creativity or divergent, inquiry, and/or critical thinking skills. Teach a section of the content from that discipline and the following creative problem-solving process and factors to the students.
	The creative problem-solving process means that you learn to defer judgments, generate many ideas even when some are not as good as you usually create, and combine unlikely ideas together.
	Paul Torrance (1960, 1962, 1964, 1966, 1968, 1977, 1981) has spent the last 25 years exploring the area of creative problem solving. In his research, five characteristics or factors have been identified for creative thinking:
	1. *Fluency or the type of thinking that produces a number of different but relevant ideas.*
	2. *Flexibility or the number of shifts in thinking or the number of categories you are able to use in solving problems.* Flexible thinking is different from linear thinking in that it involves skills of logical analysis between dissimilar categories.
	3. *Elaboration or the type of thinking ability that enables you to use significantly more different ideas to work out details of new ideas.*
	4. *Originality or the ability to generate a significantly greater number of infrequent responses than the normal person when facing a new situation.* To generate original ideas, you must produce a creative intellectual mental process (explained above).
	5. *Evaluation or the thinking ability rapidly to select, test, and revise one or more ideas when a large group of ideas has been generated.*
Modeling	Give models of each of these steps from former classroom experiences and your life.
Guided and independent practice	Create a group solution to a problem. Students then are given a problem to solve individually that relates to the content, creates an individualized, new and product, or solves a problem in the classroom or school.
Diagnostic test	Item for six-week test is written by students in another class who have had the same lesson, and vice versa.
Transition	Explain that students will have their next lesson on _____

Figure 6-2

LESSON 2

Mental set	Write the following quotation on the board: "Almost all really new ideas have a certain aspect of foolishness when they are first produced"—Alfred N. Whitehead, philosopher.
Objective	Tell the students that they are going to learn the most frequently used methods of creative problem solving used in the business community today. They are to memorize and use the five parts of brainstorming today orally in writing, in groups, and alone so as to learn the process more rapidly. They will know they have been successful when they suggest that the class use this method in the future when they face a problem and you will not have prompted your suggestion.
Rationale	Throughout life you will solve problems faster and more effectively if you learn the five skills and process taught today.
Input	Explain to the students that brainstorming is the most frequently used process for creative problem solving in our society today. Explain that they will need to recognize the five aspects of brainstorming before you explain the process. You then either show the filmstrip and listen to the audio cassette entitled "Creativity—Recognizing and Developing Your Creative Strengths" (distributed by the Claremount Educational Resource Center, P.O. Box 998, Claremount, Calif. 91711), which asks students to practice each aspect during pauses in the filmstrip, or you present the following aspects yourself, in the manner you desire:

1. *Substitution*—put one idea in place of the first solution considered or place the new idea with the first and see what evolves.
2. *Adapt*—use a slight variation of the first solution.
3. *Modify*—change one element in the idea.
4. *Magnify*—increase the size and/or impact of one dimension of the idea.
5. *Rearrange*—reorder the steps in the solution (Van Gundy, 1984).

You then explain the brainstorming process:

1. Everyone is to think of as many ideas about the topic given as they can. All ideas are written down by a recorder.
2. No one comments on any of the ideas, and no one criticizes any idea.
3. At the end of a specified time (5 to 15 minutes), the group categorizes all ideas and selects the best idea or combined idea.
4. The first four steps to an action plan, to implement the idea, are drawn up, duties assigned, and deadlines given.

Modeling	Show a model of a previous class' brainstorming activity on the overhead or on a handout.
Guided practice	Solve a problem as a whole class by brainstorming.
Independent practice	This has two parts. The class is broken into small groups and practices solving a problem orally. Then, the same small group solves a second problem, but this time each student writes down his or her ideas separately and combines them later.
Diagnostic test	Students are given a homework sheet where they brainstorm in written form, alone, and then turn in all their work along with the solution and plan they each generated.

Figure 6-3

LESSON 3

Mental set	Tell the class that individuals with a good sense of humor have been discovered to have a better ability to make connections between apparently unrelated events and to generate the fastest and best solutions in problem-solving situations.
Objective	Tell the class that they are going to learn how to improve their sense of humor today. They are to take notes from the guest speakers and to develop an individual plan for increasing their own sense of humor. They will know they have been successful when they find themself using the steps the guest speakers cited without conscious effort to do so.
Rationale	Even if someone had to start to improve his or her sense of humor by merely writing down jokes and trying to relate more jokes to situations, that person's thinking capability would increase. Today we are going to learn several ways people use humor to increse their thinking ability.
Input and modeling	Begin the lesson by telling how you increased your sense of humor and the problems you had. Also share how humor can become a catalyst to creativity as it initiates the subconscious and expands conscious insights. Your testimonial will help the student to not be as afraid to use the methods the guest spekers will next share with them. Tell your students that believing in themselves and being open to ideas, along with persistence and concentration are attributes that will make developing a sense of humor easier and faster.
	Prior to beginning the lesson, you will have asked the class to select people in their school or community that they think are funny and that they would like to invite to class to share how they came to develop this ability. The students can select sports figures, news commentators, upper classmen, and so on. You screen their choices and invite three guests to share their stories and skills and then particpate in a question and answer period with the students.
Guided practice	The class then, after the guests have left, discusses the points common to all speakers and list these on the board. Dissimilar points are also noted.
Independent practice	Students are given the assignment to develop their four-step action plan to increase their own senses of humor. Each student is to set a six-week goal.
Diagnostic test	Students' papers are returned at the end of the six-week period and they write an answer to you: Did they meet their goal to develop their sense of humor? How do they know they did or didn't?

Figure 6-4

LESSON 4

Mental set   Explain that many times people cannot identify a problem at its inception and, if they can develop this creative thinking ability, they will be happier and more productive people.

Objective   Tell the students that they will learn how to make boundary examinations and problem redefinitions. These two abilities are the best to identify what problem is emerging. They will learn how to examine the boundaries of situations and to redefine problems by following a sample of former students and by experimenting with the process themselves. They will know that they have learned the process when they can apply the process in the six-week test question you will give.

Rationale   Few people use these two processes, and learning them can help advance their capabilities in their life and career.

Input   Describe boundary examination and problem redefinition as the scrutiny of statements of problems they generate or that are given to them by someone else. Then model how to use synonyms and precise definition of words in the problem statement to point you toward the correct solution. Then give the following example taken from a group of high school students who were to be preparing to debate the causes and solution to the nuclear arms race. They write the problem statement as, "Identify the causes and possible solutions to the threat that exists due to increased nuclear arms production." To increase these students' skills in reaching effective solutions to difficult problems, the teacher could use the "boundary examination" method. Taking each phrase of the original statement and substituting more specific and exact expressions of the intent students seek will ensure the statement of purpose leads to the first step for solution. The "boundary examinations" method will increase skill in formalizing thoughts so they directly point to the first step to solving difficult situations. That is, in the example, as students worked with the separate phrases of "identifying the causes," "possible solutions," "threat that exists," "due to increased nuclear arms production," they discovered that what they really wanted to learn was "What is available or what can I, as a future leader in society, create that could circumvent all possible negative aspects of nuclear energy?" The work would then begin with increased vigor and through a growth in creative problem-solving ability.

Guided and independent practice   Students practice in groups and alone with two separate problem statements.

Diagnostic test   Each student writes a problem statement that will be answered by a fellow classmate on the six-week test and the problems are collected.

Figure 6-5

LESSON 5

Mental set

Many people claim that some students can leave the education system without having gained the ability to think. The work you will do today will better ensure that you know how to think about difficult concepts and problems.

Objective

Today you will learn about the most comprehensive thinking process we can use. The process is called attribute listing and is a systematic method of solving difficult situations and thinking about abstract or complex phenomena. You will know you have learned it if you can create an attribute listing for the problem you face at school.

Rationale

Explain to the students that this skill will be very valuable to them later in life and that it will take two days of practice to learn it.

Input and modeling and guided practice

You then present the following information and activity to the class as a whole:

Attribute listing is a systematic way of listing all the facets of a problem in one column and all the descriptors, attributes, and positive and negative features of each solution in a row to the right of each problem. These separate attribute listings can be combined to make very effective solutions.

To illustrate, you wish to study the automobile industry and its effects on the American economy. You draw a grid similar to the one here on which you and the class list all the attributes in each dimension of the cause-effect domain. After each dimension is listed, a phrase that describes one aspect of the effects or condition of the interrelationship of each two attributes. This interrelationship is written in the square that designates the intersection of the column and row of the two attributes compared.

Independent practice

Students make a grid and report on the benefits of completing the activity that they experienced. Most students should note that this activity creates an exceptional amount of creativity thinking and combines more evaluative and analytical thinking than most of the othe types of thinking processes they may use.

Diagnostic test

Each student describes a personal problem for which he or she would like a fellow classmate's opinion. Each problem is written so it can be included on the six-week examination in an anonymous manner. You note which student submitted each problem, however, so upon the end of the test, you can give each student back the response a classmate generated to the problem. Each problem is placed in a sealed envelope or otherwise hidden so that students do not see who wrote the problem they answered on the test or who answered the problem they wrote for the test.

Transition

Share with the class that they have yet to learn the last and the most recently developed creative problem-solving approach.

American Economy

Automobile Industry	Fluctuating	Based on supply and GNP	Gaining or losing strength internationally	Influenced by many different sectors of society	All people depend on its strength
Is highly competitive					
Employs a lot of people	tenure guaranteed				
Touches each person's life	planned carhood				
Uses products from many other industries	work on producing products cheaper				
Is characterized by rapidly changing technology	use technology that aids economy				
Is influenced by government	Federal auto laws change according to economy				
Projections are based on speculations of public	make parts that can be interchanged to update cars				

Figure 6-6

LESSON 6

Mental set	Tell the students that they are going to learn something that was invented only 40 years ago and that few people know about.
Objective and rationale	Tell the students that to solve some problems takes several approaches before the correct solution can be found. This creative problem-solving approach is the one some rely upon when others did not satisfy the problem. Students will practice the method and then teach it to others in the class that they select, if approved by you and the teacher of the class. They will know that they have been successful if the other students can do synectics, the creative problem-solving method they will now learn.
Input, modeling, and guided practice	Share the following information and model with the class, elaborating upon points that need to be clarified. Before you start this section of the lesson plan, you will have received approvals to have your students teach this strategy to another class and have established the date.

Synectics appears to be the newest, formally identified, creative problem-solving technique (Osborn, 1979). When given a problem the problem solver uses a *fantasy analogy,* a *direct parallel or opposite analogy,* and a *personal analogy* and "forcefits" the analogy into a realistic solution.

For example, the problem is that too many students are tardy. *Fantasy analogy:* large mechanical arms are attached to each student's bed that lift him or her up and deposits each body into his or her chair at school at the appointed time. *Force fit:* These high school students are all assigned to car pools. Each car pool that has all members at school on time for the six-week reporting period will be allowed three days of early dismissals. *Direct parallel or opposite:* What motivates high school–aged students to be places on time? Getting to see their girlfriend or boyfriend, being in charge of an activity, being interested in what is going to happen, or being embarrassed to walk in late. *Force fit:* One day a week, extracurricular activities and club meetings are scheduled to begin 15 minutes prior to the regular opening of school activities. On that day, students can come ot the cafeteria to visit with friends if their club is not meeting or they are not a member of a club. *Personal analogy:* How would I like to be treated if I were causing problems for myself and others by my always being late to school? I would like to be able to contribute to the school to pay back for the problems I caused. *Force fit:* Students who are tardy for more than three days in a reporting period must meet with other students in the same grade and subject missed and either prepare a video of the introductory materials of the lesson topics covered in the reporting period (to be viewed by students who are tardy in the future) or prepare a special mini lesson delivered to the rest of the class covering an interesting aspect of the material that was not covered in the class. All work is done after school or during the lunch period.

Independent practice	Student select the problem in their school that they wish to solve using the synectics approach. The students prepare their teaching demonstration.
Diagnostic test	Students teach synectics to the class they selected and they use the problem in the independent practice to do so. Students in the other class demonstrate in writing or orally that they learned the approach.

Ms. Septima Green, runner-up for the 1985 Teacher of the Year in Texas (sponsored by the National Education Association), gives each student in her classroom a responsibility and assists in making the following list:

Take up papers	Passing out books
Hand back papers	Line leaders
Filing papers	Taking up books
Writing on boards	Organizing art supplies
Cleaning boards	Bulletin boards
Picking up trash in corners	Calendar
Emptying trash cans during day	Door decorations
Plant care	Keeping a list of classroom supplies needs
Caring for aquarium and other pets	Thought for the day
Correspondence secretary	Classroom librarian
Photographer/scrapbook	Weatherman
Taking roll	Research person
Rearranging room	Banker (lunch money, etc.)
Cleaning sink	Windows and door
Grading papers	Waste disposal engineer
Neatness grader	Desk monitor to check for lost supplies
Office errands	Equipment repair technician
Projectionist	

Alternatives to the classroom officers program as a means of building student responsibilities follow. You can assign each student a number. Then, when a task needs to be done, a number can be drawn out of a container and the student assigned that number does the job. The difficulty with this method is that it does not develop creative problem-solving ability as students do not have the responsibility for solving difficulties that develop with a job over a period of time. Second, you can post a list of duties and assign a designated reward with each duty. Early finishers can perform the task they prefer and receive the reward designated.

A FINAL NOTE

As you begin to use these problem-solving techniques, it may be necessary to remind yourself that you should never allow a fear of failure to stand in your way. Try to remember that next to success, failure is the best thing that could happen to you. It causes you to "bump into something" that will set you on the correct path once again, and you will be farther down the road as a result.

Buzzing around uncommitted and avoiding taking the initiative to solve problems will not help you nor will problems improve. Also, when you pause and listen to all you know about time management, you can make decisions that have potential of assisting many and hold great potential for your greater growth as well. I wish you every success in increasing your problem-solving skill.

To review the ideas we've explored, let's relist each lesson you could use to develop problem-solving skills. After each, jot down an idea you have as to which curriculum area you could include the lesson plan in the next few weeks:

1. *Brainstorming* involves building a large volume of ideas with no idea rejected. You might try it in _____

2. *Substitutions, modifications, magnifications, and rearrangements* are means of taking each element of an idea and viewing it in a new way to understand more carefully how it can bear more effectively upon the solution.

   _____

   _____

3. *Brainwriting* is like brainstorming except that each idea is written down by an individual and then is included in a more specific, expanded group listing of ideas and ramifications of a plan to solve the problem.

4. *Developing one's sense of humor* can be inserted at any time of day that you can most efficiently build your own skills in conjunction with another curriculum goal and then share with the students how you developed it.

   _____

   _____

5. *Analogies* are lesson plans that compare problems to nature or natural phenomena (e.g., tests at the end of lesson plans in science classes). What problem in school, classes, or society did this scientific phenomenon remind you of? _____

6. *Boundary examinations and problem redefinitions* are when students and you write the best sentence description of a problem and synonyms and more exact phrases are supplied through word-by-word examination and study of each phrase separately. _____

7. *Attribute listing* is a lesson plan whereby problems that don't appear to have a best solution and each possible solution are listed with adjectives that describe that alternative and the positive and negative features of each plan. _____

8. *Synectics* is a lesson plan where a problem is related to a fantasy analogy, a direct parallel or opposite analogy, and a personal analogy "force fit" into a realistic solution. _____

9. *Using classroom officers is a means of developing students'* _____

   _____

Refer back to the list we made earlier in the chapter of ways you intended to avoid classroom problems. How many have you already accomplished?

In Chapter 1 (see Figure 1-1), we assessed your ability to control your classroom. Now that we've completed more than one-half of this book, refer to the first assessment you made. With a different colored pen, date today's date on the pretest and mark it "Posttest" with the new pen. Shade in the bottom section of each row marker to indicate your present assessment of skill in controlling the class using the same directions we followed in the preassessment.

REFERENCES

Bruner, Jerome. *The Process of Education*. Cambridge, Mass.: Harvard University Press, 1960.

Cross, Ray. "How to Beat the Clock: Tips on Time Management." *American School and University*, Vol. 52, September 1979–April 1980.

Guilford, J. P. *The Nature of Human Intelligence*. New York: McGraw-Hill, 1967.

Johnson, B. *Ability, Achievement and Bilingualism: A Comparative Study Involving Spanish-Speaking and English-Speaking Children at the Sixth Grade Level*. Doctoral dissertation, College Park, Maryland: University of Maryland, 1962.

Osborn, Alex F. *Applied Imagination: Principles and Procedures of Creative Problem-Solving, 3rd rev. ed*. New York: Scribners, 1979.

Roe, Anne. "A Study of Imagery in Research Scientists." *Journal of Personality*, Vol. 19, 1951, 459–470.

Torrance, E. P. "Cross-cultural Studies of Creative Development in Seven Selected Societies." In J. Gowan, J. Khatena, and E. P. Torrance (eds.), *Creativity: Its Educational Implications, 2nd ed., pp. 89–97*. Dubuque, Iowa: Kendall/Hunt, 1981.

Torrance E. P. "Creatively Gifted and Disadvantaged Gifted Students." In J. Stanley, W. George, and C. Solano, eds., *The Gifted and the Creative: A Fifty-Year Perspective*. Baltimore: The Johns Hopkins University Press, 1977.

Torrance, E. P. "Creative Positives of Disadvantaged Children and Youth." *Gifted Child Quarterly*, Vol. 13, no. 2, 1969, 71–81.

Torrance, E. P. "A Longitudinal Examination of the Fourth Grade Slump in Creativity." *Gifted Child Quarterly*, Vol. 12, no. 4, 1968, 195–199.

Torrance, E. P. *Torrance Tests of Creative Thinking: Norms—Technical Manual*. Princeton, N. J.: Personnel Press, 1966.

Torrance, E. P. "Education and Creativity." In C. W. Taylor, ed., *Creativity: Progress and Potential*. New York: McGraw-Hill, 1964.

Torrance E. P. *Guiding Creative Talent*. Englewood Cliffs, N. J.: Prentice-Hall, 1962.

Torrance, E. P. "The Minnesota Studies of Creative Thinking in the Early School Years." *University of Minnesota Research Memorandum*, No. 59-4. Minneapolis: University of Minnesota Bureau of Educational Research, 1960.

Torrance E. P., and R. Myers. "Teaching Gifted Elementary Pupils Research Concepts and Skills." *Gifted Child Quarterly*, Vol. 6, 1962, 1–16.

Torrance, E. P., and J. P. Torrance. "Educating Gifted, Talented and Creative Students for the Future." *American Middle School Education*, Vol. 4, no. 1, 1981, 39–46.

Tschudin, Ruth. "Secrets of A+ Teaching," *Instructor*, Vol. 88, September 1978, 65–74.

Van Gundy, Arthur B., *Training Your Creative Mind*. Englewood Cliffs, N. J.: Prentice-Hall, Inc. 1982.

seven

Spending Quality Time in Groups

A Teacher Comments on Chapter 7

Chapter 7 reviews the types of situations that decrease group productivity. Group settings are a common way to share opinions, build rapport, or introduce new ideas. In education, the most frequent group settings are the classroom group or subgroup discussions, faculty meetings, and classroom question-answer periods. The teacher who initiates these discussions does a great deal of preplanning, organizing, and structuring so that the groups are able to achieve the desired goal while maintaining the highest level of productivity. However, frequently unforeseen difficulties arise that decrease a group's ability to function effectively. For example, productivity in the classroom can be lessened by student arguments, rebellions, and erroneous comments and in faculty meetings by resistance to change, loquacious speakers, and prolonged discussions. These interferences occur consistently in group set-

tings and, therefore, due to the adverse effect they cause, require immediate action to maintain productivity. This action takes the form of positive leadership techniques such as negotiating, compromising, and direct questioning.

This chapter provides specific techniques for dealing with situations that decrease productivity. It will be extremely helpful to teachers when they are in group settings.

Ms. Marty Ford
Speech/Language Pathologist
Kansas City, Kansas

*Participation is a way of insuring your investments
of time in new products [students] methods, [lessons
taught], and facilities [society].*

—James T. McCoy (1959)

When class rapport is lost, consciously or subconsciously, students waste time and try to sabotage your attempts to reestablish the group unit. To make group building a faster and longer-lasting process, you can take one of the following actions, depending upon the student groups' composition:

1. Divide the group in half or into four small groups. Give them an assignment to find answers in the text to eight or so questions. The answers will be recorded and turned in to you at the end of the period.

2. Set the issue of poor discipline aside for the first three-fourths of the class period or day in which the incident occurred. As the class (or day) closes, acknowledge how well the class was able to carry on in the activities of the day, despite the incident. Then, acknowledge the class's concern and tell them that you will present your position tomorrow, if they wish to bring the topic up again. You can answer their questions and attempt to resolve the conflict at that time if you desire, telling the class that you invested a considerable amount of time and used several concerns to reach your decision. You can allow more elaboration if time permits.

3. Change the lesson plan. Shift to a lesson where students work independently and silently on a written assignment that is due at the end of the period. Then you return to the issue on a one-to-one basis or the next day, when you are not as emotionally involved with the issue. If you delay discussing the issue as an entire class, you can list all the key points in your position before the students enter the room and be better prepared to address their concerns.

METHODS OF BUILDING GROUP RAPPORT IN THE CLASSROOM

Verne Acular states that "If a burst of laughter will do you in, so will a gentle wind" (Carnes, 1980, p. 204). In other words, if you can withstand the amusement your errors provide your students, you will better be able to capitalize upon criticisms that your serious work raises. When viewed in a positive light, humor can be used to dissipate tension and break a barrier between students and the teacher. Then, rapport can be reestablished in the most efficient manner.

Method One

If a small argument erupts, involving only a few students and/or you, provide an independent practice activity for the rest of the class and step outside in the hall to discuss the issue with the few. Be honest with any students who may begin to use arguments and disruptions as a means of getting out of the classroom and of gaining your undivided attention. After confronting their inappropriate means of gaining attention, describe four different alternative actions they can select to take to improve. Tell them the methods, ask them to select the one they judge to be most appropriate for them. Ask if they have any concerns about using the new method and model a situation where they practice applying the method before the student returns to the room.

Method Two

Student groups can be used to solve individual student problems. Designing a generic lesson over a problem is one method of doing so. The lesson is presented as a part of the regular curriculum rather than because a particular student needs the information. Unfinished story starters are excellent beginnings for elementary student lessons of this type. They can be obtained from NEA Publications, 1201 16th Street, N.W., Washington, D.C. 20036. Secondary examples, such as "Composition Situations," can be obtained from the National Council of Teachers of English, 508 South Sixth Street, Champaign, Ill. 61820.

Method Three

Make time within the week for students to discuss problems. One teacher's plan to do so follows as an illustration:

Leon plans his program by helping children gain greater internal strength and increased awareness of their own identities. Fortunately the desks in his classroom are not attached to the floor. Leon asks the students to sit on cushions in a circle around him. He talks about the friendship and fun they can have as they work together. He explains that if any one of them needs extra help or is having difficulty, another child can try to help—everyone can help someone else. They will spend every Friday afternoon sitting in a circle, talking about how the class is doing and about any problems they have in learning or in any problems in their relationships with each other. He welcomes any suggestions that will help him to become a better teacher.

At the first Friday afternoon meeting, he asks if anyone is having difficulties with the subjects the class is learning. A couple of hands go up. One child says he does not clearly understand their work in arithmetic; in fact, he is beginning to feel lost. When the teacher asks if anyone feels sure of himself in arithmetic several hands go up, and a student volunteers to help the child who is having difficulty. (Carnes, 1980, p. 84)

SAVING CLASSROOM TIME WITH GOOD DISCIPLINE PRACTICES

The breadth and depth of discipline has been addressed in several books. I would like to list a few because several teachers have changed their abilities to discipline through reading a book or article that most appealed to them:

Burns, Marilyn. "Groups of Four: Solving the Management Problem." *Learning*, September 1981, p 46–50.

Erk, Jean, and Meg Hendricks. *Shortcuts for Teachers: Strategies for Reducing Classroom Workload*. Belmont, Calif., Pitman, 1981.

Evertson, Carolyn, Edmund Emmer, Julie Sanford, Barbara Clements, and Murray Worsham. *Classroom Management for Secondary Teachers. Classroom Management for Elementary Teachers*. Englewood Cliffs, N.J.: Prentice-Hall, 1984.

Gnagey, William. *Motivating Classroom Discipline*. New York: Macmillan, 1981.

Green, Judith L., and Timothy Rasinski. "Teacher Style and Classroom Management: Stability and Variation Across Instructional Events." Paper presented at the Annual Convention of the American Educational Research Association, Chicago, Ill., April 1985.

McGinnis, Ellen, and Arnold P. Goldenstein. *Skillstreaming the Elementary School Child*. Champaign, Ill.: Research Press, 1984.

Paine, Stan. *Structuring Your Classroom for Academic Success*. Champaign, Ill.: Research Press, 1983.

Wolfgang, Charles, and Carl Glickman. *Solving Discipline Problems: Strategies for Classroom Teachers*. Boston, Mass.: Allyn & Bacon, 1986.

Ineffective classroom management skills can waste more time than can any other teaching weakness. More important, poor management drains your energy and drive to make more learning time for your students. That is, if you have repeatedly watched what you had worked so hard to create in learning experiences destroyed as the class became unruly, you will not put as much time in future lesson plans.

Classroom discipline skills can be learned quickly. If reading one of the books just cited is too time consuming for you, here are a few key points from the book *How to Discipline Without Feeling Guilty* (Silberman and Wheelan, 1980).

These authors recommend that all teachers use the least energy-draining methods they can to quell conflicts. Among the methods they cite,

1. Remain silent; for example, wait students out through silence in situations where students know what is expected of them and why. Teachers must be unmoved by the students' attempts to resist the teacher.

2. Chart the number of infractions and share these with the students.

3. If the behavior is ignored, someone must think "Will tangible, harmful consequences occur before the behavior becomes sufficiently extinguished?".

4. A behavior cannot be ignored if this cannot be done without appearing or being visibly upset.

5. A behavior cannot be ignored if the teacher's attention is not important enough to the student that ignoring will make a difference.

6. Redirecting catches the student off guard and diverts his or her interest away from what he or she is doing negatively to another activity; this is not as easily accomplished with other students.

7. Say or do the opposite of what a child expects—even if the child once delighted in pushing us around, the teacher can now remove himself or herself as objects of battle and allow the student to make a clear decision about how he or she wants to act. This works best if the teacher wishes to show the child that he or she has the power to choose a different course of action.

8. Make the teacher expectations attractive by making it more attractive to comply with the rules of the class than not to comply.

Silberman and Wheelan also state that teachers should remember that if only they compromise, students will take advantage. If the teacher is exclusively a penalizer, students will become immune to the teacher's authority, and teachers should not vacillate between the two, such as negotiating free time with the class one minute and threatening punishment the next. To avoid each of these negative responses, the teacher should:

1. Say no to a request but provide alternatives.

2. Ask the student to make a suggested solution.

3. Jointly look for a mutual solution.

4. Ask students to figure out a plan for changing their behavior.

5. Have a few standard consequences that students and the teacher are aware exist and have agreed in advance that they will be used.

DEVELOPING YOUR GROUP LEADERSHIP SKILLS IN THE CLASSROOM

Silberman and Wheelan go on to state that one of the best ways for teachers to gain support is by establishing themselves as the group leaders of their classrooms. Find ways of making the total group attractive to its members and help group members share information and help each other, as emphasized in our previous discussion. This technique is effective because socially integrative behavior in one person will tend to induce socially integrative behavior in others. Since some students cannot learn through this mentoring and osmotic process, they will tend to be more domineering than their peers; they will also lack the ability to integrate their own behavior into new group settings. Because of this inability they will not know how to act in socially acceptable and accepting ways, on many occasions. Frank Farley (1985) is doing research to identify the causes and cures of these types of students. His research has identified several causes, and it appears that these students have a special personality type (labeled T type) that requires frequent environmental stimulation. The need is related to the metabolism of the student.

These T type personalities seek new experiences. If they are guided to seek novelty through positive and creative leadership developing responsibilities, they become innovative and productive contributors in the classroom and, subsequently, in society. If they are not trained to invest their talents in creating new ideas, they often begin to release their needs for experiences in easier, more continuously present methods of breaking established rules of order, in the classroom and society.

Chapter 6 was structured as it was so as to assist us in reducing disciplinary problems, developing students' creative problem-solving skills and our own simultaneously. Creativity, when used in connection with developing problem-solving skills, is best defined as a tool that more closely integrates your personal skill and means of using personal power to integrate effectively with others and things.

As a final point, a teacher must have the self-confidence that he or she can be a leader because a "lack of self-trust will keep us from using whatever skills are suggested and render them useless" (Silberman and Wheelan, 1980, p. 5). Teachers "cannot protect and guide without, at the same time, controlling and restricting. Students cannot grow and become individuals without rejecting and attacking. The process [in a classroom] is inherently conflictual" (Silberman and Wheelan, 1980, p. 17). Addressing this conflict in an open and honest, firm, direct and objective manner appears to be the fastest and most effective means, for example:

> Student: Do we have to diagram sentences again?
> Teacher: I'm not sure if you feel that it's hard or boring or just silly. What do you feel?
> Student: I can't do this stuff.
> Teacher: Do you want to call it quits for just now or do you really feel hopeless about it?
>
> (Silberman and Wheelan, 1980, pp. 64–65)

MAKING MORE TIME FOR PROFESSIONAL ADVANCEMENT VIA FACULTY MEETINGS

> With thee conversing I forget all time.
>
> John Milton, *Paradise Lost*, 1667

Being able to contribute effectively in faculty meetings (and with groups of teachers) as well as being able to lead productive one-to-one parent/student/colleague conferences is a way to make time for other purposes.

Prior to each meeting, you should have the answer to three fundamental questions: What the agenda will be? What you need to bring to the meeting? and How long the meeting is scheduled to last. If these questions are not clear, you can assist each member present by asking them as near to the opening of the meeting as possible.

REDUCING THE AMOUNT OF TIME
SPENT IN INFORMAL MEETINGS

Often an informal meeting between two or more people takes longer than you would like. To eliminate this eventuality, before you start a discussion, stand as you talk. Tell your colleague how much time you have before you begin to talk. Conversely, if you have to interrupt a colleague, ask if you could take only _____ minutes of his or her time and then stick to this time limit and leave.

Politely mention that you might meet in the other person's room so that you can leave as soon as the issue is resolved. Informal meetings should never be the format used to discuss personal or large issues. Interruptions should involve easy-to-solve problems such as issues concerning rules, procedures or materials.

REFRAINING FROM SAYING TOO MUCH DURING FACULTY MEETINGS

The ability to speak is a shortcut to distinction.

Lowell Thomas

Hasn't there been a time when you wished someone would have gently nudged you to keep you from having given a long oration or having engaged in an argument during a faculty meeting? All teachers will profit and should work to help each colleague refrain from saying too much. The tips in Figure 7-1 can help faculty meetings be more productive.

You may wish to practice to see if you have learned each of the tips given. The scenario in Figure 7-2 will take you approximately 3 minutes to read and complete. The time and work you do will help you develop your skills in faculty meetings.

We will simulate a meeting and ask you or one of the members of the inservice meeting to handle each of the four problems in communication that were discussed in the scenario. Although today's practice session was designed for small groups, you may enjoy and would benefit from acting out the roles, separately, yourself. Grade yourself by referring back to the answers, or have someone serve as a judge for you. Throughout the scenario, blanks have been inserted so specific points concerning your organization can be inserted so you can create a personalized scenario. If such a personalized scenario is made, role-playing participants might find it easier to identify with the characters and enjoy the activity more.

As you do this activity, reflect upon a true situation that will occur: teachers who have not responded to the body language several colleagues exhibit in a faculty meeting need to be directly instructed, somehow, in the techniques of interacting in a faculty meeting. If they are not, the annoying speaking habits of this single member will drain the energy of all faculty and can rapidly decrease the amount of time and quality of goals set by the entire group collectively and individually.

Figure 7-1

MAKING FACULTY MEETINGS MOVE ALONG MORE PRODUCTIVELY

1. Stop extended speeches by asking the speaker a direct question.

2. Keep yourselves from rambling by answering each question directly. Then, if clarification is needed, someone will ask you a question.

3. Never argue with a speaker. If a point of view is expressed that is opposite to the consensus or to your personal opinion, instead of arguing, ask one of the following questions:

   a. "Could you give an example so I can be certain I understand what you are saying?"

   b. "What effect would this point or opinion have on the decision/problem being discussed?"

   c. "Why should we accept this idea?" "What should we expect to see as a result?"

4. As the participant, be concerned about which questions are being debated. You can turn the decision of a minor point back to one of the major objectives without offending those deeply concerned with the tangential point by using one of the following techniques:

   a. "I really believe (think, or feel) that one of the reasons we are having difficulty resolving this issue is that we have not made a firm decision or established a clear direction/procedure for the larger objective of _____ . I move that we allow each person concerned about this _____ (minor point) to take 30 seconds to tell us what impact his or her point of view (concerning this minor point) would have upon the _____ (larger objective)."

   b. "Although it seems as if we have spent a lot of time in discussion of minor points without resolving the issue, the discussion has helped me to clarify one thing concerning _____ (the larger issue) now and allow _____ , _____ , and _____ (names of three people concerned with the minor point) study the _____ (minor point) in more detail and report back to us at a later time." After making this point, if the majority of people seem to agree, you might make a motion that a question calling for any additional discussion of the main issue that _____ , _____ , and _____ be appointed as a task force to explore the _____ (minor point) and present a motion to the next meeting.

   c. "I believe people on both sides of this (minor point) discussion are presenting good points. I would make a better decision on _____ (minor point) after I am clearer concerning the procedures we need to follow in _____ (the larger objective). Could a person from each of the points of view concerning _____ (minor point) help me understand at what point and how this issue (minor point) will impact the decision we are making concerning the _____ (larger objective)?"

If the answer you receive shows that impact from the minor point will come early in the implementation process, you might make a motion that a field test begin.

5. If the impasse does not come until nearer the middle or end of the process, suggest that committee members contact other programs that are successfully using the minor point and construct a list of strengths and weaknesses being experienced. Prior to the next meeting, these lists could be distributed to each teacher, and all could be better prepared to respond objectively to the issue.

Figure 7-2

SCENARIO IN INCREASING THE EFFECTIVENESS OF FACULTY MEETINGS

A school has decided to change its language arts curriculum. In previous years, the school has used English, handwriting, spelling, and reading textbooks. It now intends to discontinue use of all texts except the reading basals, supplementary reading textbooks, and library books. The original two 50-minute periods have been changed to be a 1-hour, 45-minute ongoing language arts block.

If this scenario is going to be enacted by you alone, place someone you know in each of the following roles, and respond to each of the people trying to use every appropriate technique. If the scenario is to be enacted in a group setting, allow each person to select a role as main character or as a responder. Responders will use as many appropriate techniques as possible to correct the action being taken by the main character to which he or she has been assigned. The main character will perform the action described, and after the scenario, describe how he or she felt and responded, and the reasons he or she saw for the successes and weaknesses in the respondent's approaches and interactions with him or her. In a group setting, it would be advantageous to set the stage also, placing people in a typical arrangement. In a scenario done by only one person, it would be valuable to jot down key phrases that you would say in the space following respondent 2. In this way, it will be easier for you to go back to check your responses after the scenario is over.

Scenario

1. The principal, _____, continues to give a ponderous description of the problem. Most people in the room already know everything he or she is saying. Several people are fidgeting and most are very bored.
   Respondent (as a member of the group, not as a chairperson for the meeting):
   _____
   _____

2. The head of the language arts department begins a long oration concerning (the history of English instruction) in the United States. You wish to change the course of this discussion from this minor point that has been stated to the major concern:
   Respondent 1 (as a member of the group): _____
   _____
   Respondent 2 (as the chairperson for the meeting): _____
   _____

continued

Figure 7-2 continued

3. The president of the Parent/Teacher Organization or Association presents a petition signed by 35 parents in opposition to the new program. They are particularly alarmed at the probable decline in spelling ability of students who are not given instruction from a spelling textbook. You wish to respond to this point so as to challenge the validity of his or her argument without arguing with the speaker:

   Respondent 1 (as a member of the group: _____

   _____

   Respondent 2 (as chairperson of the meeting): _____

   _____

4. You become very concerned that four of the five first and second grade teachers are not going to include (grammar instruction) in their (language arts) objectives. As the only one of two third grade teachers, you are opposed to this decision. You, unwittingly, begin an oration as to all the reasons why six- and seven-year-old students need instruction in grammar.

   Stop yourself from continuing your long oration: _____

   _____

   Respondent 2 (state what the chairperson for the meeting should say to you):

   _____

   _____

   Respondent 3 (what could a member of the meeting say to you?): _____

   _____

   _____

   _____

   _____

5. Give a good summary and closing for this meeting: _____

   _____

   _____

6. List or discuss the techniques that will or could be used in the future to keep meetings of your particular group of educators (a) moving smoothly and efficiently; (b) on time; (c) capitalizing upon strengthens, needs, plans, and problems of all members; and (d) enjoyable while providing maximum productivity.

7. Critique each other or check your responses by referring back to the notes in this chapter.

WHEN FACULTY ARE RESISTANT TO CHANGE

> We live in an era when rapid change breeds fear, and fear too often congeals into a rigidity which we mistake for stability.
>
> Lynn White, Jr. (1985)

This statement summarizes many reasons for inability to change. Methods of helping one or more teachers, administrators, students, or parents to change follow.

1. When faculty appear unchanging "a good analogy is often worth three hours' discussion" (McCoy, 1959, p. 135).
2. People have very clever ways of sheltering innovations, using personal charisma and relationships to further a discussion away from important issues when they feel they are gaining ground on their side issues.
3. People also gravitate to those things they feel do the best (Hall, 1985).
4. Using well-chosen words and gentle examples that point out how each faculty member can contribute the talents they most enjoy giving to eliminate a need they feel appears to be the most effective way to prepare for all meetings.

Without question, working on "building" group energy for accomplishing large change actions builds personal skill growth and efficiency. It increases productive and positive climate. It multiplies successes and raises the level of openness for future opportunities that pass before the group and the person. Each meeting will profit all doubly!

At meetings where changes are being proposed you will play a role whether you choose to do so or not. For this reason it is important for teachers to recognize the roles they play and to assist other teachers to learn to serve a beneficial group role. You can test your present knowledge concerning small-group dynamics in the next paragraph.

To do so, circle the following group roles that you judge to be beneficial in group meetings: citing personal experiences, returning to topics discussed previously, being self-appointed notetaker, conversing privately, talking more than most faculty at the meeting, being the first to change the subject usually, asserting authority, telling stories, talking about one's own feelings, being the devil's advocate, using humor to draw off negative feelings, yielding when necessary for progress, reconciling points of view, supporting others, encouraging others, keeping communiation open, summarizing a discussion, or testing whether the group has reached a decision. According to the research of Sanford (1983), the roles that contribute positively to groups are:

1. Using humor to draw off negative feelings.
2. Yielding when necessary for progress.
3. Reconciling points of view.

4. Supporting others.

5. Encouraging others.

6. Keeping communication open.

7. Summarizing a discussion at the close of the discussion.

8. Testing whether the group has reached a decision.

I hope you were able to identify at least six of these contributions you can make. If you weren't able to identify that many, you may have gained increased insight into reasons why your faculty meetings are not progressing as smoothly as you would like. You might want to present this information at your next meeting or begin to play some of these roles yourself.

In addition to grooming yourself and others to be aware of the ways they can contribute to the groups' productivity, you should guard against the tendency to carry a grudge against any one who takes an opposing position in a meeting. No matter how right you may be, another day you may be wrong and you can model for other teachers how you would hope to be treated on that day. If you do otherwise, you will do yourself, your boss, or "that" person who opposed you no favors by trying to even the score. One of the skills I most admire in someone is if they offer points of disagreement in supportive ways, such as by pointing out which part of my original idea has merit and which part they believe they can help make more productive. Then after the meeting, they show me that this disagreement was only a cognitive exchange, and they soothe our affective connections.

SIX POINTS TO MAKE YOUR TEACHING MORE PLEASURABLE

Many teachers find they enjoy teaching less than they wish. Enjoyable experiences are often absent for simple, yet enmeshing, reasons. The following points could explain why you may feel your efforts are futile and frustrating at times. Compliment yourself if you have already identified one of the following factors as having diminished your professional success. As you read the list, you may find another simple, daily means of enhancing your work.

1. Break all cliques. Form strong support groups that don't gripe about the profession or cut down others or talk about negative things.

2. Allow an idea to reach a priority level before beginning work on it if you are having trouble adding the level of quality work you desire to add. When it does rise to the top priority, don't worry that the wait will have been wasted time. It won't, because by doing it as soon as it rises to this level, you will do it so rapidly that it will almost seem to finish itself, with the tiniest effort on your part because your highest levels of creativity, affective energy, and efficiency are in action.

3. Be patient with yourself. Know that the new skills you are developing are being developed and will soon be in place.

4. Saying "no" to some people and some things may always be more difficult than you'd like, but by thinking ahead that they or the situation may demand something you'd rather not do, you can make an alternative commitment in advance (if even to yourself) to ensure that you will invest your talents in the most productive ways.

5. Those teachers who do the activities in the next chapter have proven to engage in a significantly greater number of productive, innovative "thought experiments" than those who do not.

6. Malcolm Forbes's view may be encouraging: "Those who enjoy responsibility usually get it; those who merely like exercising authority usually lose it."

AVOIDING INTERRUPTIONS IN GROUPS

Are you available to the right people and students often enough? Interruptions often appear legitimate. Four actions can limit the negative interferences interruptions can have upon your teaching.

First, as we discussed, select a time to work on project when you are not likely to be distracted by the "grass fire" needs of others (e.g., working 10 minutes in your room before you go to the lunchroom for your lunch break); and then work where objects around you do not initiate thoughts of smaller goals that could cause you to stop and do something else, "right now, just for a little break," so that you do not return to the task at hand.

Second, begin your work as near to the time you had planned to begin as possible. As you work, be aware of the special feelings you have and the moments of self-achievement and creativity you experience and that you created for yourself!

Last, if an interruption occurs, do not be angry. Being upset at yourself or the interruption wastes time. Instead take care of the matter in a way that you will be proud to recall. Then, if you can, literally force yourself to begin your work again. If you must leave your task, tell yourself the next block of time you will return to it and make an appointment with yourself to do so.

By doing these four actions, you will not be affected negatively by interruptions. That is, if you are thinking of interruptions in a positive way, they can even assist in completing large tasks you are doing. In fact, you will probably finish your larger task sooner because the interruption was a purposeful break that dealt with something that have had to be done later, probably. You probably also allowed your body to relax before you continued to complete your larger goal. Finally, you feel so good about your manner of handling of the interruption and the fact that you were able to help someone that your attitude toward work is improved.

If the interruption comes from a person who continually just "drops in" to "kill time," a different approach is required, however. You could direct the person to an activity that will be beneficial for him or her. You could share a part of your work. Work will discourage a person who is "masquerading his or her interruption under a disguise of legitimacy." Work will help those who truly care about teaching but are not as skilled in time-use skills. You can help them better themselves to value their time and yours more highly through the model you project.

How to Handle Different Interruptions

Now, you may be saying to yourself, "How can I distinguish between profitable and distracting interruptions? Interruptions are interruptions and they are unavoidable!" But there is an indicator to help you distinguish between the two: *if an interruption occurs very rarely, the interruption probably is necessary and should be handled immediately, if an interruption occurs regularly, a change in your scheduling pattern or approach to the interruption will eliminate it.* One type of interruption warrants special treatment. Neither of the foregoing strategies should be used when you find that one activity interrupts your plans more and more frequently. That activity needs an extended period of attention. That is, you need to set a definite period aside to identify the cause for the interruption. In this way, you can eliminate the cause instead of continuing to address the surfacing manifestations or interruptions that are not the true need. In these types of interruptions, you cannot eliminate the problem regardless of the number of times you stop your work in an attempt to satisfy the surface, interrupting, "disguised" request.

One student always lags behind the rest of the class and has a different question for you each day before he leaves for the day. The time spent with you is increasing each day. Nothing is being accomplished as you answer each new question. Instead, you ask the student's reasons for wanting to be around you and find the cause and devise a plan so the student learns more productive ways to meet his need with future figures of authority.

Further, if you consider the blocks of time set aside as appointments with yourself, if you follow an automatic routine each morning, if you visualize the next step needed on the next task in advance, and if you assess and reward/rechannel your energy toward important goals each day, fewer interruptions will occur. Leas (1978) points out that if you do not learn to remove the tension associated with interruptions, you will hear only your cries for help and these will be so loud that you may not clearly and correctly hear the underlying need the other person had for demanding the time. Alternatively, when your needs for order and/or solitude are too highly valued, it is usually that you have not developed the skills of avoiding interruptions and a segment of joy in the teaching profession will not be possible.

The pestering student, the one who continually seeks to have your attention, sometimes can be handled by stating:

"I'm up against a deadline now; could we discuss this as we walk to lunch?"

"I'm in the middle of preparing for our science class right now. This sounds like something you can handle, but if you run into some trouble, I will be available immediately after class, during the passing period."

"I'd like to hear more about this, but I can't give you the concentrated listening (or the time) I'd like to give right now. Why don't you jot down your thoughts as your creative writing journal entry tomorrow and I can read all the details when I can really concentrate on them."

"I wish I could tell you how my experience with that was so much like yours. However, you have to go to social studies class. When you have time, you probably would enjoy hearing Robert's [another student in the class] experience. I wonder if his feelings are the same as yours. I think he saw it differently, and I think you will be surprised, and he will be as well, when you share your experience."

HANDLING A GROUP'S INCORRECT ANSWERS

> When children give a wrong answer it is not so often that they are wrong as they are answering another question, and our job is to find out what question they are in fact answering.
>
> Jerome Bruner (1985)

Most teachers more frequently tell slower-learning students the correct answers and give slower students less time to solve a problem before supplying the correct answer. Alternatively, teachers who have been trained to handle incorrect answers can cover more content in less time and use the following types of responses equitably for all students. These responses keep students from wandering off the track and help students (and themselves) learn as much, if not more, from student errors as from their correct answers. These same teachers also tend to be the ones who realize the importance of being a strong leader during discussions.

You probably have created several effective strategies to respond to your students' answers effectively. The following list may help you increase your skill and promote more active participation of your students in even less time.

Question-Asking Skills

When asking questions, you will create more learning if you state the question first and then allow about 3 to 5 seconds for all students to think and then call on a student to answer. As you may be aware already, calling a student's name before you ask the question causes many students to not think as they realize they won't be called upon. The "6 second" wait time for an answer has almost become a trademark in the profession, but have you ever timed yourself to see if you wait that long for an answer? Six seconds seems like such a short time, but you may be as surprised as I was when I timed my wait time. I discovered how hard it is for me to be still and wait one-tenth of a minute before I prompt! This wait time convinces students that they have the responsibility and capability to learn. When they know you are not hurrying answers, they will not expect that if they just delay their thinking that you will rush in with the answer.

Responding to Correct Answers

Acknowledging that a student's answer is correct seems like an easy task. To not be repetitive or insincere is the difficult part. While you are aware that the reinforcement that the student's answer is correct is valuable to the student responding, such statements also inform the rest of the class that the answer is correct and allows their minds to be free of doubts and open to the next question. The most skillful teachers that I have observed acknowledge correctness by adding a detail to the statement the student made, telling what part was most original in thinking or adding a personal comment relative to their own lives or thoughts that the student's response generated for them. Saying "That's right" or restating the student's answer appear to be less effective and interesting ways of sustaining a discussion period.

Responding to Incorrect Answers

If a wrong answer is given, you can use one of the following strategies, depending upon the student who gave the answer.

1. *Supply the question the student was answering.* Try to let the student down easy and permit him or her to retain dignity. If you recognize why the answer was wrong, you might wish to supply the question for which the student's answer would have been correct. For example, if the question was, "What is the capital of the United States?" and the student answered "Sacramento," you could respond, "Sacramento would be correct if I had asked for the capital of California, but I am asking for the capital city of the entire 50 states."

2. *Allow time for the student to think.* You can use this strategy when the student who gave the incorrect answer has the background to answer the question and you judge that he or she would be able to give the correct answer if only given more time to think. To illustrate, a student gave an incorrect answer to a question about the subject matter you emphasized yesterday in class. You respond by saying, "I know you know the correct answer. You just need a minute to think." Then you allow the 6 second wait time and implement strategy 3, 6, or 8 below. This response works better with older students as younger students tend to lose their trains of thought and become frustrated with additional time allotted.

3. *Prompting.* Use this strategy when students have a partial answer or when the student needs the teacher's guidance or structure for thinking. This structure brings about a sense of comfort and the additional reassurance needed to be able to perform. All prompts should be related to the content and not to incidental clues. For example, prompt names of geometric procedures with aspects within the procedure rather than by words that rhyme with that name.

4. *Differential reinforcement.* Use this strategy when you can tell the part of the answer that was correct. It is used to reinforce a student's first

attempt to contribute to class discussions. This is another form of prompting; however, it reduces the student's temptations to guess. It gives the student more information with which to modify his or her thinking. For example, you could say, "You almost have the idea. The first part was exactly correct. There was an error in your second part. Do you want me to lead you through the second part, or do you think you can get that part yourself?" "That was correct. It sounds as if you have been doing some original thinking. How would _____ fit in with your conclusion?" "That's almost 100 percent accurate. Consider this and then tell me what you think: _____."

5. *Paraphrasing the question.* You can use this strategy when an irrelevant answer has been given or when students begin to ramble. This strategy is also effective if the question you have to ask is a long one. This strategy helps students to rethink the answer they gave. Many times, this strategy affords the student an opportunity to recognize his or her mistake before the teacher points it out to him or her. To illustrate, you might say, "I'm sorry, I wasn't clear"; "Let me clarify my question"; "Let me give another example"; or "I wasn't as specific as I wanted to be in my question."

6. *Expand upon the answer.* Use this strategy when you are not clear why the student answered the way he or she did. This strategy asks students to tell the teacher why they answered as they did or why they felt their answers were correct. This strategy is used when an answer is partially correct or when the answer is completely incorrect.

7. *Tell the student the answer and express the need for him or her to remember the answer.* The strategy could be labeled "making the student accountable" as you will tell the student the correct answer and then return to the student and reask the same question again before the period is over. For example, "The correct answer is Washington, D.C. Now, I know you will remember it. I will ask you to tell me what the capitol of the United States is before this period is over. Be prepared." (You might then also wink, just to add a light touch to the response). You cannot forget to return to the student, however, as if you do the strategy will lose its effectiveness in the future for other students. This strategy gives the student the responsibility for having a successful contribution, the incentive to remember the information, but the risk to achieve success is not great.

8. *Ask a fellow student to give clues.* You can use this strategy with strong groups that possess good rapport. This strategy works well because of the support given by students to each other. When other students assist one another, the pressure and fear of failure is alleviated.

9. *Give examples of the possible answer.* You can use this strategy at the close of a unit or lesson or as a review. This strategy assists students to focus upon the material in which many different types of content could have been present. For example, you could have asked, "What type of imports do we receive in the United States?" Then you could give an

oral multiple choice answer of very plausible choices but only one is correct. Students are to select the correct answer from the choices given. As a second example, you have just asked the question, "Who discovered the "fountain of youth," and no one gave a correct response. You then say "_____ discovered the fountain of youth— Balboa, Cabasa De Vaca, Ponce de Leon."

10. *Use nonexamples or opposites of the answer.* In using this strategy, you tell what the answer is not. It is used effectively when no student raises his or her hand to answer a question. Other students can use this strategy by calling upon students who raise their hands first to tell classmates what the answer is not, allowing other students time to think.

In closing, try to avoid questioning patterns that allow students to predict when they will be called upon. The questioning pattern should be random yet provide equal opportunities for all to participate. Figure 7-3 might help you to call on all students rather than to focus more upon those in the front/center of the class or those with hands raised. Use the sheet by writing the students names in the left-hand column and a tally for each correct answer they gave on the day the information was introduced (recall) or days after the information was introduced (retention). The columns to the right correspond to the level of difficulty of the question asked: information, comprehension, application, analysis, synthesis, and evaluation levels from Bloom's Taxonomy. Circle each tally when a student misses a question, making a record of students' areas of weakness at the same time you counterbalance the number of questions each student has an opportunity to answer.

HANDLING OFF-THE-TRACK ANSWERS AND THE STUDENT WHO RAMBLES

If students are giving an extended, incorrect answer and are leading the interaction away from the objective of the lesson, consider saying

1. Yes, I understand that.
2. That seems reasonable to me!
3. I think I see the idea you are getting at!
4. That certainly makes sense!
5. I have not thought of that before!
6. That's a possibility. Are there others, class?
7. Hold on to that thought for a minute (and then return when this student is in less need of attention and will give a shorter reply).
8. That's a different thought; an interesting idea.

Figure 7-3

Teacher's Name _____ Activity _____
Date _____ Subject _____
Time of Day _____

	I	C	Ap	An	S	E
Recall						
Retention						
Recall						
Retention						
Recall						
Retention						
Recall						
Retention						
Recall						
Retention						
Recall						
Retention						
Recall						
Retention						
Recall						
Retention						
Recall						
Retention						
Recall						
Retention						
Recall						
Retention						
Recall						
Retention						
Recall						
Retention						
Recall						
Retention						

If one of these statements isn't strong enough and students continue to ramble on, to have side conversations, offer erroneous comments, interrupt, or exhibit an oral, hostile reaction, the techniques in Figure 7-4 will draw the students back on task.

TECHNIQUES THAT INTERFERE WITH EFFECTIVE QUESTIONING PRACTICES

A group of more than 50 third grade students were asked to tell me the things their teachers have done that interfered with their ability to give correct answers in class. Their answers were solicited in the hope they can be used as a checklist to strengthen your questioning practices:

_____ "When my teacher repeats the question before he or she gives a student a chance to answer. When he or she does this, the question is usually asked in a slightly different way and it confuses me. I don't know exactly what answer he or she wants."

_____ "When he or she answers his or her own questions because I don't want to raise my hand then because I know that if I don't he or she will answer the question for us. I even get mad when other students raise their hands. I want all of us to just wait and let the teacher answer all his or her own questions."

_____ "When he or she calls on me and I didn't have my hand raised. I get so embarrassed because I don't know the answer."

_____ "When he or she tells me 'No, that's not right' and then calls on someone else and they seem to get it right away."

_____ "When he or she repeats the students' answers, even when the answers were given loudly by the students."

_____ "When he or she tries to make us guess what's on his or her mind and it could be one of many things."

_____ "When he or she does not listen well enough to my answer and doesn't ask me to clarify or justify an answer that I think is really deep."

_____ "He or she doesn't state the question clearly or says a sentence and then, immediately, asks a question about that sentence."

_____ "He or she uses hard words I can't understand."

_____ "He or she doesn't repeat the question louder."

_____ "He or she changes the question after I answer it."

_____ "He or she doesn't say anything after I'm finished with my answer."

SEVEN LEADERSHIP SKILLS THAT MAXIMIZE THE BENEFITS OF TIME SPENT IN GROUP DISCUSSIONS

1. Before asking a question that needs considerable thought, you can suggest that you do not want an immediate answer. This discourages the more aggressive students from intimidating quieter students who have valuable observations to add, e.g., "Now, I don't want an immediate answer. Take your time to think about this carefully: _____."

Figure 7-4

STRATEGIES FOR HANDLING OFF-THE-RACK ANSWERS AND RAMBLING

Rambling

1. Ask a specific question that requires a "yes" or "no" answer.

2. Clarify a point made by rephrasing the last sentence and tying it to the student's first sentence and to the objective. For example, "The reference you made to the 'early days' was well taken. It is a second example of the main point of our discussion, that pioneer values are evident in our society today in many ways."

3. Thank the student and then move on.

4. Paraphrase an idea you have that the student's extended answer caused you to think about that could be used to bring the rest of the class back to the objective.

Side Conversations

1. Pause in the subject delivery, take a few seconds to survey the entire class, and then continue.

2. Ask one of the students involved in a conversation to be prepared to answer the next question, for example, "Susan will answer the next question after Robert finishes," so that the student has time to regain the content drift and is not humiliated in front of peers.

3. Set a time to meet with them to discuss the problem.

4. Move to their desks and continue the discussion from that point in the room.

Erroneous Comments and Comments off the Subject

1. Clarify the reason why the comment was made by asking, "Why do you ask" (say) that? "What were you thinking, more specifically?"

2. Emphasize with the feelings that underlie the comment by stating, "Although Jerry's comments may surprise some of you, I've felt that way before as well." Or "I wasn't thinking of it in just that way. Interesting."

3. Restate or summarize the part of the extraneous information that was correct. If possible, relate it back to the subject. If not, present the next point in your lesson plan as if the student's comment was the beginning of a new point and you are continuing with his or her thought. This will provide a feeling of closure of a section of the discussion and a new section of content to be learned and the student will have his or her previous pattern of thinking interrupted. He or she will not be tempted to continue to mindwander and will have been able to have done so without losing face with the other students in the class.

continued

Figure 7-4 continued

Interrupting Your Talk

1. Redirect the class discussion to another issue or to another student.
2. After acknowledging the interruption, ask the person who interrupted to summarize the points up to that point in your talk and then move on to the next point yourself.
3. Pause, make a reference to the amount of information the class has already covered up to the point of the interruption, and, if you wish, praise the class; then go on or point out the amount that remains to be covered as if you were offering a challenge and not a threat.

Hostile Reactions

1. Compliment the courage the student had in disagreeing and then assign that student an important function in relation to the topic he or she raised, for example, "Julie, would you like to tell us how you gained so much information about _____ at the close of class tomorrow? You can bring any materials you wish."
2. Admit that the problem the student pointed out is a valid one that was related to the point you were making. State the reason why you did not mention it, for example, that the point was one that was too advanced except for only the most capable. This praises the student, if done in a proper manner, without offending the remainder of the class.

Drawing Students into a Discussion

1. Ask a shy student the following question, "If I understood what you told me yesterday when the class was not here, you seem to have strong feelings about _____ . Would you share your feelings with us?"
2. Provide a disclaimer for the student at the beginning so he or she will not feel as if they have to give a profound series of statements on the rare occasions that they do contribute orally, for example, "Wanda, I know you haven't had much time to think about this, but would you tell us one of your opinions?"
3. Make the task a simple one by providing a major portion of the information for the student, for example, "Wayne, what is your understanding of (you give the main point of the discussion)?
4. You give a plan or action or a series of facts and ask the student to just tell if they seem reasonable or correct, for example, "JoAnn, this is the work I plan to do next week in this class. How realistic does it seem to you or do you have any suggestions for improvement?"
5. Ask a student a hypothetical question or questions where there are no single, correct answers, for example, "What do you see for the future?"

2. Calling on nonvolunteers in a productive and predictable manner. That is, announce that you will call on four people who have not yet raised their hands to participate in the next few questions you ask to close the lesson. When using this skill, be certain the students receive a question they can at least be partly successful in answering, so as to heed the advice of the third graders given earlier.

3. Use redirection. This involves your planning questions that can elicit several correct responses or opinions. You can cue the group by saying, "This question has many parts. Please give only one when you answer. I will ask several people to give their viewpoints before I comment upon them." Redirection encourages students to respond to each other.

4. Allow students to lead discussions of correct answers to homework or work common to the group of students.

5. Dignify even the simplest statements. To do so quickly, add a statement of your own at the end of the smallest student contributions, making the statement more interesting to the class. This strategy helps the shy student to feel more important and other students begin to want to listen to each other better. They are learning from you that anything said can be important. They enjoy seeing how you so ingeniously tie everyone's comments together. As you do this, students begin to model your behavior and extend the respect you have shown to their peers as well. Class rapport increases.

6. Tape one of your lessons as a check on your questioning techniques. An immediate benefit is the realization that you are a stronger discussion leader than you may presently believe yourself to be. That is, while leading a discussion you "hear" all the self-talk and all the thinking you decide to reject. You do not get a clear picture of what the students hear while you conduct class discussions.

7. When a student misunderstands, reteach and do not just rephrase the previous statement. The reteaching can take the form of (a) pointing out features of the task that you originally judged to be self-evident, (b) giving an analogy of the learning to nature, (c) discussing common previous experiences of your class as an example of the concept, (d) moving to a different level of thought on Bloom's taxonomy and ask different questions covering the same concept, and (e) allowing another student to paraphrase what you meant in the question and/or the concept that would answer the question.

A SUMMARY OF THIS CHAPTER'S MAIN POINTS

1. If the class appears to balk at a teacher's decision, the teacher can make a group assignment that is due at the end of the period, defer the issue to a student task force to present their position on the subsequent day, or change the lesson plan as students do written work independently for the remainder of the period.

2. Student small-group work can solve individual student problems.

3. Discipline skills can be developed, and if they aren't in place a classroom will decrease the amount of time spent productively as much as a lack of self-discipline reduces one's personal satisfactions and accomplishments.

4. Hold as many informal meetings as possible "on your feet."

5. Learn to refrain from saying too much at faculty meetings and serve the role of either using humor to draw off negative feelings, yielding when necessary for progress, reconciling points of view, supporting others, keeping communication open, summarizing a discussion or testing whether the faculty has reached a decision, whichever is within your area of talent.

6. Being available to the right people and students often enough attests to the skill you have learned that if an interruption occurs very rarely, it is usually a necessary one and should be handled without negative responses on your part. If an interruption occurs regularly and creates resentment in you, change your organization or approach the problem directly, by setting aside a block of time to eliminate the interruptions.

7. There are ten time-saving and student ego-saving methods of changing incorrect answers to productive, valuable learning experiences.

8. By memorizing key response phrases, one can reduce the amount of time wasted in handling off-the-track answers, students who ramble, students who demand your attention continually, hostile reactions, and incomplete answers.

In Chapter 1 you wrote one talent-centered goal. As you reread it, note if it has been attained. It will also be interesting to note why some were achieved in a different way than you first expected. After rereading your goal, do you feel differently about yourself? Do you see a new capability? Do you feel strange, humbled, or perplexed?

REFERENCES

Bruner, Jerome. "The Model of A Learner." Educational Researcher, June/July 1985 Vol. 14, No. 6 p. 5-8.

Carnes, William T. Effective Meetings for Busy People: Let's Decide It and Go Home. New York: McGraw-Hill, 1980.

Farley, Frank. "The T-Type Personality." Paper presented at the annual convention of the American Educational Research Association in Chicago, April 1985.

Hall, Gene. "Teacher Change Process." Paper presented at the annual convention of the American Educational Research Association in Chicago, April 1985.

Leas, Speed: B. Time Management: A Working Guide for Church Leaders, Nashville, Tenn. Abingdon, 1978.

McCoy, James T. *Management of Time*. Englewood Cliffs, N.J.: Prentice-Hall, 1959.

Sanford, Julie P. "Time Use and Activities in Junior High Classes." *Journal of Educational Research*, Vol. 76, no. 3, January–February 1983, 140–147.

Silberman, M. L., and S. A. Wheelan. *How to Discipline Without Feeling Guilty: Assertive Relationships with Children*. Champaign, Ill.: Research Press, 1980.

White, Lynn, Jr. "Understanding Change." In Leslie Huling-Austin and Shirley Hord, (EDS). *Understanding How Teachers Experience School Change*. Austin, Tex.: Research and Development Center for Teacher Education, 1985.

eight

Designing Times for Self-Improvement

A Teacher's Comments on Chapter 8

I reacted to Chapter 8 on a Saturday afternoon in September just following seven sweltering northern Illinois days of dealing with a new crop of 24 little "corks" in a first grade classroom and just 51 hours before my doctoral-level classes would begin again. "Chapter 8: Self-Improvement, indeed!" I thought, as I procrastinated over two weeks' ironing, floors to be scrubbed, and a new word processor to be mastered before Monday morning. There were also lesson plans to write, a pear tree bending with ripening fruit, and green beans, planted late, indicating that they must be frozen "now or never." These tasks must be completed before I ventured forth on the next step of my great personal mental improvement.

My next independent thoughts were "How appropriate!" Reading the chapter provided exactly the impetus I needed to get up and get moving. It followed me to the ironing board, through the picking of the pears, and to the figuring out of the final important mystery of the computer. Lesson plans will be finished. The othr tasks are low priority and can wait. The chapter (1) provides just the kind of consolation we need to realize that our reactions to the demands of our profession are normal, and within the realm of human tendencies, and (2) sets forth a means of resetting goals to provide time for self-improvement. It is the kind of inspiration we need to experience time and again as we move through the mundane tasks of our lives.

Grace S. J. Vyduna
Johnsburg Community Unit School
District 12 Elementary Teacher
McHenry County, Illinois

"Man wants to rise above his limited duration,
above the course of history, above the fact of what
is determined in his life. Sometimes he does reach
the point of losing all awareness of time. He is
elated in ecstasy; He possesses himself in one single
moment.

—*William Butler Yeats*

Last night as I began revisions of this chapter I thought, "This chapter is going to be so short. I think I'll combine it with Chapter 9. If I just make the discussion more generic, the chapters would be closely related and, after all, teachers already know that we need to spend time in self-improvement. This is the message I want to bring. All I can possibly add is a stronger rationale to do so and suggest ways of making it easier."

The reason this short chapter remains is that I judge that a strong program of self-improvement warrants a separate emphasis. The amount to be gained in increased time through use of the information, in my judgment, is equal to the information in other chapters. As a matter of fact, the feat of setting time aside for your personal self-improvement may be very difficult for you to accomplish, making the next discussion even more vital, and distinct.

I compare this chapter to a coach who is thrusting you into a physical fitness improvement program. Prior to "meeting your coach," you will have heard several reasons why such a program is valuable. It may be that only after reading this chapter will you be completely convinced that expending the effort in professional, self-improvement, on a continuous basis, will indeed bring the promised gains. May this chapter be the "coach" that assisted you to gain the courage to begin and sustain your program.

THE RATIONALES FOR SELF-IMPROVEMENT

My intent is to collect the reasons and methods of "making time for self-improvement" so it can provide the support to increase the quality of your self-improvement efforts.

1. "When you develop your own personal resources, you will have enough time to do what you want to do" (McCoy, 1959, p. 84).
2. The most successful teachers have a more positive outlook on life and a significantly greater desire to advance themselves (Meade, 1966; and McClelland, 1961).

3. People who experience personal growth and who receive information about the rate of their growth will increase their job satisfaction and job achievements (Meade, 1966).

4. Principals report that the planning and reflection they do away from the school site are just as valuable in creating an effective and efficient learning experience as the continual problem-solving decisions they spend time responding to at school (Nur, 1985).

5. As a continuous self-improvement program accumulates you will be forced to act upon new information and to reject and recognize obsolete knowledge and skills. Without a continuous self-improvement program, you will more easily use obsolete tools, and take longer on professional tasks than other, more recently trained or "improved" teachers.

6. With a continuous professional development program in action, you will avoid the feeling that everyone else is "gaining ground" and perhaps passing you professionally. Rather, you will be able to use more numerous practical experiences you have accumulated in passing years to enhance your veteran wisdom and capacity to provide strongest leadership in the profession.

WHAT SHOULD BE IN A SELF-IMPROVEMENT PROGRAM

The content for your improvement program is simple: you should include only the goals you want and/or believe you need, period! Because growth in one skill enhances others, you should never hesitate to focus upon the highest-priority need or desire you have at the moment. The only condition upon the goals you select is that the program must center on those you can have full power to achieve and control. That is, each personal improvement goal should not be under the influence of other people. For example, a goal of having students working so hard in your class that none fail is not a goal to include on your self-improvement program. For such goals to be reached, other people must agree to it, and they are not under your complete control. Sample goals over which you hold complete control include writing a letter to ask to be a member of the task force to plan means of increasing the district's effectiveness in _____, volunteering to be building representative for your professional organization, making a new bulletin board, learning to water/cross-country ski, getting a new hair style, or any goal that would make you more productive and happy.

Although the "rules" of beginning a program are simple, I have found that many of us need to first design a routine or "goal process." Setting a standard time to work on your professional development adds to the commitment and makes it easier to "make time to do it."

With the exception of the job analysis routine that follows later in this chapter, each of the processes in the next discussion have been used by hundreds of teachers to build a stronger professional life. They have been very effective in breaking down inertia and fears of starting to improve on a regular basis. May you try several and design combinations of the processes until you find a method that you enjoy initiating systematically. At some point you may go for a few days and then realize that you haven't made time for self-improvement. You can change your process and method of scheduling time to do so, and your program will become even better for you. In essence, you can experiment with each process until you find the best fit in your unique, and ever-changing life-style.

Finally, as you begin, you will discover many things about yourself. Each discovery in and of itself will make more time for you. That is, once each new dimension of your talent is uncovered it will be permanent self-knowledge to aid in future decisions. This self-knowledge will make your decisions more successful, and you will never need to invest time learning this point about your character again. Therefore, it will become increasingly easier and faster to reach professional goals in each passing day and as the time your program has been in place increases.

Some of the first discoveries, you make will include

1. Which time of the day/week/month is best or is your peak time for various types of activities?

2. What time of the day or week is best for your self-improvement program?

3. How much time you enjoy and feel is valuable to allocate to self-improvement?

4. What will you do if you miss a time you had set aside to work "for you"?

5. What motivates you to keep going?

6. Should you include other people as consultants, observers, or partners in areas of needed improvement?

7. Do you work best alone, in small groups, or should you schedule less frequent, larger-group settings to try new things?

8. What resources and tools do you need or do you need for your jobs to produce greatest benefits?

9. Should you expand your sphere of reference so more and more people benefit from the work you are doing to improve yourself?

PROCEDURES THAT MAKE IT EASIER TO "MAKE TIME" FOR SELF-IMPROVEMENT

There are seven procedures you can follow for making time for your self-improvement.

Take One Risk a Month

Three years ago, I met a remarkable man. At the age of 52, he had become very wealthy and had retired. He had been president of one of the largest insurance companies in America, served as a professor in graduate business schools across the country, was a member of the board of directors for three large companies, and was a state's business advisor. This man's only formal education was to have completed a bachelor's degree in elementary education.

While he was lecturing at our university's School of Business, I invited him to speak to my graduate students in a course entitled "Advanced Human Growth and Development." I specifically asked Don to analyze his own life and to share his "pearls of wisdom," those things to which he most attributed his success. Although he shared a list of 16 different factors, he gave 1 factor extra emphasis and credit.

Don attributed a great deal of his success in life to the fact that he forced himself to take risks. He did something that he wanted to do but would take courage to accomplish each month. He reported that, at times, his risk was more than he could handle but he would just "pull back, regroup, get a little more information, and then try again."

I began to use his suggestion. If I hadn't tried it, I wouldn't have believed what it can do to enrich a teacher's development.

I thought it might be easier for you to understand what kinds of risks can improve you professionally if I list the first risks I took after meeting Don. I was surprised how even the most seemingly unrelated risk tied in to aspects of my professional goals and competence.

> May: Climbed a 12-foot fence and discovered I was braver than I realized I was. I did have courage.
> June: Read a book and studied film history and added this new hobby in my life.
> July: Began a physical fitness program.
> August: Read a book; discoursed with three students on the subject of "color me beautiful"; had my coloring "done"; and began a new wardrobe based on my summer colors.
> September: Did two things I didn't want to do.
> October: Attended a Dallas Cowboy football game (The personal risk in this will not be obvious as will be some of the risks you take because some will take a courage only known to you, privately. Even such "private risks" create a level of self-confidence that spills over into each teaching day and a level of confidence that would not be possible had you not taken the risk.)
> November: Undertook a 30-day vocabulary improvement program.
> December: Began piano lessons.
> January: Went downhill skiing for the first time. As I successfully completed the run that scared me to death, I realized that I would never be afraid to speak before large audiences again.

Write One Action Letter a Week

This method is based on a principle taught in business management courses. The process encourages you to initiate cycles of action you believe are needed. You may use the plan by scheduling a time (such as Friday afternoons) where you write a letter to advance an idea concerning our profession. The letter is not one asking for information, a friendly letter that you've been wanting to answer, or a letter to request a preview of new teaching materials. The letter is one designed to help you implement your ideas. It is not necessarily one where you ask someone else to advance another person's idea. The types of action letters you might consider are letters telling someone an idea where you volunteer to serve as the chair of the committee to explore the idea, requesting an item that could enhance your work, or offering an opportunity to use a talent you would like to use.

The "Write-an-Action Letter-a-Week" procedure may not even be a letter but any action you take to advance your professional life in a direction you wish it to go. For example, your "Write-an-Action-Letter-a-Week" could be an oral interaction to advance your ideas and goals for the profession or a thank-you letter designed to establish an ongoing professional relationship with a business or to relay specific skills you have.

As an illustration, a teacher once gave a speech at a state convention. A member of the audience asked her to give an inservice training session on the same topic to teachers in the member's district. After doing so, she wrote an action letter expressing her gratitude for the opportunity of working with the teachers. In the letter, she also listed talks in other inservice topics she had delivered in other districts in the event that her new professional acquaintance might know of teachers who needed training in these topics as well. Because of this letter, this teacher returned to the district twice and was able to establish new friendships with some of the best teachers she has ever known.

In closing, an action letter doesn't have to be a formal letter. A note to the principal, curriculum director, or colleague or even a brief meeting to discuss your request and ideas, done on a regularly scheduled, basis will enable you to grow very rapidly. A principal in Arizona shared with me that the most important characteristic she values in teachers is that they volunteer to help her. Some will even project a professional need ahead of the time of the need and say, "I'll do it for you." These are the types of "action letters" that will benefit your professional growth and skills.

Do Something Special for Yourself Once a Month

This plan is exceptionally effective during times, such as holiday seasons, when you have many professional and personal projects in action and must fill all your daily schedules and time commitments to accommodate them. Using this self-improvement plan, you can easily put your own professional development program on the back burner for a little while and not miss a day! Without this plan you might feel as if you have to place yourself and your needs out of the way when large school-related responsibilities emerge. This need not happen. Prior to using this procedure, some teachers told me that they didn't enjoy having extra school-related responsibilities because they were disappointed that they couldn't stick to their own personal schedule and goals while doing them. Further, they explained, once they had "gone off their self-improvement plans," they found it easier to make excuses for not going back to them after the project was finished. With the following "once-a-month plan" you will find it easier to stay on track with your own professional growth even when other goals are pressing.

Whenever you have pressing goals, block out a day after the goal will have been reached that is only for yourself. You will do those things you want to do for yourself before you begin a second major project for the school. It won't matter if "the day" is not even an eight-hour period. The principle is that you keep track of how many times you postponed your program and then you just pay yourself back all at one time. In this way you do not miss any time for yourself; you just schedule it in a larger block.

Spend a Set Amount of Money on Your Self-improvement Program Each Day

It seems that this method works regardless of the amount of money committed. There may be two reasons why this method is so effective. Consider the adage, "Where a man's money lies, therein lies his heart." Somehow we seem to have an increased motivation and commitment toward goals when we make a concrete, monetary investment in them. Second, as we often hear, "Money is power." With a pool of money to use for your growth and your self-improvement your goal will be easier to reach. This monetary commitment also seems to make it more difficult to place other things as higher priorities.

Believe That There Are No Failures, Only Delays

Each time we don't reach a subgoal within our program, we tell ourselves that we have just been detained, we have not failed. We then reanalyze our goal. We begin a different procedure, and we go on. This plan, it seems, allows our conscious and subconscious minds to emphasize all past days we have returned to goals and have been successful. Without this attitude, we emphasize our past inabilities to succeed in meeting our plan, and we label it as one of many "failures" we have had to stick to a self-improvement program. This "no-failures-only-delays" plan will keep you from emphasizing your human frailties and interferences that are beyond your control. Instead, this plan helps to validate the increased strength, self-will, and wisdom you have gained from setting and resetting your goals. This process also increases your perserverance as you develop the ability to plan around obstacles and to meet demands of others while maintaining your perspective.

Capitalize Upon Opportunities and Situations

You may have already realized that some of the difficulties you have when a "problem" develops or you seem to regress to a lower ability level is that you are not viewing the problem as merely a new situation. You can often gain strength or overcome problems by increasing your positive approach, which relabeling a problem as a new situation can cause. Once you've done this, you can begin to see if the situation exists mainly because you had a very specific expectation that someone else or something else didn't meet. By realizing that sometimes what you want or expect is not the best that could be, you will be freed to see the positives you are experiencing. This step sometimes eliminates your problem because the "real problem" you were experiencing was that you were suffering a loss—a loss of not having the wish or desire you had expected to realize. Using this procedure may create a second benefit for you. You may begin to realize how the reality you are experiencing has more benefits than would have been possible had your expectation been actualized.

Perform a Job Analysis

In a job analysis you dissect your performance that you wish to improve from three different perspectives. First, you think about what you think you are doing about the goal you wish. Second, you think about what you ought to be doing. Last, you think about what you actually are doing. You then write five steps to take in the next five weeks and perform the job analysis again.

Some teachers benefit from including a goal for *personality or character development in their self-improvement program.* Figure 8-1 lists characteristics that you might select as goals. The first 35 were taken from studies by Douglass and Douglass (1980, pp. 211–212) that identified the personal characteristics most admired in management-related jobs. The next 26 were taken from a research study where I asked practicing teachers to identify the most outstanding characteristics of the teacher they most admired. The last 21 are the hierarchically ranked qualities that 255 students in grades 2 to 12 from Wisconsin cited as what made a good teacher, in their opinion, as recorded in the master's thesis of Nancy Wichtel entitled "The Characteristics of a Good Teacher as Judged by Students" (1972).

SELF-GOVERNING THE MANNER IN WHICH WE ALLOCATE TIME

Certain aspects of human nature reduce the effective use of time. By becoming more aware of the influences these tendencies have upon the way you allocate time, you can gain more control over your decisions and your day. The list in Figure 8-2 identifies the ten most prominent human tendencies that reduce the amount of time you have for your own pursuits. Following each entry is a description of one method you can use to overcome the effect of this tendency. As you read each item, you may realize that you also have used a specific method of overcoming the difficulties associated with that tendency. If you have, describe the method below the item on the line provided. By so doing you will reaffirm its value and "reprogram it more automatically, as a habitual function in your life."

If you do not have a method of combating a specific tendency, reflect upon previous discussions in this book, mentors in your life, and use the suggestion following each item to help set a goal you will use to overcome each tendency. In your goal, tell what you want and what you will do to get it. Write this on the lines provided.

I wanted to be able to close this chapter by telling you how long you should expect for self-improvement goals to be actualized, but there has not been any

Figure 8-1

GOALS THAT COULD BE USED
IN PROFESSIONAL DEVELOPMENT PROGRAMS

A. Personal Characteristics Most Admired in Management Jobs

1. Energetic and hardworking.
2. Accepts success gracefully.
3. Accepts defeat gracefully.
4. Takes responsibility for mistakes and errors of judgment.
5. Is open to constructive criticism.
6. Has good leadership ability.
7. Is a good judge of character.
8. Is a good parent.
9. Recognizes own prejudices.
10. Is trustworthy.
11. Likes to work on a team.
12. Is a loner.
13. Has a good sense of humor.
14. Takes pleasure in the accomplishments and successes of family and friends and co-workers.
15. Keeps temper under control.
16. Is highly motivated.
17. Doesn't need to get own way all the time.
18. Can accept people, including children and parents, whose values are different from own values.
19. Is growing, and accepts the pain and disruptions involved in the process of development.
20. Likes challenges, even at the risk of failure.
21. Is well qualified for the present (or proposed) job.
22. Likes to work with people.
23. Is not satisfied until having done his or her best on any given task.
24. Is creative in finding other solutions when one method doesn't work.
25. Asserts own needs and isn't victimized by others.
26. Is a "doer" who likes to get at what needs to be done.
27. Likes to analyze and plan tasks carefully to be done.
28. Works well under pressure.
29. Likes to work wtih reports, figures, data.
30. Prefers a lot of structure and organization.
31. Has an excellent educational background.
32. Has much valuable experience.
33. Takes good care of own body and possessions.
34. Has a pleasing personality.
35. Knows what he or she wants and generally gets it.
36. Strives for knowledge, delicacy, and precision in use of words (this characteristic is taken from McCoy, 1959).

B. Characteristics of "most admired teachers"

1. Is calm, not easily upset or loses his or her temper.
2. Is patient, willing to give student time to assimilate new material.

continued

Figure 8-1 continued

3. Is knowledgeable about his or her subject.
4. Seems to never get frustrated even when asked the same question repeatedly.
5. Makes the rules and sticks with them.
6. Organizes himself or herself and his or her work.
7. Is interested in students and kind.
8. Is nice looking.
9. Is friendly, but stern.
10. Is concerned with all students.
11. Never raises his or her voice.
12. Makes students feel special.
13. Is soft-spoken.
14. Lets students know he or she likes and cares about them.
15. Is sincerely interested in each child's progress.
16. Is willing to give extra time to work with students.
17. Loves his or her work and being with children.
18. Always listens to what a child had to say.
19. Expects everyone to do his or her best work.
20. Is friendly.
21. Is concerned with students outside problems, had personal conversations.
22. Has an aura of serenity.
23. Solves problems with fairness.
24. States clearly the duty to be performed.
25. Praises often.

C. Characteristics of a good teacher as judged by elementary and secondary students' opinions concerning good teachers:

1. Enjoys teaching and students.
2. Understands students' problems and helps them.
3. Spends time after school to help students.
4. Knows subject matter.
5. Deserves respect through mutual respect with students.
6. Strives for "student-centered" classroom.
7. Puts less stress on grades and more on knowledge gained.
8. Has reputation for difficult and challenging work and tests.
9. Gives extra credit to raise grades.
10. Is relaxed in class and makes students feel at home.
11. Gives students a say in class curriculum.
12. Uses an organized teaching method.
13. Gives students a "second chance" when disciplining.
14. Has good room displays.
15. Has sense of humor.
15. Uses audio visual equipment often.
17. Lets students do what they want during free time.
18. Holds classes outside in nicer weather.
19. Repeats directions until fully explained.
20. Sees competition as a motivation to work harder.
21. Is strict in discipline.

Figure 8-2

**ASPECTS OF HUMAN NATURE THAT INFLUENCE
THE WAY WE ALLOCATE TIME**

1. You will do what you like to do before you do what you do not like to do (e.g., "I find that I like jobs better when my friends work with me or when I push a little harder and do the difficult things in order"). Tell how you will try to overcome this tendency in a statement similar to the one just given.) _____

2. You do the things you know how to do faster than the things you do not know how to do, and you do things for which the resources are available. _____

3. You do the things that are easiest before doing things that are difficult. You tackle small jobs before you tackle large jobs, and you do things that provide the most immediate closure. You can do one easy thing as a "priming of the pump" to get a big task going. _____

4. You do things that require a little time before the things that require a large amount of time. You do the things that are urgent before you do things that are important.

5. You do scheduled activities before nonscheduled ones. _____

6. You respond to demands of others before demands from yourself. You work on the basis of the consequences to the group. _____

7. You will readily respond to crises and emergencies, and wait until a deadline approaches before you get moving. _____

8. You do interesting things before uninteresting ones. _____

   (It could only take a very small and simple thing, like using a brand, new mechanical pencil to make an uninteresting task more appealing.)

9. You respond in the order of your personal objectives and to the consequences of doing or not doing something. _____

10. You work on things in order of their arrival. You do things that make the most noise. _____

research to answer this question. Personally, however, I set the following three goals, fours years ago, to overcome three of the foregoing tendencies:

1. Improve my ability to do the things I don't like by breaking them down into smaller tasks
2. Become more aware of when my pace of work slows down and get more information about the topic or break away from the work for a while to rest and reflect
3. Overcome the "squeaky wheel principle" by asking a person why they came to me or what resource/talent I have that they feel I have that will alleviate their concerns and problems.

After four years, I have achieved the first goal. I no longer avoid tasks I value but dislike. I have not yet achieved the second goal as a habit but feel as if I am almost there. I have not yet met the third goal. I'm still working on it. This sample is not intended as a guide, but only as a case study in the attempt to help you establish and meet your goals as rapidly as you can. It has been valuable to me to have set my goals even with the long period it took for me to realize them.

Now, before we push off on a voyage of self-discovery and improvement, you may have a more satisfying and productive experience if you build a mechanism in your improvement plan to ensure that you continuously add new resources and new people's ideas as to ways in which you can improve. Two means of doing so is to read how good time managers build and continue to revise their self-improvement programs and to set aside time for planning, evaluating, and improving your own time management/self-improvement program. You might also want to refer to the 61 tips Alan Lakein lists in his book and uses in his self-improvement program (Lakein, 1973).

> In the introduction to Chapter 4, we analyzed the commonalities among the types of time wasters that most disturb your work. Also, we closed our discussion by setting a few methods of overcoming the most difficult ones for you. If you would like to see how many you have mastered, you might enjoy turning to your notes in that chapter and reading what you wrote at that time. You could also make a checkmark in the third column of the list of time wasters in Figure 4-1. This second checklist will show which aspects of wasted time were easiest for you to overcome. You may decide to analyze what types of characteristics the remaining have and set a new goal. I remember how happy I was when I first did a posttest like this. I want you to experience the growth you have attained.

REFERENCES

Douglass, Merrill, and Donna Douglass. *Manage Your Time, Manage Your Work, Manage Yourself*. New York: Amacon, 1980.

Lakein, Alan. *How to Get Control of Your Time and Your Life.* New York: New American Library, 1973.

McClelland, D. C. *The Achieving Society.* Princeton, N.J.: Van Nostrand, 1961.

McCoy, James T. *Management of Time.* Englewood Cliffs, N.J.: Prentice-Hall, 1959.

Meade, R. D. "Achievement, Motivation and Psychological Time." *Journal of Personality and Social Psychology*, Vol. 4, no. 5, 1966, 577–580.

Nur, M. M. "The Role of Research-Oriented Universities in School Change." Paper presented at the annual convention of the American Association of Colleges of Teacher Education in Denver, March 1985.

Wichtel, Nancy. "The Characteristics of a Good Teacher as Judged by Students." Master's thesis, Department of Curriculum and Instruction, University of Wisconsin, Madison, 1972.

nine

Changing Burnout to Superproduction

A Teacher Comments on Chapter 9

Dr. Collins, through research, observations of others, and personal experiences, gives us excellent and specific ideas concerning burnout. Take a warm bath. Recognize your classroom. Plan special activities to make your day more exciting. These and the other suggestions she gives will help you avoid burnout. I hope "avoid" burnout accurately describes your need. If "cure" burnout reflects your condition, you should begin implementing the activities as quickly as possible.

No one can be in a euphoric state all the time. As Dr. Collins suggested, we all have straws which will break us. Conditions can, and do, affect burnout. Some of us, in spite of or because of conditions, do experience happiness and satisfaction in our careers. I, personally—a nineteen-year veteran teacher, have not experienced burnout, yet! I believe working with people, as opposed to objects, inspires and rewards me.

Ms. Septima Green
Teacher of Gifted and Talented Students
Forth Worth, Texas

*The deepest personal sorrow suffered by human
beings consists of the difference between what one
was capable of becoming and what one has, in fact,
become.*

—*Ashley Montague*

Burnout is a complex phenomenon as it appears to have both an attitudinal and a behavioral dimension (Wiggers, Forney, and Wallace-Schutzman, 1983). The attitudinal dimension involves a loss of motivation and energy. The behavioral dimension is marked by a dramatic departure from one's previous normal level of work and/or the development of nonwork habits.

There are four types of burnout: (1) all pervasive; (2) periodic or situational; (3) activity based, where you have become drained from having had to perform one task for too long; and (4) boredom. This fourth type appears to be derived from a complex feeling arising from a dissatisfaction with yourself or a dissatisfaction that others don't fill your needs and emptinesses.

SEVEN WAYS TO OVERCOME OR PREVENT BURNOUT

The following methods can help you understand all four types of burnout and overcome the negative influences they have upon classroom learning time.

Get Away from It All

If you occasionally focus attention on activities outside work, you will eliminate type 2, or periodic, burnout. This approach can also be used as the first step in combatting type 1, or all-pervasive, burnout.

This method works for many reasons. First, monotony is broken. When you dislike what you are doing, it is often not so much because it is causing difficulty but because you are unable to express other feelings or to engage in other activities. It is the frustration caused by these suppressed outlets of activity and feelings that creates type 2 burnout.

If repetition creates negative emotions, why are so many values and procedures centered around it? Repetition and organization do enable us to waste as little time as possible and make it almost impossible to escape the details needed in standardization. Reflect upon this first value each time you tend to persecute yourself or think that fatigue, boredom, and burnout have been caused by your lack of dedication, devotion, and self-will. These latter characteristics are not the cause of burnout; rather, they are the results of human responses to suppression and monotony. Thus, you cannot cure burnout by enrolling in a course to strengthen self-will or by becoming angry that you use certain defenses to call our attention to the other needs you have that are not being met.

A second reason that just looking away, taking a few minutes away from grading the papers, or taking a weekend trip works to overcome burnout is that it increases your alertness and observation skills. These strengths transfer to the work you were previously engaged in so you make up for the time spent away. Moreover, breaking away from teaching, as you may have already discovered, is one of the fastest ways to add reflective insight to it.

With each new period of reflection, your skills to stick with a commitment grow so you will better sustain initial commitments and postpone future periodic burnout.

There are other reasons that removing yourself from "the forest" enables you more easily to see the trees. The opportunities clothed beneath our problem emerge. Curiosity develops. You become more open and positive toward the kaleidoscope of complexities, changes, and joys in the rest of you life. Thus perspective is rapidly restored. These absences of curiosities could seriously alter your perception of your teaching ability. Specifically, if you begin to see teaching as mundane, you may express this view by decreasing your emotional investment; using rigidity to cling to past, established procedures; believing the fantasy that others abandon you; wallowing in trivia; or becoming satisfied with boring activities. We are very vulnerable to boredom, and boredom appears to be the crack in our emotional makeup by which burnout first seeps in and begins to overshadow all our work.

Reflective time can provide an opportunity for you to uncover the causes for time-wasting habits. One vivid example was shared by a man, who, on his vacation, took the time to reflect upon his work. He discovered that he had done many things to aggravate others at school because he wanted to compensate for the lack of appreciation he thought he should be receiving for the extra hours he was investing at school.

Last, breaking away provides rest. Rest is more vital to production than you may realize. I am repeatedly shocked by the power fatigue has over all aspects of my cognitions, emotions, and physical output. As a matter of fact, research has demonstrated that placebos and hospital rest cured ulcers as well as would the standard medication in use today.

When rest is not possible, its absence alone can create problems and waste time. When you rest, you not only build energy, but you change the energy flow patterns within your body. You switch to a different set of support muscles and stress ones not exercised in regular teaching activities. In addition, by "laying around" you create an increased need for productive, efficient work. Such work will take away the monotony that you will begin to experience from having had too much rest!

Take Time Out to Make the Classroom More Attractive

Taking the time to make the classroom more aesthetic and attractive (especially your desk and working spaces) increases organization and time. An added benefit is that it makes the classroom more comfortable and increases the positive feelings students have when they enter.

Students can be taught to apply this principle in their lives by helping to decide and to make objects to add to the room. For example, one tenth grade art class designed ways in which rooms in their high school could be used more effectively. The architectural and interior design drawings were approved by the school board and were enacted by Parent-Teacher Organization funds.

You might wish to use the space here to list the five things you would especially like to do to your room and designate a means of doing it. You could even take the first step today:

	Areas to Improve	Date	How I'll Do It	Date Completed
1.				
2.				
3.				
4.				
5.				

The following lists given by teachers and administrators in the Southwest may help to stimulate your thoughts on the activity:

Which method, cited in Chapter 2, could you use to make time to add beauty to the school: begin not at the beginning, leave it lying around, set a deadline, do it better, 7–11 method, building a set of training wheels, making an assembly line, and/or changing the procedure or structure of the task?

Areas to Improve	How I'll Do It
1. Bulletin board	1. Have students make string art to put on the bulletin boards.
2. Walls in the lunchroom or auditorium	2. Have the art department paint one wall with geometric designs.
3. The room in general	3. Put some plants in the room.
4. The teacher's desk area	4. Keep the desk area clean and uncluttered with colorful objects about the desk.
5. The ceiling	5. Students can make soda-straw solids that can be suspended from the ceiling.
6. Equipment	6. Let students repair some equipment.
7. Trash-can color	7. Let students paint the trash cans.
8. Bulletin boards in locker rooms	8. Color code each _____ activity.
9. Two bookcases with peeling paint	9. Paint with a bright latex.
10. Reading area	10. Get a rug, tables, several chairs.
11. The walls	11. Posters—use pictures of the students to make a collage.
12. Bookcases on three walls that look rather junky	12. Rearranging books or kits to make the room look more spacious.

Areas to Improve	How I'll Do It
13. Two large tables in the room that are badly scarred.	13. See if maintenance could refinish the tops of the tables.
14. Area above blackboard	14. Put sayings on different-colored and different-shaped paper in this area.
15. Inside of door	15. Each month fix door to look like a face, animal, scene, holiday.
16. Picture center	16. Take camera to school, take pictures, develop, put up on picture center, change often.
17. Windows	17. Fall leaves (different colors), winter—snowflakes (different colors), spring—flowers (different colors).
18. Desk	18. Use sayings or posters.

Set Aside Quiet Time

Setting aside a certain amount of time where you will not be interrupted is one of the only ways you can give yourself time to meet the needs of your emotions. Without such time you will be able to meet these needs only with great personal stress if at all. In addition if you do not target some time for your emotional needs, you may begin to demand or expect your students or someone else to satisfy these needs. If you begin to lose sight of the value of "quiet periods alone," you may try a technique others have used. When tempted to give up your quiet times as time wasters, try to remember the saying, "Many old nags began as people who prided themselves in being self-sacrificing martyrs for others."

Educators who have set aside quiet time report that they use the time to write letters, jog, read a favorite book, soak in a warm bath, pet their cat, take a walk, or work on a hobby.

The suggestions found in the following books can also be helpful in restoring the soul and refreshing your attitude toward work:

Benson, Herbert. *The Relaxation Response.* New York: William Morrow, 1975.
Craven, Margaret. *I Heard the Owl Call My Name.* Garden City, N.Y.: Doubleday, 1973.
Pirsig, Robert. *Zen and the Art of Motorcycle Maintenance.* New York: William Morrow, 1974.
Rogers, Dale Evans. *Angel Unaware.* Los Angeles: Rogers, 1949.

You may want to give yourself the following assignment (you can complete it in a few moments, and it will pay big dividends): stop right now and select the best time for you to have a quiet time to meet your emotional needs each week. Make this a time that you can use as your own, private, uninterrupted, luxurious oasis.

Overcome Monday Morning "Blues"

If it is becoming more and more difficult to go to work on Monday, perhaps your days off have not provided you with enough variety and change of pace.

Some teachers find if they (1) become busier in professional activities after hours (taking an active role in educational or professional community projects, school activities' sponsors), (2) plan one special event each weekend/month, or (3) wear their favorite clothes on the first day back to school each week, Monday morning blues are reduced.

Also, ask yourself, what is the most important thing that someone could make, buy, or do for you that would make your job more enjoyable? What could you do now to do the thing or secure the thing for yourself?

By asking questions such as these, you can also discover if boredom or dissatisfaction at work is stemming from a single, camouflaged cause. By increasing small factors of enjoyment that you receive, major, job-related frustrations can be avoided. For example, a teacher center associate began to dislike coming to work. She loved the people she was with, but it seemed as if each day was becoming filled with one menial task after another. She couldn't place her finger on exactly what was happening. Then one day, during "the quiet time" she had set aside, she began thinking about her growing discontent. As she pondered, it dawned on her that she began to feel a sense of dissatisfaction shortly after a teacher gave her a used, portable typewriter so she could type the correspondence in her job, instead of writing short memos in longhand. But by typing memos, she had decreased the amount of time she had as she made so many typing errors. And with every correction she made, her work was becoming more and more tedious, menial, and frustrating to her. That day, the teacher center associate removed the typewriter and her "Monday morning blues" vanished.

Such small things can have dramatic impacts upon attitudes. An accumulation of tiny, thin straws can break a camel's back. Is there some aspect of your job that could be changed to affect positively other aspects of your work? You may want to use a few moments to analyze the specific, tiny aspects of your job that are dissatisfying. Perhaps you can change one of these. You will be greatly rewarded for doing so. What is the greatest dissatisfaction you face? _____ _____You may wish to record today's date. _____

Children seem to have created another technique for avoiding temporary burnout. This technique could be labeled the "counting the pages till the end." "How much farther do we have to go?" they ask. "How many more pages do we have to do?" Children seem to have discovered that when they become enmeshed in the middle of a difficult or boring task, getting an idea of how much farther ahead the end will be revitalizes them. There are times when you may want to borrow their strategy.

Finally, Jay Forrester, professor at Massachusetts Institute of Technology, estimates that middle management (e.g., curriculum directors and team leaders) have an average lifetime effectiveness ratio that is only one-tenth of the maximum that could be achieved. (Meade, 1963). He adds that insofar as lifetime performance is concerned, an individual literally need make only one significant contribution in his or her entire 40 years of professional service to raise this personal overall effectiveness rating from the average of 10 percent to a level of 50 percent of the maximum possible. You can begin to increase your effectiveness ratio by studying what ideas should be left to incubate before you begin action. You can also increase by identifying what needs to be done with a wider perspective and which tasks hold potential for greatest contribution.

Make Each Day on the Job as Exciting as Possible

A few classroom teachers shared a special technique they created to avoid task specific burnout. I have found it to be so valuable that I would like for you to try it today, if possible. Whenever they became bored, they either reflected alone or asked someone else to list the answer for the following question they asked for themselves: "What are the two most special teaching activities that they have really enjoyed?" As they answer this question for themselves they find that the next direction the conversation or self-reflection takes is to begin planning a special activity that they wanted to use by the end of the week to brighten their class's routine. To give you a better understanding of how this technique works, I asked four of these teachers to list the activities they liked.

As you read the list in Figure 9-1, think about the most special activities that you have done and the periods in the day where these activities or the ones listed could alleviate task specific burnout. In the margin of the list you may wish to jot a special note on adaptations you would like to make upon these teachers' ideas.

Prevent Boredom in Routine Tasks

Some activities, done regularly, involve either small goals or ones you have already mastered. Because these activities will demand only a part of your thinking ability, yet need repeated attention, some type of external motivation to sustain your careful attention will be necessary. That is, when a task does not captivate your full attention, you can avoid task-specific burnout by creating a new challenge for yourself or your students.

The chart in Figure 9-2 will help and can be referenced whenever you begin to feel boredom in your teaching. You will use it to identify ways in which routine tasks can be changed to become more productive, efficient, and enjoyable. That is, any small task can be made more appealing and growth producing if it is:

1. Combined with a second activity.
2. Performed in a different spot or room.
3. Rescheduled to be done at a different time.
4. Afforded more time, perfecting a detail that develops a personal or student talent you or he or she values.
5. Afforded less time designing a more efficient procedure to complete it.
6. Afforded less space (e.g., the activity is moved to smaller conference room or the activity takes less space to be stored).
7. Assigned more work space, (e.g., the group is moved into a larger circle, room, or table).
8. Made smaller in terms of the number of people involved.
9. Made larger in terms of the number of people involved.
10. Assigned new content, depth, or breadth by diversifying one aspect in a manner that will be beneficial or aesthetically pleasing to others.

Figure 9-1

RECALLING PAST SUCCESSES

Activities other teachers shared and used to relieve burnout:

1. Researching math history.
2. Using straws (soda) to make three-dimensional figures.
3. Using geoboards.
4. Using plastic models to explain solids.
5. Allowing students to attempt to draw solids.
6. Allowing students to critique each other's proofs.
7. Taking field trip to the planetarium to later discuss the mathematical aspects in space.
8. Undertaking special projects.
9. Working with the computer.
10. Using paper folding to show and explain about different geometric objects.
11. Bringing in resource people to explain how they use geometry in their jobs.
12. Taking a field trip to the office of an architect.
13. Allowing the better students to examine the works of Euclid.
14. Working with the physics department to team teach some aspects of geometry relating to science.
15. Using more constructions and practical applications.
16. Taking a field trip to an Air Force base to see the use of geometry in navigation.
17. Having the art teacher explain the use of and relations of geometry to art.
18. Utilizing string art.
19. Encouraging reserach in the library into fields of geometry.
20. Introducing and encourage study of other geometric systems.
21. Using a map and making a game of learning how to read a map.
22. Using "Strike Out" vocabulary game by Dexter Wesbrook.
23. Using "Point 31" reading lab.
24. Using "Now Age" illustrated series.
25. Using Pal paperback libraries.
26. Using "Know Your World" (magazine).
27. Using "Flash Gordon" remedial reading kit.
28. Using scope kit "Survival".
29. Using "Sprint" magazine.
30. Using target comprehension.

Special activities:

31. Using news lab kit.
32. Developing an in-depth program on using the local newspaper.
33. Imagining and writing at the accelerated level.
34. Using map skill games.
35. Learning to use the library (The Hunt stories).

continued

Figure 9-1 continued

36. Using more plays.
37. Using scope kit "Comedy."
38. Assigning Read magazine for high-level students.
39. Buying a kit on building a rocket.
40. Offering insights about America.
41. Having guest speaker.
42. Having student teaching the class.
43. Having student-led Master of Ceremonies Program.
44. Team teaching.
45. Having students select activities.
46. Making a 4-day units—choice of activites on Fridays.
47. Making inter-class activities.
48. Making extramural activities.
49. Making interschool activities.
50. Making interdiscipline activities.
51. Going on field trip to activities that we are learning.
52. Letting class observe other schools (field trip).
53. Engaging in interdependent group activities.
54. Showing likeness and differences—feeling objects in a sack.
55. Guessing what's in the box—describe what is in the box to students, they guess; then reverse roles.
56. Playing blindfold games—five objects on table, blindfold student, take one object away; student must guess which one was removed.
57. Having spelling bee—use sign alphabet.
58. Having spelling bee race—two students race to board to spell word.
59. Having spelling bee—use magnetic letters.
60. Having sentence and/or paragraph word mixup—put in proper sequence.
61. Guessing occupations—student says, signs, or finger spells vocabulary words about occupations one at a time; class uses words to guess occupation.
62. Learning song in hula language.
63. Having students compose small books about themselves, using pictures throughout their lives.
64. Making an insect collection.
65. Learning flags and symbols of countries.
66. Learning flags and symbols of states.
67. Engaging in picture study—show picture, take away, ask what they saw.
68. Developing word-picture-word stories for high school deaf students to read.
69. Developing large-sized current events map in room—to show where news and history are being made today.
70. Getting feature-length movie to show to honor roll students.
71. Having high school students compose reading books for younger students in program.
72. Making video tapes of students doing different projects.
73. Having special project on energy conservation.

Figure 9-2

USING SELF-REFLECTION TO CIRCUMVENT BURNOUT

Special Activities of My Day That Make the Day More Exciting

1. _____
2. _____
3. _____
4. _____
5. _____
6. _____
7. _____
8. _____
9. _____
10. _____

Special Aptitudes/Interests of My Students or Staff Individually and as a Group That I Want to Include in My Plans

1. _____   8. _____
2. _____   9. _____
3. _____   10. _____
4. _____   11. _____
5. _____   12. _____
6. _____   13. _____
7. _____   14. _____

Special Interests I Have That Could Be Used in My Day Better

1. _____
2. _____
3. _____
4. _____
5. _____
6. _____
7. _____
8. _____
9. _____

---

11. Given decreased concentrated attention by giving a more general, oral outline or direct response instead of the traditional plan followed. Given more concentrated attention so more details are explicitly and creatively planned and implemented and the activity becomes a more vivid expression of your professional uniqueness.

12. Changed in its mode of delivery (e.g., if done in writing, switch to oral, dramatic, or an artistic representation).

13. Given more motivational appeal.

14. Designed to allow staff or students to direct or plan the activity.

15. Changed to one personally directed alone or as a team.

16. Taken to colleagues and subordinates for their new ideas.

Be Creative

One powerful way a person can capture time and make it endure is through artistic efforts, through creation of writings, poetry, and music. Creativity appears to be an eternalization. That is, while creating, people also build time. Instead of just adjusting to the world, you force the world to adjust to you. Time seems to become irrelevant when filled with new dreams, new activities, and creative deeds. However, those who are most creative have discovered that self-discipline is the price of freedom, and this freedom is necessary to be creative.

Sturt (1925), in one of the first studies of time, wrote: "A compromise is, however, possible; a certain limited freedom from [monotony] can be achieved without a complete severance of our connexion [sic] with external objects." He goes on to tell how. The first and second methods are, "A mind supplied with stories of the past and dreams of the future has a certain freedom. Supposing the affairs of everyday do not press too heavily on it [the mind], it can slip away for many hours and walk with poets, long dead in the green dusk of a twilight wood, or pass to the calm, unchanging regions of speculation where the roar of the passing centuries dies as a whisper on the air" (p. 150).

Increasing your ability to create has other benefits. You will soon be able to become absorbed in the eustress of "creation" and the creative process. Whenever you feel bored, if you can create something in the moment that will cause you instant satisfaction, your boredom is eliminated. You could also spark a lasting innovation.

A FINAL WORD

In summary, to overcome each type of burnout often ask yourself (1) "What type of burnout am I feeling"? (2) "What causes your burnout at this time?" and (3) "What can I do to reverse this process?" You may decide (1) to get away from it all, (2) take a few minutes to make the classroom more attractive, (3) use a period of quiet time alone to meet emotional needs, (4) add a special event in the teaching day, (5), make a routine task more enjoyable, or (6) create something innovative for yourself, your students, school, or school district.

At the end of Chapter 5 (in Figure 5-3), you completed a ten-item check on the growth of your delegation skill. Check the response to each item that best describes your present abilities.

1. Are your students taking more initiative in your room as exemplified by requesting to do some of the jobs you normally do? Yes _____ No _____

2. Are you more frequently asking yourself, "Does this task lend itself to students' leadership?" or "Does this task come within those that my class officers could plan?" Yes _____ No _____

3. Have you given a task to one of your students or adult aides that you really would have enjoyed doing and one that freed you to do a task that was difficult for you to do? Yes _____ No _____

4. Has a student or aide commented to you that they were glad you gave them a particular job to do; that the job made them grow? Yes _____ No _____

5. Do you use students' ideas in planning your lessons? Yes _____ No _____

6. Have you refrained from making more than one example of individual needs of students (e.g., if each student is to have a separate folder you do not spend one planning period writing each students' name on a separate folder but allow students to do it)? Yes _____ No _____

7. All but three of your students have had a task delegated to them so far? Yes _____ No _____

8. You feel you are evaluating what tasks you personally will do more often than prior to reading this book. Yes _____ No _____

9. Someone else has led a class discussion or taught a lesson beside yourself (e.g., you've invited a specialist in a field in to speak to the class.)? Yes _____ No _____

10. Students are beginning to volunteer ways in which assignments and tasks could be evaluated and graded? Yes _____ No _____

If you scored eight "yes" answers, you have made outstanding progress!

REFERENCES

Meade, R. D. "Effect of Motivation and Progress on the Estimation of Longer Time Intervals." *Journal of Experimental Psychology*, Vol. 65, 1963, 564–567.

Sturt, Mary. *The Psychology of Time*. New York: Harcourt Brace, 1925.

Wiggers, Thomas, Deanna Forney, and Fran Wallace-Schutzman. "Burnout Is Not Necessary: Prevention and Recovery." *NASPA Journal*, Vol. 29, no. 7, 1983, 23–27.

ten

Spending Less Time on Paperwork

A Teacher Comments On Chapter 10

Why did you become a teacher? I bet it wasn't because you enjoy answering letters and memoranda, writing reports, or grading papers! It's important that we learn good organizational and time management skills so we can have quality time to teach children—the true joy of our profession. Chapter 10 teaches us to reduce the paperwork and other tasks that interfere with our teaching.

Mrs. Ann Huber
Elementary Teacher
Norwalk, Ohio

No one has enough time, yet everyone has all the time there is. This is the great "paradox" of time. It is the one resource that is distributed equally to all.

—Bob Rundell, **Time Management Worksheets,** *1979*

In a recent, free-response survey by Louis Harris for Metropolitan Life Insurance Company, the most common point of agreement between more than 1,200 teachers surveyed was that they "loved to teach" and 96 percent of the sample stated so (NEA, *Today's Education*, November 1985). The second most frequent response, however, was that they judged they had to spend too much of their time doing paperwork and administrative tasks (92 percent of the teachers surveyed). These excessive tasks were identified as:

Grading papers
Writing unanswered notes to parents
Completing administrator's reports
Sending letters of inquiry
Ordering new materials
Answering mail
Completing written requests for information from professional organizations
Planning lessons
Monitoring school rules
Checking attendance
Taking lunch counts
Collecting money
Scoring tests that are not used in subsequent instruction
Interacting with sales representatives
Reading publishing company mailings
Completing inventory sheets
Reinitiating instruction following distractions or misbehavior
Encountering principal interruptions and office messenger's notes
Dealing with absences and tardiness of students

SHUFFLING PAPER EFFECTIVELY

Business managers have developed an effective system for processing information quickly and efficiently. They never handle a piece of paper more than once. As a result, successful managers rarely have large stacks of things on their desks to be sorted. They file information in its proper place the first time it is in hand.

Teachers who have specific locations for papers of several different topics and who file completed lessons and manuals in their proper locations during the time in which students are putting up their materials rarely have an unorganized desk calling for their attention at the end of the day.

Another strategy used in large corporations can be followed in the school setting. The next time you get a memorandum that is due on the same day, or soon thereafter, to exercise self-discipline and to not succumb to the tendency to postpone a reply, answer it in the office immediately after you read it. You will not have to carry it back to clutter your desks; if back in the room, fill it out before you leave that day and put it in your drawer or basket of things to go to the office the next day. You will have developed an automatic system where you never miss your principal's deadline, a practice he or she will value. To reduce paperwork, you can

1. Take action now, jotting the answer right on the paper itself if you wish.
2. File it for later reference, and be sure all papers are filed by the end of each week.
3. Stack notes of phone calls so you can make all phone calls together.
4. Throw unimportant papers away.

It seems to also be helpful if you always open mail at the same location and respond to as many pieces of mail as possible immediately after opening. That is, if you read a letter and put it aside, you may find yourself reading it again and again as long as it lies on your desk. Also, you will have it completed and will not waste any subconscious and conscious energy trying to remember to do it.

STORING MATERIALS IN THEIR MOST CONVENIENT PLACE

Storing manuals, books, and materials in the location where instruction will be given, instead of in a single bookcase at the back of the room, or at your desk, saves time moving "paper" and books each day from one space in the classroom to another. For example, planning materials, lesson materials, and teacher's manuals can placed in a cabinet near the area where you lead the lesson. In addition, you will be surprised at how much time and irritation is saved when most frequently used materials are stored at eye level, in easy reach, near you.

Today's work in time management is to look at the top shelves in your room. Look at all storage places. Put frequently used objects at locations that are from waist height to eye level. All objects of irregular size should be on shelves that are below waist level. Objects stored on the top shelf are light weight. Objects left in view are aesthetically appealing. Take objects off the top of any cabinet or large bookcase. By scanning the room now, you can select a spot that can be reorganized and improve your time use. In less than 5 minutes you can make your materials more accessible. Use this time now.

REDUCING THE AMOUNT OF TIME SPENT RUNNING ERRANDS

Running errands, filing, and finding papers can be three of the most unproductive activities, can't they? Do you complete errands on each trip out of your room? Do you place objects you plan to take home near the door so you won't forget them? Do you have your files and materials organized according to priority and convenience?

Do you keep the materials that you use every day in front of you, within arm's reach? Do you get everything ready for the next day on the previous day, right before you leave, so your first hour of the day will be a productive one? Are you tired of rushing from corridor to corridor and then back again with those papers you forgot the first time? The next three instructions can eliminate these frustrations forever.

Decide on the time of the day that is best for you to go to the office, resource room, copy area, and/or library. If you use the same time to go to all these places, you will save even more time. Now set that time firmly in your mind and write it on your schedule, and go *only* at that time each day. What time(s) will you go?
_____.

Now, so you will not have to rush around gathering things before you go to the office, resource room, and so on, designate a specific spot to collect papers, books, memos, and reminders that you need to take with you. You may prefer to use a colorful bag, or basket with a handle, or just specify a convenient place on your shelf to stack these items.

SAVING TIME BY NOT TRYING TO FIND THINGS ALL THE TIME

As mentioned earlier, materials for the same topic should be stored or be placed at the same location. For example, if the staple gun is almost exclusively used when bulletin boards are made, but you are storing bulletin board paper in the closet near the board and the staple gun in the desk drawer at the back of the room, you will spend time and energy just getting your materials together and then putting them back. Stop. Mentally record changes that you want to make in the way your materials are organized. You will quickly discover many pieces of material are stored as they are because it is the spot that it has been stored traditionally even when it is inconvenient.

Another example: How long will it take you to gather materials if you decide to use the overhead transparency and pens as you lecture; or begin to introduce a once-a-year unit, such as "Introduction to Calculus?" Do you have Christmas books in two places, Christmas activities in a card file, transparencies in a folder, and Christmas films and records stored in the corner cabinet? Or, how many times have you run across some forgotten materials and thoughts, "I wish I had remembered to use this when I did that _____ unit"?

Storing units of study materials together will eliminate one of the greatest time wasters in classrooms.

CUTTING DOWN ON PAPERWORK

Educators have studied why paperwork is so time consuming. One reason appears to predominate. The characteristics of the duties of educators interfere with efficient paperwork completion. That is, teacher's duties are unique; teachers must constantly place priority upon spontaneously meeting individual needs, while addressing crises and being guardians of several youths daily. They are masters of many diverse topics and subjects. Their first priority is to transport our culture and literacy to a younger generation in a manner that will be best understood and sustained. These tasks, almost of necessity, leave many types of written work unfinished, as interruptions concerning any of these higher-priority duties will force a teacher to leave his or her first attempt to complete a document. If a person has to go back and reconstruct his or her thoughts at a second sitting, much time is wasted and one has had to be concerned with paperwork for two periods of time instead of one. Teachers need strategies for finishing paperwork. The strategies are given in Figure 10-1.

Additional ideas to assist you include

1. Use colored dots on book backs to keep from having to check books off an end-of-year inventory (e.g., each dot has a number and you can note which books are missing).
2. Use post cards instead of sheets of stationary for notes to parents and others.
3. File only one important sample of each thing; clean out all teaching examples once a year.

Today, we'll begin to reduce the amount of time you'll spend doing paperwork. Write down two ways you learned and would like to use tomorrow. As stated earlier in your reading, by writing these two new ideas here you will employ your subconscious to aid in doing them.

STACKING WITH A PURPOSE

As you read earlier, stacks of paper should appear on your desk less and less frequently. There will be times when paperwork needs to be stored within easy reach or within eye range; however, these stacks will be high priorities for you. They will need your immediate attention and they will have deadlines for the end of the present week. Each stack will be related to a single goal or project.

Here are 12 good rules to follow about stacks of paper:

1. Do not store stacks on you desk for longer than one week.
2. If a week passes and the stack has remained the same, file the stack to be referenced at a much later time.
3. Keep stacks coming and going.
4. Never stack any two topics upon each other so no time is wasted in trying to find a specific piece of paper.
5. Answer individual correspondences immediately and file them.

Figure 10-1

STRATEGIES FOR EFFICIENTLY HANDLING PAPERWORK

Type of Paperwork	What to Do: Strategies That Are Efficient	What Not to Do: Less Effective Methods
Letters or junk mail that do not interest you	Throw away after quickest possible skimming. (Reason: Mail is the most timely paperwork you have. If mail does not address your specific concern at the time, it will become outdated too quickly to save. Clutter most rapidly arises when timely papers are allowed to remain on table and desk tops.)	Set aside to read quietly with coffee when you feel that you need a break. (Reason: Break times should be saved for important self-initiated actions to meet present needs. A danger can develop if you do unnecessary paperwork or read low-priority mail during your periods of slowdowns, relaxations, and breaks. After you have relaxed, you tend to take more action and might act upon a tangential issue or respond to a request from junk mail during this time that would begin a cycle of correspondence and paperwork on issues outside your immediate concerns and needs.)
Letters or memoranda that require brief answers	Answer it as soon as you finish reading it, while the letter is still in your hand. Jot your note on the bottom of the letter or memo that you received. (Reason: It is so much faster to address an envelope and jot a note to someone than to compose an entire letter and have it typed. Second, if you mail a letter that you composed to respond to specific questions to someone, they may have forgotten their initial concerns and,	Set aside and write a letter later. (Reason: Tomorrow may never come, and you may be viewed as incompetent by those who wait for your reply. Second, as soon as you let go of a piece of paper, it lays somewhere and takes up space, cluttering your mind with unfinished business. Third, any time you do not answer a letter immediately, you have to reread the letter before answering, and this second reading time is wasted motion that is repetitive and is not an advantageous use of that present moment.)

continued

Type of Paperwork	What to Do: Strategies That Are Efficient	What Not to Do: Less Effective Methods
	with your answers on the letter with the questions, the communication will most likely be understood.)	
Letters or memoranda that require a new composition as an answer	As you read the paper, begin your outline of responses that you wish to make. If the letter or memo is well organized, you can make these notations by stopping after key points to write the outline. If the letter is not well organized, you may need to make notes for categories on the letter as you read and then go back and make your outline. As soon as your outline is finished, you can carry it around with you if you wish to think on the points for the remainder of the day. You can tape-record your response so you or the secretary can type the letter. In the opening paragraph of your letter, give the date of the letter to which you are responding and paraphrase/restate the concerns addressed in that letter. (Reason: Realizing that a letter is the most timely piece of paper you hold, delayed responses to actions require explanations as to why the response was delayed, making a postponed	Lay aside until the office is quiet, when you can think about it, or until you gain more information about the requests. (Reason: The letter will tend to become buried in other paper. Carry the letter with you until you have made enough decisions that you are ready to write the letter if you need more information before answering. At any rate, always make your outlined response on your initial reading.)

continued

Type of Paperwork	What to Do: Strategies That Are Efficient	What Not to Do: Less Effective Methods
	letter more difficult to write, longer in length, and more time consuming.)	
Reports that can be completed in a 1-hour setting or less	Set aside this amount of time and allow no interruptions by carefullly selecting a time and place in which paperwork will be completed. Be certain you have given enough thought to the issue tht you can truly sit down and begin to write as soon as you begin your hour's work. If you get "bogged down" on a point during that time, (1) get up and walk around the room for a moment or step outdoors if interruptions will not interfere and (2) either return to that point or a new point when you return. (Reason: Most people can sustain a highly intense 50-minute period of concentration before fatigue overtakes their drive. A report written in a single sitting will have more cohesion even if a second period is needed for editing and final touches. One writing and one editing period is preferable to two periods of writing/ editing one-half of a report because intervention of time is one of the most valuable aids to	Start the task; stop because of lack of preparation, lack of prior thought, or interruptions. Start again. Stop again, prior to 1 hour's on-task time. (Reason: The first 5-minute period in writing is the most susceptible time for unproductiveness and interruptions due to the effects of inertia. Force yourself to not begin to write the report before you are ready and stick with the task at least 10 minutes before deciding to set a new time to do it.)

continued

Type of Paperwork	What to Do: Strategies That Are Efficient	What Not to Do: Less Effective Methods
	objective editing and, when the report has pieces left unfinished after the first sitting, the task of returning to that piece of paperwork will require more motivation and self-discipline to break inertia than will returning to the proofreading of a finished product. Many educators have reported that implementing this single technique has changed their perceptions about "paperwork" so drastically that they now look forward to the periods of variety that tasks invovling important paperwork provide for them.)	
Periodical reports	Put someone else in charge of these reports. Store these reports in convenient places so ongoing records can be made in spare moments. Many administrators keep these records on the counter by the telephone so that, during telephone conversations, records can be added to the report. Many teachers keep periodic records on the stand near the door so time while students are getting ready to line up or getting ready to pass from class can be	Store these reports and all information relating to them in various places in the room, dependent upon where you were when you received them. Then, prior to the time the report is due, collect them all and move them to your desk to organize them and to write. (Reason: Although this solution sounds ludicrous, many of us use this method without realizing it. Let's try this experiment to see: (1.) Think of the next periodic report that you have to complete. (2.) Picture the spot where all of the materials are that you need to complete it—including paper, pen, clips, and so

continued

Type of Paperwork	What to Do: Strategies That Are Efficient	What Not to Do: Less Effective Methods
	used to record grades, mark absences, or count money. (Reason: If periodic reports are left unattended until the time in which they are due, separate pieces of information can be lost, requiring valuable, burdensome time to reconstruct. Second, reports that have to be completed more than twice yearly can become tedious and boring if attempted in single blocks of time. With boredom comes an increased probability of error.)	on. (3.) Will you have to move to more than one spot before you finish the report? How much of the report will you have to spend time reconstructing because of the amount of time that has intervened since your last notations? Organization and capturing spare moments that would otherwise be wasted is the key to minimizing the time spent writing periodic reports.)
Reports, papers, curriculum that require more than one session to write	This type of paperwork is delayed most frequently. There is a very successful and satisfying technique to use. Follow all the guidelines given under completing reports that require only one sitting to complete. At the end of that session, collect all your materials, in order, placing the paper where you had just written your last thought on top. Store the report as a unit and carry it with you if possible in a satchel or briefcase, without any other types of paperwork, until you are ready to begin your second session. (Reason: Although this technique may sound	Work on the report for a few minutes, thumbing through notes and making big goals. Then, restack the material back in the order of the first piece of paper seen on top. Leave this on the desk or, worse, out of sight in a drawer. (Reason: You will begin to feel that you are not making progress and abandon the task or, worse yet, postpone it until its timeliness has past and every moments of time that you had invested will have been entirely wasted.)

continued

Type of Paperwork	What to Do: Strategies That Are Efficient	What Not to Do: Less Effective Methods
	simple and sensible, deviations from it have decreased the benefits of the system. Each step is designed to help you overcome inertia. By unpacking your materials each time, you can have completed an easy task [getting ready] before starting [increasing momentum] instead of just leaving all the papers on a table and returning to a big, hard task first thing. By organizing your materials at the end of each session rather than at the beginning, you do not waste the freshest moments of your working periods by doing an organizational task that does not require a deep level of your professional judgment and skill.)	

6. Make stacks by topics, i.e. put all notes, papers and books concerning unresolved issues, projects, or single topics in a stack separate from others so that all information on a particular topic is together.

7. Keep a mental note of the first place where you put a piece of paper by reviewing to yourself as it is put away.

8. Always return that paper to that spot every time you refer to it in the future.

9. We are often not aware that our brain has stored the first location of the paper and, rather than scurrying around searching, it would be much more valuable to pause and walk through the last time we had a piece of paper, reconstructing the incident stimulating recall of the information needed.

10. Try to file information in distinct categories to avoid subject overlaps.

11. Establish a place to keep information that you may not need again. To illustrate, one teacher has a large cabinet where he puts all materials that he may not need again but does not yet want to throw away. Then, in June of each year, all materials still stored in that cabinet will be thrown out in one fell swoop. By doing this he also has a clean space for new ideas for the new school year. He feels less encumbered, and new issues of interest are undertaken more rapidly.

12. Keep and use only the materials that are *best* for specific activities. If you receive a pamphlet that describes a topic almost as well as a larger, more attractive poster you already have, you may be tempted to keep the pamphlet because "you might need it some day." "What if a slow learner or a gifted student wanted to work on the topic?" You might think to yourself. But, when the time comes where you are tempted to use the second best piece of material, you will probably end up saying to yourself, "I'll want José to have the best, so I'll give him the poster, not this pamphlet." Thus, if mediocre materials are stored with more superior teaching aids, your files may become cumbersome. Today, think about the file of materials that you least like to rummage through when it is time to teach that topic. Get that file now; throw away all mediocre and duplicate materials. If you have time, do three files today. Spend your time tomorrow and for the next few days condensing mediocre files into valuable reference folders, if you can.

Look around your class now. Do two more things before moving on in your reading. Do you have stacks with purpose. Rearrange your paperwork for the next few minutes so you apply the 12 rules. First, make a spot to place the material that you may not use again. Second, you will be amazed at the amount of time you are able to save by never saving mediocre materials. Two closing notes: (1) some teachers like to use different colored pens to highlight different components in the grading system and in their lesson plan book, and (2) many teachers keep carbons in their drawers and a rubber stamp with their name and address for use in a wide variety of time-saving ways.

COLLECTING MONEY, NOTES, AND FORMS EFFICIENTLY

Finding an effective way to spend less time collecting notes and things is an important quest. For today, let's pick one or two of the following methods that may help you in these types of tasks:

Method A: Volunteers keep unofficial student and school records as well as collect student money during periods of the day when students are working at their desks independently.

Method B: Frequently the process of collecting money, objects, or forms from students involves too much time if each student moves from his or her desk to the teacher's desk and back. By asking a high school student or parent volunteer to move from one student to another to collect the papers or money much time is saved.

Method C: Many schools have overcome the problem of spending those valuable early-morning hours on paperwork. These schools move homeroom period to later in the day, such as 10:30–10:45 each day. If your school could change in this way the benefits transfer to increased student learning and reduction in tardiness. The potential benefits outweigh the time that would be invested in discussing the matter with the principal.

Method D: For records that must be completed by the teacher, begin the records by asking a volunteer or student with exceptionally good handwriting to complete the routine information such as names and addresses. Individual students can even do their own as one meaningful handwriting lesson that their parents will see. Second, design a system where one report card is handled only once; for example, record all grades for all subjects on a single sheet so that the averages are computed and transposed from only one paper to the report. If possible, allow enough time during the report-making process so that you will not have to do more than seven reports in any single setting.

Method E: If you must collect money or make a record first thing in the morning, do so as soon as the first early bird comes, even before the bell rings, or take your record (envelope) with you to playground duty. Your day will probably be much more relaxed. Any records or checking/collecting that must be done first thing in the morning can be more easily begun if the checklists are laid open on the top of the desk before leaving for home the previous day.

How many principles for managing paperwork do you use presently? _____ How many do you realistically estimate you will be using one year from today? Write that number here _____. Write the date one year from today _____. Refer back to your prediction on the date.

GRADING PAPERS

The following methods have been used by teachers to decrease the amount of time they spend grading. I hope some can help you.

1. Delegate some types of grading to Future Teachers of America Organization.

2. Get a date stamp so a classroom monitor can date late papers and class papers and place the first in an absentee folder.

3. Have students respond to other students' creative writing assignments as a critic and you grade only one of the selections written in a specified period of time.

4. Grade written compositions for originality, for correct sentence structure, and so on, or allow students to grade the latter.

5. Give homework assignments only to those who have not yet learned the assignment material and those who can will review the concepts by grading the homework of classmates on the next day. Some spend homework time to prepare for examples you will use in the next day's lesson.

6. Check with a red pencil the number of problems you were able to check on each child's paper as you walked around the room monitoring the written work so that when the papers are collected you only grade below the red checkmarks.

7. Use more oral drill.

8. Ask more oral extended-thinking questions that require two or more days reflection before answering or give written assignments that require two weeks of work to answer.

9. Ask each student to give an answer to an example of a concept before he or she leaves the class that day.

10. Schedule a time for students to tell you what they learned and what they do not know.

11. Use charts and checklists to record progress as you monitor individual practice.

12. Spread out due dates for papers.

13. Grade only one major paper per week. This paper could involve a synthesis and an evaluation of the lower-level thinking tasks you've done during the week.

14. Students check their own papers by going to see separate answer keys for each problem worked, with the keys being posted on the bulletin board or blackboard. As soon as a student finishes, let him or her come to the answer key and check it. Only one student at a time would be allowed to come to the sheet, and a colored marker is used to correct

the errors. The teacher checks the last two problems to see if the students have mastered the concept. In doing so, both these last answers can be memorized by the teacher, and he or she can quickly see which students know the concept and which do not, placing papers with both answers incorrect in one pile and those with both answers correct in another. Students needing additional instruction are then identified at the same time the papers are collected without future time being spent in grouping students for remedial follow-up instruction.

15. Place questions on strips for students. Students then ask each other questions orally with other students responding orally.

16. Grade only every fourth practice exercise in a series of problems.

17. Carry a clipboard around the room as you monitor each student's progress, placing checkmark, "ab" in squares that have been specified for individual assessments and absences that you wish to note.

18. Student monitors, as row or group leaders, are very effective graders of homework practice sheets.

19. Post answers on the blackboard to each problem on separate sheets of paper that have a cover sheet. As soon as a student finishes the first problem, he or she can go to the answer sheet marked "1" and check that problem, making corrections needed. He or she then works the second problem, at his or her desk, and goes to the answer sheet marked "2" as soon as the second problem is finished, and so on. Each answer sheet is worked by a team of students who had been assigned the problem the night before. This procedure continues until the last four problems. Students do not have answer sheets for these answers and work them without checking the correct answer. When the students finish and turn in their papers, place the papers in two stacks— one for papers with more than 80 percent of the unchecked problems correct and another for papers with less than 80 percent (or missing 2 of the 4, for example) of those problems correct. In this way, you can memorize the correct answers to the last four problems in advance and students will have practiced many more. You will have not only graded but also diagnosed needs and formed your two instructional groups for the next day—those who will work on the same concept again and those who are ready for formal testing of the concept or for moving on to the next aspect of the concept.

20. Most important, allow yourself only one or two times during the semester to grade stacks of papers at home. By spacing the times at which written work will be done and by planning how students will be graded while planning instructional methods, you will develop a habit of planning your grading time. Because of this prior planning, the grading that you do will become more valuable, more important to the students, and more comprehensively administered.

21. Grade in class, with students writing all correct answers on their paper in red pencils.

22. Use timed math tests, learning center work, practice spelling tests, and questions at the end of the chapter, and when the time is up, have students grade these daily works. Then, to be dismissed, have each student rewrite any incorrect answer so that each will turn in a 100 percent correct paper. Grades are not recorded but a checkmark can be placed in the grade book if desired.

23. Individual student or one large chart is used where students record their own grades.

24. Make individual blackboards using 8"x11" pieces of cardboard, painted with blackboard paint, available at a paint store. You ask a question and have students hold up the answer they wrote on their blackboard. You check the whole class at once.

A FINAL WORD

In closing this chapter, I would like to list two small actions I have taken to reduce the amount of time I spend doing paperwork:

1. You may want to begin doing less important paperwork at low points in your day, biorhythmically. For example, I plan my big paperwork periods during the times when I feel my best, and by using these "best times" to do the important tasks, I do not waste energy and work as hard to motivate myself to continue the task; between 3:00 and 4:00 in the afternoon I try to do less demanding paperwork.

2. You may want to do unimportant paperwork in conjunction with other things—while you listen to music, while you wait for a student who is a few minutes late for an appointment, while standing in line, and so on.

In conclusion, the less paperwork you do, the greater the satisfaction you will have in teaching. Keeping this principle in mind may make it easier for you to monitor your actions so you continually seek new ways of reducing the paperwork load through creative time management methods.

eleven

Helping Colleagues and Students Manage Their Time Better

A Teacher Comments on Chapter 11

Chapter 11 contains many valuable methods for teaching time management principles to students. Two especially appealed to me. The overview sheet for "Aspects of a Topic" is a most creative means to involve my first grade students in planning as well as introducing the value of time scheduling. I will add pictures, shapes, and so on to the "Aspects of the Topic" chart to stimulate thinking.

The "Student Planned Project" sheet will also be a valuable tool for me. I will use this sheet for varied subjects, but I am especially excited about using it for social studies when we study homes and communities.

Breaking the project down into parts with a deadline date for each step is a unique feature of the plan. Knowing what is expected and when, and approaching the work a step at a time, will allow my students an opportunity to internalize, "I can do it." Each successfully completed step helps a student gain enthusiasm for doing the work on the next step properly and on time. This approach allows the teacher to affirm, encourage, spot problems, and guide students to evaluate how to correct them after each step.

Ms. Donna M. McAdoo
Teacher, Grade 1
Longview, Texas

We are born helpless. As soon as we are fully
conscious we discover loneliness. We need others
physically, emotionally, intellectually; we need
them if we are to know anything, even ourselves.

—C. S. *Lewis,* **The Four Loves**

Before we discuss helping others, I believe it is important to remember that no one can force someone else to improve. That is, I have found it very valuable to remember the principle so graphically depicted in the following anonymous quotation:

Never try to teach a pig to sing;
It wastes your time and
It annoys the pig.

One of the leading causes for fellow teachers' misuse of time that you can assist them to overcome is a lack of motivation to improve. This absence could stem from a feeling that they are not involved in planning new tasks for the school. Figure 11-1 is a worksheet that can be used to help teachers become more involved in school goal-setting activities. The sheet can be used in faculty meetings or in memorandum form.

HELPING SOMEONE ELSE HAVE MORE TIME BY SETTING PRIORITIES

A second major source of faculty time wasters occurs when teachers do not feel as if they are a vital part of their educational unit. This can be eliminated by analyzing which segments of the ongoing educational process could be asigned to them. Then, as the person becomes more comfortable with the new assignment, he or she will begin to add creative ideas and plans on his or her own initiative. At this point, specific techniques of managing time during that task can be suggested. Then, as each job is passed to another teacher, the "old" teacher can suggest methods of doing the tasks that were most efficient for him or her. To set this process in motion, you can model by asking predecessors about their best methods of doing a new schoolwide task that has just been assigned to you. You could also identify areas in your school's management system and procedures where time is being wasted and suggest methods of change. By asking for your suggestion to be placed on the agenda for the next faculty meeting, the faculty can then begin to practice and feel more comfortable discussing other time management problems.

As priorities are set in a faculty meeting, it will be important that teachers needing time management are praised for slightest improvements.

Figure 11-1

SCHOOL GOALS AND PLANNING GUIDE

Name: _____

1. What parts of your job are most interesting to you?

2. What do you think would make you feel better about yourself and your place in our educational system?

3. What would you like to be able to do this year that you could not do last year?

4. What would you like to see our educational system do this year that we did not do last year?

5. What talent would you like to contribute to our school or to another aspect of our educational program?

6. What part of your work or the work of our educational unit do you think might better be performed in a group rather than individual basis, or vice versa?

7. What reward would you like to receive for a job well done?

8. What keeps you from doing as well as you would like in your job?

(You can include other items more specific to concerns, problems, or plans that have already been set for the coming year, to which you desire their input.)

WORKING WITH COLLEAGUES

Colleagues will best begin to think about their time use when they select the aspect of time management upon which they most wish to improve. There are three steps to improving one's time management skills. Stress these three points in a faculty meeting, formal presentation, or informal introductions to others.

People can improve how well they (1) *conserve time*. The tasks they do can take less time, for example, use of form (or standardized) letters, speed reading, and reducing meeting times through prior planning.

Teachers can improve how well they (2) *control the time available to them*. That is, they can learn to make flexible time and appointments made with themselves, such as controlling overcommitment as well as making more effective decisions.

Teachers can improve upon their (3) *ability to make time*. Examples of making time are to work more predominately in areas of personal skill, interest, talent, developing skill in delegation, and spending more time in activities that require their professional judgments.

After a discussion of these three points, each teacher could select the area in which he or she prefers to concentrate. Turning the discussion to rewards that could be given for people who learn to use their time more wisely, those who get "more done better in less time" could be selected, on an individual or group basis, the type of reward they desire.

SETTING GOALS WITH STUDENTS

At the beginning of your next term, discuss with students the many areas that you could cover within the subject. Tell your students the three learning goals that you have set for the term. Then let them choose three of their own. Take the next 10 minutes of class time and use the worksheet in Figure 11-2 to list your three most important goals for your students and some suggestions for goals they may set for themselves this term or for a specified time period. While being open to the students' suggestions as they set their own goals, also help them be realistic so they can successfully reach those goals.

ALLOWING STUDENTS TO CHOOSE ASPECTS OF A TOPIC THEY WISH TO MANAGE

When you begin a new topic of study, give students an overview of the aspects you could cover under that topic. Then let students decide which aspects they especially want to emphasize. For example, aspects your class may want to emphasize in a chapter on money might range from place value, to making change, and to inflation. You could spend 10 minutes of your planning period tomorrow making the overview for your next topic of study and listing some aspects the students may choose to emphasize. Use Figure 11-3 and make multiple copies for future use before you first use it tomorrow.

Figure 11-2

SETTING GOALS WITH STUDENTS

1. What parts of this subject are the most interesting to you?
2. What skill would you like to be able to do in this class by the end of the semester? This year?
3. You think you could best learn this skill if we did _____ (e.g., an experiment, small-group work, reading about it, interviewing an authority on the topic, taking a field trip, working in class, practicing at home)?
4. What kinds of work do you like to do in groups?

   With a partner?

   Alone
5. What reward would you like to receive when you reach the goal of this project?
6. What keeps you from doing as well as you would like to in this subject?
7. How can you learn best in this class?

Figure 11-3

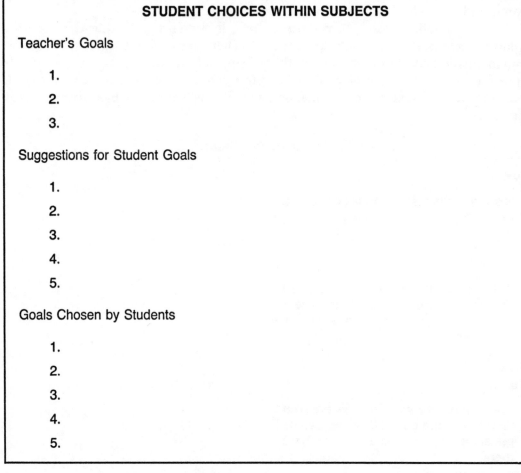

STUDENT CHOICES WITHIN SUBJECTS

Teacher's Goals

    1.

    2.

    3.

Suggestions for Student Goals

    1.

    2.

    3.

    4.

    5.

Goals Chosen by Students

    1.

    2.

    3.

    4.

    5.

Equally effective is listing all the topics covered in the text in a particular curriculum area. These could be listed in the first section on a page that has been divided into thirds, as shown in Figure 11-4. Students are then asked to suggest related topics or questions they wish to explore. These are recorded in the second section of the worksheet. These lists of 20 items could then be ranked in the third section of the sheet with a designation of the student's name who will lead the study of each topic. The name(s) are cited after each topic. Deadline dates are also given.

You can then give an overview of the format each group is to follow in their teaching of basic principles within their concept. Also, you could give suggestions for teaching strategies by distributing the master lesson plan given in Chapter 3.

Challenge students to improve by teaching them how to improve their scheduling abilities and to eliminate problems they have in wasting time, based on the skills you have learned.

TEACHING TIME MANAGEMENT PRINCIPLES TO STUDENTS

As soon as possible near the beginning of your next unit or trimester, give your students a written copy of the final plan for their work with clear instructions. Go over the plans with your students and ask what they wish to learn or what they want to add or change. Students who know what is expected can be better prepared and waste less time waiting for you to start every lesson.

In your final plan, be certain to include a column for due dates and a column for checking if deadlines are met. Then help your students overcome procrastination and improve their study skills by helping them set their own deadlines for each step of a project as well as the due date. In so doing, you will be teaching your students time management skills as well as subject content; for example,

Project—Letter Carrier

Part 1

Read and discuss with class book on the letter carrier and his job.

           3/8   _____

Part 2

Write a letter to mail to yourself (remember your address?) or write a letter to the classmate whose name you draw.

           3/9   _____

Part 3

List things you want to see on your field trip to the post office, as well as questions to ask. Mail your letters there.

           3/11   _____

Project—Propaganda

Part 1	Due Date	Check
Read and discuss in class pp. 209—211 on propaganda techniques.	3/4	————
Part 2		
Bring newspapers or magazines to class and find an example of each propaganda technique with a partner. Share with the class.	3/5	————
Part 3		
Write your own advertisement or campaign slogan and tell which device you used.	3/6	————
Part 4		
Read your advertisement or slogan in class and discuss positive and negative aspects of propaganda.	3/7	————

Figure 11-5 can be used as you plan your next project for students. Use the rest of your 10 minutes of study time to write in your plan book when and how you will use this planning method with your students on their next project. Primary teachers may want to use a flip chart for planning with the entire class rather than giving worksheets to individual students. The last part of this worksheet is a sample of types of projects students could use to complete the project.

TEACHING STUDENTS TO USE MATERIALS EFFICIENTLY

By preparing specific instructions for students on the location, use, and storage room materials, you will have a more efficient classroom. The next time you are introducing a new procedure, piece of equipment, or classroom process, instead of writing directions on the board as you introduce it, write them on a posterboard that can be placed near the materials students use as a reminder of wise time use. Posting these instructions near the materials and discussing how to care for and put materials away at the beginning of the year are good time investments for the entire year. A good time for this discussion is immediately preceding the first time you use the materials. You will need to remind students of proper use of materials occasionally, and by doing it with an emphasis upon your evaluation

Figure 11-4

STUDENT INVOLVEMENT IN PLANNING

Topic _____

Circle those areas that students show most interest in learning for the topic above.

1.	6.
2.	7.
3.	8.
4.	9.
5.	10.

1.	6.
2.	7.
3.	8.
4.	9.
5.	10.

1.	6.
2.	7.
3.	8.
4.	9.
5.	10.

Figure 11-5

STUDENT-PLANNED PROJECTS

Name _____

	Due Date	Check
Part 1	_____	_____
Part 2	_____	_____
Part 3	_____	_____
Part 4	_____	_____
Final Due Date	_____	_____
Reward	_____	_____

Task:		
Differentiated Task:		
Setting:		

	Lecture	Learning center	Role playing
	Film	Community mentor	Independent study
	Task card	Simulation	Worksheet
	Game	Peer group (committee)	Library
	Tutor	Small group teacher-directed lesson	Programmed textbook

that they are responsible and that you trust them eliminates their viewing the discussion as a reprimand.

For primary student you may wish to use a combination of words and pictures on your poster(s) and list five or fewer instructions for third graders and three and fewer for kindergarten students. Intermediate students can decorate or make the poster(s) for an art project after you have written the instructions, if you prefer. Intermediate students have seven or fewer instructions to follow.

TEACHING STUDENTS TO HELP THEIR PEERS MANAGE THEIR TIME BETTER

Some students learn to manage their time better by leading groups in learning activities. Because these students must assume the leadership duties of planning and preparing activities, they improve their time use skills through practice. Learning activities include

1. If reviews before unit tests have become a drudgery, use student committees to liven them up. Give each committee the responsibility for one section of the unit to review the rest of the class over. Suggest that they use such review methods as acting out a part of the reading, a debate over historical political issue, a game, or relay, a pretest, or an experiment. Be sure that you share a few leaders in each group and that they know how much time they will have to prepare and to present their section. Also be sure to be available to help guide their planning.

2. To interest children in reading, choose high-interest books or a series of books and read one section each day. Good readers can read to the class after they have preread the book alone.

3. Let a student make the model for an art project a day early and demonstrate it to the class while you have time for checking off their oral skills or planning ahead.

4. Have students raise their own money for their spirit squads and school improvement projects.

UPDATING YOUR STUDENTS' STANDARDS OF PERFORMANCE

By updating standards of performance for your students and for your teaching, you make more time for higher-order activities. Asking students to tell you specific things you do or don't do that act as barriers to them doing their best provides an opportunity for you to ask students to answer the same question concerning themselves. Videotaping their present level of performance or viewing a class at a higher level of skill are also effective methods of raising students' expectations. A third means of obtaining this end is to ask students to write their own job description for a certain section of class content. Another means is to solicit the aid of the parents. India Podsen, in an article entitled ''My Child Has

Poor Study Habits: Academic Excellence Begins at Home" (1984), has many suggestions about how this could be accomplished.

Lastly, you may wish to call students' attention to the fact that there is a great need for new generations to design better schools for the students of the future. Your students could begin plans that would address such issues as

1. Determining how schools can increase people's communicative skills, creative problem—solving skills, inventing skills, negotiating skills, planning and forecasting skills, and self-directed skill development.

2. Developing methods of validating expertise that is obtained from experimental learning.

3. Designing a curriculum format whereby as soon as a new technology or fact is uncovered, it is channeled into the educational system at the point of best use.

4. Developing methods that help students to better actualize their unique talents.

A FINAL WORD

In summary, it is important that you assist colleagues and students to increase their talents through increased time management. They will grow by following the model you set as you improve. One method of increasing this sense of ownership is to Build learning goals that they form and value, and ask students/ colleagues to be in charge of one aspect of a group management project. You can design faculty meeting presentations and classroom lessons to teach time management principles to colleagues and students. By making success more predictable, students and colleagues can do their best more efficiently. Higher-order and more productive work can often be the by-product of updating and increasing the standards of performance for students and colleagues.

REFERENCE

Podsen, India. "My Child Has Poor Study Habits: Academic Excellence Begins at Home." *American Education*, August-September 1984, 28-32.

INDEX